2-4

# TRACTS ON
# SLAVERY and LIBERTY

## The Just Limitation of Slavery in the Laws of God... The Law of Passive Obedience... The Law of Liberty...

NEGRO UNIVERSITIES PRESS
WESTPORT, CONNECTICUT

Originally published in 1776, London

Reprinted 1969 by
Negro Universities Press
A Division of Greenwood Publishing Corp.
New York

SBN 8371-2382-8

PRINTED IN UNITED STATES OF AMERICA

# THE

## JUST LIMITATION of SLAVERY

### IN THE

# LAWS of GOD,

#### COMPARED WITH

The unbounded Claims of the AFRICAN
TRADERS and BRITISH AMERICAN
SLAVEHOLDERS.

## BY GRANVILLE SHARP.

With a copious APPENDIX:

##### CONTAINING,

An Anfwer to the Rev. Mr. Thompfon's Tract in
favour of the *African Slave Trade.*—Letters concerning *the lineal Defcent of the Negroes* from the
Sons of HAM.—The Spanifh Regulations for the
gradual Enfranchifement of Slaves.—A Propofal
on the fame Principles for the gradual Enfranchifement of Slaves in *America.*—Reports of Determinations in the feveral COURTS OF LAW
AGAINST SLAVERY, &c.

----Take away your Exactions from my People, SAITH
THE LORD GOD! Ezekiel xlv. 9.

# T R A C T I.

## T H E

# Juſt Limitation of Slavery.

THE opinion of the lords Hardwick
and Talbot, which I laboured to
refute in my Tract againſt *Slavery in En-*
*gland* (1), (printed in 1769,) has ſince
been effectually ſet aſide by a clear determination, in the Court of King's-Bench
(2), in favour of *James Somerſett, a Ne-*
*gro,* againſt his former Maſter, C******
S******, eſq. in the year 1772.

B

But

(1) A Repreſentation of the Injuſtice and dangerous
Tendency of tolerating Slavery in *England.*

(2) See Appendix.

But it is not enough, that the Laws of England exclude *Slavery* merely *from this island*, whilft the grand Enemy of mankind triumphs in a toleration, *throughout our Colonies*, of the moft monftrous *oppreffion* to which human nature can be fubjected!

And yet this abominable wickednefs has not wanted advocates, who, in a variety of late publications, have attempted to palliate the guilt, and have even ventured to appeal to Scripture for the fupport of their uncharitable pretenfions: fo that I am laid under a double obligation to anfwer them, becaufe it is not the caufe of *Liberty* alone for which I now contend, but for that which I have ftill much more at heart, the honour of the holy Scriptures, the principles of which are entirely oppofite to the felfifh and uncharitable

uncharitable pretenſions of our American Slaveholders and African Traders.

A late anonymous writer, who calls himſelf "*An African Merchant*," remarks, that,—"By the Law of Moſes, "the Iſraelites might purchaſe Slaves "from the Heathens, and even their "own people might become Slaves to "their brethren." *A Treatiſe on the Trade from Great-Britain to Africa, &c. by an African Merchant.* P. 8 *and* 9.

Now, with reſpect to the firſt part of his obſervation, it is true, indeed, that the Iſraelites were expreſſly permitted to keep Bond-Servants, or Slaves, "of the "*Heathen*, (or, more properly, of the "*Nations* הגוים) that *were round about*" them, and of "the children of the ſtran- "gers that ſojourned among" them. (Levit. xxv. 44 to 46.) But we muſt remember, that theſe *Heathen*, or "*Na-* "*tions*

# [ 4 ]

" *tions that were round about them,*" were an abandoned race of people, already *Slaves* and *worſhippers* of devils, and by them led to debaſe *human nature*, and to pollute themſelves with the moſt un‐ natural and abominable vices: " For in " all theſe," (ſaid the Almighty,) " the " nations are defiled which I caſt out " before you: and the Land is defiled; " THEREFORE I do viſit the iniquity " thereof upon it, and the land itſelf vo‐ " miteth out her inhabitants,"*&c.* Again; " For all theſe abominations have " the men of the land done which " were before you, and the land is defi‐ " led," *&c.* See Levit. xviii. And the " *children of the ſtrangers,*" abovemen‐ tioned, were (probably) alſo of the ſame deteſtable nations of Paleſtine, the Amo‐ rites, Canaanites, *&c.* which were ex‐ preſſly doomed to deſtruction (3), and

that

(3) " Obſerve thou that which I command thee " this day: behold, I drive out before thee the Amo‐

rite,

that by the hand of the Ifraelites, *who were commanded to ſhew them no pity* (4).

But no doctrine muſt be drawn from theſe commands to *execute God's vengeance* upon the ſaid wicked *ſtrangers*, without confidering, at the ſame time, *that very contrary treatment of ſtrangers* which was *equally* enjoined in the Law : for the Ifraelites were pofitively commanded not to *vex* or *oppreſs* a *Stranger*. " *Thou* " *ſhalt*

" rite, and the Canaanite, and the Hittite, and the
" Perizzite, and the Hivite, and the Jebufite. Take
" heed to thyſelf, leſt thou make a covenant with the
" inhabitants of the land whither thou goeſt, leſt it be
" for a ſnare in the midſt of thee," *&c.* Exod. xxxiv.
11 and 12.

(4) " And thou ſhalt confume all the people which
" the Lord thy God ſhall deliver thee : thine eye ſhall
" have *no pity upon them*," *&c.* Deut. vii. 16. " The
" Lord thy God will put out thoſe nations by little and
" little," *&c.* " The Lord thy God ſhall deliver
" them unto thee, and ſhall deſtroy them with a migh-
" ty deſtruction until they be deſtroyed. And he ſhall
" deliver their kings into thine hand, and thou ſhalt
" deſtroy their name from under heaven : there ſhall
" no man be able to ſtand before thee until thou have
" deſtroyed them." Deut. vii. 23 and 24.

" *ſhalt love him as thyſelf,*" ſaid Moſes,
by the exprefs command of God. " If a
" Stranger ſojourn with thee in your
" land, ye *ſhall not vex*" (or *oppreſs)*
" him. But *the Stranger* that dwelleth
" with you ſhall be unto you as one born
" among you, and *thou ſhalt love him as*
" *thyſelf:* for ye were *Strangers* in the
" land of Egypt." Levit. xix. 33. 34.
And again : " The Lord your God is
" God of gods and Lord of lords, a great
" God, a mighty and a terrible, which
" *regardeth not perſons* nor taketh reward:
" he doth execute the judgement of the
" fatherleſs and widow, and *loveth the*
" *Stranger,* in giving him food and rai-
" ment. *Love ye,* therefore, *the Stran-*
" *ger* ; for ye *were Strangers* in the land
" of Egypt." Deut. x. 17 to 19. In all
theſe paſſages, and many others, the Iſraelites were reminded of their *Bondage*
*in Egypt :* for ſo the almighty *Deli-*
*verer* from *Slavery* warned his people
**to**

to *limit* and moderate the *bondage*, which
the Law permitted, by the remembrance
of *their own former bondage* in a foreign
land, and by a remembrance alfo of his
great mercy *in delivering them* from that
*bondage*: and he expreſsly referred them
to *their own feelings,* as they themſelves
had experienced the intolerable yoke of
Egyptian Tyranny! " Thou ſhalt not
" *oppreſs a Stranger*; for ye know the
" heart of *a ſtranger*, feeing ye were
" *ſtrangers* in the land of Egypt." Exod.
xxiii. 9.     And again: " Thou ſhalt
" remember that *thou* waſt *a Bond-man*
" in the land of Egypt, and the Lord thy
" God *redeemed thee:*" Deut. xv. 15.

We muſt, therefore, neceſſarily conclude, when theſe very oppoſite commands are conſidered, that the *Heathen,*
or *nations* that were " ROUND ABOUT,"
or in the *environs* of the promiſed land,
and alſo the *children of the ſtrangers*, that
dwelt

dwelt among them, mentioned at the
fame time, whom the Ifraelites were permitted to retain *in perpetual bondage,*
were not intended to be included and
ranked under that general denomination
of *Strangers,* to whom fo much real *affection, benevolence,* and *confideration,* are
ftrictly commanded, in the texts to
which I have juft now referred. And,
confequently, it muft be allowed, that
the particular nations, (the feven nations
of Paleftine, fee Deut. vii. 1.) which
were exprefsly devoted to deftruction,
were the only *Strangers* whom the Jews
were permitted to hold in *abfolute Slavery;*
fo that the wicked practice of *enflaving*
the poor *African Negroes* would have
been as *unlawful,* under the Jewifh
Difpenfation, as it certainly is, now
a-days, to Englifhmen, and other fubjects of Great-Britain, that profefs *the
Chriftian Religion; in whofe confideration,*
ALL STRANGERS, from every
other

other part of the world, are, without
doubt, entitled to be ranked, efteemed,
and beloved, *as brethren*, which I have
elfewhere particularly demonftrated; and
which even the law of Mofes exprefsly
commanded : — " But *the ftranger*, that
" dwelleth with you, fhall be unto you *as*
" *one born among you*, and THOU
" SHALT LOVE HIM AS THY-
" SELF ; for *ye were ftrangers* in the
" land of Egypt : I am the Lord your
" God." Levit. xix. 33 and 34.

This excellent fyftem of benevolence to
*ftrangers*, which the Ifraelites were fo
ftrictly enjoined to obferve, cannot, I apprehend, be otherwife reconciled with the
permiffion to the Ifraelites of retaining in
perpetual bondage *the heathen that were
round about them*, and the children of *the
ftrangers* that fojourned among them :
for, if this permiffion were. to be extended to *ftrangers in general*, it would
fubvert

fubvert the exprefs command concerning *brotherly love* due to *ftrangers*; becaufe a man cannot be faid *to love the ftranger as himfelf* if he holds *the ftranger* and his progeny in a perpetual *involuntary fervitude.* The obfervation therefore of the African Merchant, that " THE ISRAELITES *might* " *purchafe Slaves from the heathens,*" will by no means juftify the *enflaving* of *modern heathens*, by *Englifhmen*, or by any other nation now fubfifting. The Ifraelites, at that time, might not only purchafe Slaves of thofe particular heathen nations, but they might alfo *drive out thefe heathen;* (I mean, thefe which were particularly named;) nay, even *kill* (5) and *extirpate* them, and *take poffeffion of their cities, houfes,* and *lands.* All thefe acts of violence *might* the Ifraelites do *without fin,* though the like would juftly be efteemed

*murder*

(5) " But of the cities of thefe people, which the " Lord thy God doth give thee for an inheritance, " thou *fhalt fave alive nothing that breatheth.*" Deut. xx. 16.

*murder* and *robbery*, if practifed by any
other nation, not under the like peculiar
circumftances : fo that the example of the
Ifraelites affords no excufe for the uncharitable practices of the *African Merchant*
and *Weft-India Planter!* The Ifraelites
had an exprefs commiffion (6) to execute
God's vengeance, *without remorfe* (7), upon
feveral populous nations, which had rendered themfelves *abominable in the fight of*

C 2 God,

(6) " Now, therefore, kill every male among the
" little ones, and kill every woman that hath known
" man by lying with him." Numbers xxxi. 17. This
was the judgement againft the Midianitiñ prifoners.
The feven nations of Paleftine were likewife fubjected
to the fame condemnation. " Thou fhalt fmite them
" and utterly deftroy them : thou fhalt make no cove-
" nant with them, *nor fhew mercy unto them.*" Deut.
vii. 2. And a reafon for this condemnation was plainly delivered in the fourth verfe, to confirm the juftice of
it : " For they will turn away thy fon from follow-
" ing me, that they may ferve other gods."
The Amalekites were alfo doomed to deftruction in
the like manner : " Thou fhalt *blot out the remembrance*
" *of Amalek from under heaven* ; *thou fhalt not forget it.*
Deut. xxv. 19.

(7) " And thou fhalt *confume all the people* which
" the Lord thy God fhall deliver thee ; thine eye
" fhall have *no pity* upon them. Deut. vii. 16.

*God,* and therefore deferved no confideration; fo that *even mercy,* in the Ifraelites,
was a fin (8), when it interfered with this
pofitive command of God!

The commiffion there given, however,
was but *temporary;* and no other nation,
except

(8) " But, if ye will not drive out the inhabitants of the
" land from before you, then it fhall come to pafs, that
" thofe, which ye let remain of them, fhall be pricks in
" your eyes and thorns in your fides, and fhall vex you
" in the land wherein ye dwell. Moreover, it fhall
" come to pafs, that *I fhall do unto you* as *I thought to do*
" *unto them.*" Numb. xxxiii. 55 and 56. And the
Ifraelites were exprefsly told, that it was not on their
own account that this extraordinary authority was put
into their hands, but on account of the *abominable wick-*
*ednefs* of thofe who poffeffed the promifed land.—"The
" land is defiled; therefore I do vifit *the iniquity there-*
" *of upon it, and the land itfelf vomiteth out her inhabit-*
" *ants.*" Levit. xviii. 25.

" For all thefe abominations" (unnatural lufts,
mentioned in the former part of the fame chapter)
" have the men of the land done which were before
" you; and the land is defiled." Levit. xviii. 27. And
the Ifraelites were warned againft prefumption, left fuch
extraordinary authority fhould occafion fpiritual pride.
" Not for thy righteoufnefs, or for the uprightnefs of
" thine heart, aoft thou go to poffefs the land, but for
" the *wickednefs of thofe nations the Lord God doth drive*
" *them out from before thee,*" &c. Deut. ix. 5.

except God's peculiar people, was charged with the execution of it; and therefore, though the Europeans have taken
upon themfelves, for a long time paft, *to
attack, deftroy, drive out, difpoffefs, and
enflave*, the poor ignorant *Heathen*, in
many diftant parts of the world, and
may, perhaps, plead cuftom and prefcription (to their fhame be it faid) for their
actions, yet, as they cannot, like the Ifraelites, produce an *authentic written
commandment from God* for fuch proceedings, the offenders can no otherwife be
efteemed than as *lawlefs robbers* and *oppreffors*, who have reafon to expect *a fevere retribution* from God for their tyranny and oppreffion. It is unreafonable,
therefore, to fuppofe that the fevere treatment of the *ancient Heathen*, by the Ifraelites, under *the difpenfation of the Law*,
either in *killing, difpoffeffing*, or *enflaving*,
them, fhould juftify our *modern* acts of

*violence*

*violence* and *oppreſſion*, now that we profeſs obedience to the *Goſpel of Peace.*

And, with reſpect to the ſecond part of the African Merchant's obſervation, concerning the Iſraelites, *(viz.* that even " their own people might become Slaves " to their brethren,") I muſt remark, that he does not deal fairly by the Jewiſh Law, to quote that circumſtance, without mentioning, at the ſame time, " *the* " *Juſt Limitation*" to which it was ſubject, and the admirable proviſion, in the ſame Law, againſt *the involuntary ſervitude of brethren*; becauſe no Hebrew could be made *a Slave* without *his own conſent,* and even *deſire,* which was to be " *plainly*" and *openly* declared in a court of *record :* — " if the ſervant ſhall *plainly* " *ſay,* I love my maſter, my wife, and " my children, *I will not go out free,* then" (ſays the text) " his maſter ſhall bring " him *unto the Judges,*" *&c.* (whereby

an

an acknowledgement *in a court of re-cord* is plainly implied,) " and his mafter
" fhall bore his ear through with an aul;
" and he fhall ferve him for ever." Exod.
xxi. 5. 6. But, without that *public ac-knowledgement* of *voluntary confent before
the Judges*, the Hebrew mafter had no
authority to bore the fervant's ear (9) in
token of bondage: and, in every other
cafe, it was *abfolutely unlawful* for the If-raelite to hold a *Brother Ifraelite in Sla-very!* The Law exprefly declares, " If
" thy *Brother*, (*that dwelleth*) by thee, be
" waxen poor, and *be fold unto thee*; *thou
" fhalt not* compel him to ferve as a *bond
" fervant: (but)* as an *hired fervant*;
" and

(9) Yet our inconfiderate Weft-Indian and American
Planters make no fcruple even of *branding* their poor
Negro-fervants with a *hot iron*, to mark them *for per-petual Bondmen, againft their will*, though they are cer-tainly their *Brethren* in the eyes of God. But God
hath declared, *exprefsly*, concerning the crimes of thefe
men, *who enflave the poor*, —— " SURELY, *I will ne-
" ver forget any of their works! Shall not the land trem-
" ble for this!*" &c,! &c.! &c.! Amos, viii. 7. 8.
See alfo the whole context, from the 4th verfe.

" and as a *fojourner* he fhall be with
" thee ; *(and)* fhall ferve thee unto the
" year of jubilee: and *(then)* fhall he
" depart from thee, *(both)* he *and his chil-*
" *dren* with him ;" *&c.* (and the reafon
of this command immediately follows ;)
" for they are *my fervants,*" (faid the
Lord,) " which I brought forth out of
" the land of Egypt:" (i. e. *which God
himfelf delivered, from Slavery:)* " they
" *fhall not be fold as Bond-men:* thou fhalt
" not rule over him with rigour, but
" *fhalt fear thy God.*" Levit. xxv. 39
to 43. And again, in the 55th verfe,
" For *unto me*" (faid the Lord) " the
" children of *Ifrael are fervants* ; *they are*
" *my fervants,* whom I brought out of
" the land of Egypt: *I am the Lord*
" *your God.*"

Thus it appears that the *involuntary
fervitude* of *brethren* is entirely inconfiftent with the Jewifh Law ; which, therefore,

fore, is so far from *justifying* the *African Merchant*, that it absolutely *condemns* him. But he is still more mistaken, when he insinuates that Slavery is not inconsistent with the Gospel. " Jesus Christ, the " Saviour of mankind and Founder of " our religion," (says he,) " left the " moral laws and civil rights of mankind " upon their old foundations: his king- " dom was not of this world, nor did he " interfere with national laws: *he did* " *not repeal that of slaves*, nor assert an " universal freedom, except from sin: " with him bond and free were accepted, " if they behaved *righteously*." *&c.* p. 9.

But how can a man be said to " behave " *righteously*," who sells his *brethren*, or holds them in Slavery *against their will?* For, though, with Christ, " *bond* and *free* " are accepted," yet it behoves *the African Merchant* very diligently to examine, whether he is not likely to forfeit his *own* *acceptance*,

*acceptance,* if he does not moſt heartily repent of having *enſlaved his brethren,* and of having encouraged others to the ſame *uncharitable practices,* by miſinterpreting the holy Scriptures.

Under the Goſpel Diſpenſation, *all mankind* are to be eſteemed *our brethren.* Chriſt commanded his diſciples to go and teach (or make diſciples of) *all nations,* " παντα τα εθνη." Matth. xxviii. 19. So that *men of all nations* (who, indeed, were *brethren* before, by *natural* deſcent from *one common father*) are now, undoubtedly, capable of being doubly related to us, by a *farther* tie of *of brotherhood,* which the law of Moſes ſeemed to deny them, and of which the peculiar people of God (jealous of their own adoption) once thought them incapable; I mean, the ineſtimable privilege of becoming ſons, alſo, to *one almighty Father, by adoption,* as well as the Jews, and, conſequently, of

being

being *our brethren*, through Chrift, by a
*fpiritual*, as well as a *natural*, relation-
fhip.

The promifes of God, likewife, in every other part of the New Teftament,
are made to *all mankind in general, without exception*; fo that a Negro, as well as
any other man, is capable of becoming
" *an adopted fon of God*;" an " *heir of God*
" *through Chrift*" (10); a " *temple of the*
" *Holy-Ghoft*" (11); " *an heir* (12) *of*
D 2 " *falva-*

(10)—" that we might receive the *adoption of* Sons."
(faid the apoftle, to the Galatians:) " And, becaufe
" *ye are Sons*, God-hath fent forth the fpirit of *his Son*
" into your hearts, crying *Abba, Father :* wherefore
" thou art *no more a fervant, but a Son* ; and, *if a Son,*
" then AN HEIR OF GOD THROUGH CHRIST."
Galat. iv. 5. 6. and 7.

(11) " Know ye not that ye are the Temple of
" God, and that the Spirit of God dwelleth in you ?
" If any man defile the temple of God, him fhall God
" deftroy ; for the *Temple* of God *is holy*, which *Tem-
" ple ye are.*" 1 Corinth. iii. 16. 17. See alfo chap.
vi. 19. 20.

(12) " That the Gentiles fhould be *fellow-heirs,*
" and of the fame body, and partakers of his promife
" in Chrift *by the Gofpel.*" Ephef. iii. 6.

" *falvation*;" a partaker of *the divine nature* (13); " a *joint-heir with Chrift* (14);
and capable, alfo, of being joined to that
glorious company of Saints, who fhall one
day " *come with him to judge the world*;"
for " the *Saints fhall judge the world*."
1 Cor. vi. 2. 3. — And, therefore, how
can any man, who calls himfelf a Chriftian, prefume to retain, as a mere chattel,
or *private property*, his fellow man and
*brother*, who is equally capable with
himfelf of attaining the high dignities
abovementioned! Let Slaveholders be
mindful of the approaching confumma-
tion of all earthly things, when, perhaps,
they will fee thoufands of thofe men,
who were formerly efteemed mere *chattels*

(13) —" through the knowledge of him that hath
" called us to *glory* and *virtue*: whereby are given unto
" us exceeding great and precious promifes ; that by
" thefe ye might *be partakers* of the *divine nature*."
*&c.* 2 Pet. i. 3 and 4.

(14) " If children, then heirs ; heirs of God and
" joint-heirs with Chrift :" *&c.* Rom. viii. 17

*tels* and *private property*, coming (15) in
the clouds (16), with their heavenly
Mafter, to judge tyrants and oppreffors,
and to call them to account for their want
of *brotherly love !*

The Ethiopians, or Negroes, received
the Chriftian faith *much fooner* than the
Europeans themfelves: their *early* converfion was foretold by the Pfalmift:
(Pfalm

(15) — " at the *coming* of our Lord Jesus Christ
" *with all his Saints.*" 1 Theff. iii. 13.
— " And Enoch alfo, the feventh from Adam, pro-
" phefied of thefe, faying, Behold, the Lord *cometh,*
" with *ten thoufands of his faints, to execute judgement upon*
" *all,* and to convince all that are ungodly among them,
" of all their ungodly deeds," *&c.* Jude, xiv. 15.

(16) — " and then fhall all the tribes of the earth
" mourn, and they fhall fee the Son of man coming in
" the clouds of heaven, with power and great glory."
Matt. xxiv. 30.
" Behold, he cometh with clouds, and every eye
" fhall fee him : and they alfo *which pierced him :*"
Rev. i. 7. And thofe men, alfo, who have worn out
their brethren in flavery, may furely be ranked with the
wretches that *pierced their Lord.* " — in as much as ye
" have done it *unto one of the leaft of thefe my brethren,*"
(faid our Lord,) " *ye have done it unto me.*" Matt. xxv.
40. (See the conclufion of my Tract on the Law of
Liberty.)

(Pfalm lxviii. 31.) " Princes fhall come
" out of Egypt," (or from *Mizraim)* ;
" and Ethiopia" (17) (or *Cufh*) " *fhall*
" *foon ftretch out her hands unto God.*"
And, accordingly, we find the *Ethiopian*
Eunuch (18) particularly mentioned in
Scripture among the firft converts to
Chriftianity:

(17) Wherever we find mention made, in the Old
Teftament, of *Ethiopians,* (though a general name for
Negroes,) yet we fhall find them exprefled, in the
Hebrew, by the name of the eldeft branch of Ham, *viz.*
*Chus,* כוש. However, we muft remember, that all
Ethiopians are not *Cufhites.* The prodigious army, of a
million of *Ethiopians,* which was overthrown by Afa,
were not all defcendants of *Chus,* though mentioned
under the general name of כושים *Chufim,* in 2 Chron.
chap. xiv. for we read, in the 16th chap. 8th verfe,
that part of that vaft body were *Lubims.* " Were not
" the *Ethiopians* and *Lubims*" (הכושים והלובים)
" a huge hoft?" faid the prophet Hanani, when he
reminded Afa of his former fuccefs. The *Lubims,* or
*Libyans,* were a great nation, from whom the internal
part of Africa receives its name of *Libya,* and were defcended from Mizraim, the fecond fon of Ham, who
was alfo the father of the Egyptians.

(18) Who might juftly be efteemed *a Prince* of that
country, being Δυνασης, *a Lord,* or one " *of great autho-*
" *rity* under Candace, Queen of the Ethiopians, *who*
" *had the charge of all her Treafure,*" &c.

Chriftianity: and that extraordinary exertion of the HOLY SPIRIT, in favour of
the eunuch, was, perhaps, the foundation
of the ancient Church of Habaffinia (19), which, notwithftanding
all worldly difadvantages, remains in
fome degree of *purity* to this day,
as a lafting monument of *Chriftianity
among the fons of Ham*, even in the moft
remote and inacceffible part of Africa!(20)

Certain

(19) The learned Lutholf was of a different opinion,
and fuppofed that the Habaffinians were not converted
till the time of Conftantine the Great, about the year
330; and, though it is not clear whether this latter period was the time of their firft converfion or not, yet,
certain it is, that, ever fince that time, they have
maintained the Chriftian faith, and the facramental in-
ftitutions of Chrift, without yielding to the adultera-
tions of the church of Rome, though the fame were
preffed upon them with all the authority that one of their
own Emperors could exert! Lutholf has given a full
and clear account (printed in 1691) of thefe Chriftian
Negroes and their church, which feems to be referved,
by the providence of God, as a *Witnefs* of the purity
of his holy Religion : a *Witnefs* not lefs remarkable
than the church of the Vaudois!

(20) They ftill retain Water-Baptifm and the holy
Communion in *both kinds*, and drove out the Portuguefe

Jefuits

" Certain it is, (fay the learned Affembly
" of Divines,) that Ethiopia, according
" to this unqueftionable prophecy,"
(Pfalms, lxviii. 31.) " was one of the
" firft kingdoms that was converted to
" the Chriftian faith ; the occafion and
" means whereof we read of Acts viii.
" 27, 28." &c.

The progrefs of the truth muft have
been very rapid in Africa, becaufe we
read of a council of African and Numi-
dian Bifhops, held at Carthage, fo early
as the year of Chrift 215 (21) ; (though
our Anglo-Saxon anceftors remained in
the groffeft pagan darknefs near 400 years
afterwards;) and, in the year 240, a
council of 99 Bifhops was affembled at
Lambefa,

Jefuits for attempting, by force, to pervert and corrupt
thefe *primitive rites.*

(21) " Carthaginenfe 1. circa annum ccxv. fub A-
" grippino, epifcopo Carthaginenfi, ab *Africæ* et *Nu-*
" *midiæ* epifcopis, *de rebaptizandis hæreticis habitum.*"
Dr. Cave's Hift. Literaria, p. 99.

Lambefa, an *inland city of Africa*, on
the confines of Biledulgerid, againſt
Privatus Biſhop of Lambefa on a charge
of Herefie. (22)  The fourth Council
of Carthage in the year 253 was held
by 66 Biſhops, concerning the Baptiſm
of Infants. (23)  And in the eighth
Council at that place (anno 256) befides (24) Prieſts, Deacons and Laymen,
there were prefent 87 Biſhops.  In
another council of Carthage, about the
year 308, no lefs than 270 Biſhops of
the Sect of the Donatiſts (25) were pre-
.fent; and in the year 394, at Baga, an
inland City of Africa, 310 (26) Biſhops
were collected together, though the
E                fame

____

(22) Dr. Cave's Hiſt. Literaria, p. 99.    (23) Ibid.

(24) " Prefentes erant preter Prefbyteros, Diaconos
maximamque plebis partem, Epifcopi lxxxvii, &c.  See
Dr. Cave's Hiſt. Literaria, p. 100.  alfo Bohun's Geog.
Dict. p. 219, under the word *Lambefa*.

(25) Dr. Cave's Hiſt. Lit. p. 222.    (26) Ibid. p. 234.

fame was long before the converfion of the Englifh and Dutch, the great traders in *African flaves* ; and though the Africans have, fince, lamentably fallen back into grofs ignorance, yet we muft not, on that account, look upon them in the fame light that the Jews did upon " *the children of the ftrangers*," whom they were permitted to hold in flavery (Levit. xxv. 45.) becaufe we cannot do fo without becoming *ftrangers* ourfelves to *Chriftianity* ; and haftening *our own apoftacy*, which feems already too near at hand. (27) We may la-ment

(27) The alarming increafe of infidelity, and the open declarations of Deifts, Arians, Socinians, and others, who deny the Divinity of Chrift, and of the Holy Ghoft, are lamentable proofs of the growing apoftacy! The African Church fell away by degrees in the fame manner, till it was totally loft in the moft barbarous ignorance, (except in Habeffinia) for even thofe Africans who are free from idolatry, and profefs to worfhip *the true God*, are, neverthelefs, enfnared and enflaved

ment the fallen ſtate of our unhappy
brethren, but we have *no commiſſion
under*

enſlaved in the groſs errors of *Mahometaniſm*, to which
a neglect of the neceſſary Faith in the *Divinity of Chriſt*,
and of the *Holy Ghoſt*, has an apparent tendency !
We have likewiſe a remarkable inſtance of *infidelity*, or
at leaſt of a total neglect of Scripture authority and re-
velation, in the attempt of two late writers to prove
that Negroes are " *an inferior ſpecies of men :*" but the
learned Dr. *Beattie*, in his *Eſſay on Truth*, has fully
refuted the inſinuations of Mr. *Hume*, the firſt broacher
of that uncharitable doctrine, as well as Ariſtotle's fu-
tile attempt to juſtify *ſlavery ;* ſo that Mr. *Eſtwick's*
ſubſequent attempt, which was prompted only by the
authority of Mr. *Hume*, needs no further confutation.
" That I may not be thought a blind admirer of anti-
" quity, (ſays Dr. Beattie) I would here crave the read-
" er's indulgence for one ſhort digreſſion more, in order
" to put him in mind of an important error in morals,
" inferred from partial and inaccurate experience, by
" no leſs a perſon than Ariſtotle himſelf. He ar-
" gues, ' That men of little genius, and great bodily
" *ſtrength, are by nature deſtined to ſerve*, and thoſe of
" *better capacity to command*; and that the natives of
" Greece, and of ſome other countries, being natu-
" rally ſuperior in genius, have *a natural right to* em-
" pire ;

*under the Gospel* to punish them for it,
as the Israelites had to punish the
*Heathens*

" pire; and that the rest of mankind, being *naturally*
" *stupid,* are destined to *labour and slavery,*' (De Republ.
" lib. 1. cap. 5, 6 ) This reasoning is now, alas! of
" little advantage *to Aristotle's countrymen, who have*
" *for many ages been doomed to that slavery,* which, *in*
" *his* judgment, *nature had destined them to impose on*
" *others*; and many nations whom he would have con-
" signed *to everlasting stupidity,* have shown themselves
" *equal* in genius to the most *exalted of human kind.* It
" would have been more worthy of Aristotle, to have
" inferred man's natural and universal right to liberty,
" from that natural and universal passion with which
" men desire it. He wanted, perhaps, to *devise some*
" *excuse for servitude*; a practice which, to *their eternal*
" *reproach,* both Greeks and Romans tolerated even
" in the days of their glory.
" Mr. *Hume* argues nearly in the same manner in
" regard to the superiority of white men over black. ' I
" am apt to suspect,' says he, ' the negroes, and in
" general all the other species of men, (for there are
" four or five different kinds) to be naturally inferior
" to the whites. There *never was* a civilized nation
" of any other complexion than white, *nor even any in-*
" *dividual* eminent either in action or speculation. *No*
" ingenious

*Heathens* that were condemned in the law! Our endeavour fhould be rather

to

" ingenious manufactures among them, *no* arts, *no* fci-
" ences.—There are negro flaves difperfed all over
" Europe, of which *none* ever difcovered any fymptoms
" of ingenuity.' (Hume's Effay on National Charac-
" ters.)—Thefe affertions are ftrong ; but I know not
" whether they have any thing elfe to recommend
" them. For, firft, though true, they would *not prove*
" *the point in queftion,* except it were alfo proved, that
" the Africans and Americans, even though arts and
" fciences were introduced among them, would ftill re-
" main unfufceptible of cultivation. The *inhabitants*
" *of Great Britain and France were as favage two thou-*
" *fand years ago,* as thofe *of Africa and America are at*
" *this day.* To civilize a nation, is a work which it
" requires long time to accomplifh. And one may as
" *well fay of an infant, that he can never become a man,*
" *as of a nation now barbarous, that it never can be civi-*
" *lized.* Secondly, of the facts here afferted, *no man*
" *could have fufficient evidence, except from a perfonal ac-*
" *quaintance with all the negroes that now are, or ever*
" *were, on the face of the earth.* Thofe people write
" no hiftories ; and all the reports of all the travellers
" that ever vifited them, will not amount to any thing
" like a proof of what is here affirmed- BUT, THIRD-

" LY,

to reſtore the *Heathens* to their loſt
privileges, than to harden them in
their

" LY, WE KNOW THAT THESE ASSERTIONS ARE NOT
" TRUE. The empires of Peru and Mexico could not
" have been governed, nor the metropolis of the latter
" built after ſo ſingular a manner, in the middle of a
" lake, *without men eminent both for action and ſpecula-*
" *tion.* Every body has heard of the magnificence,
" good government, and ingenuity, of the ancient Pe-
" ruvians. *The Africans and Americans are known to*
" *have many ingenious manufactures and arts among them,*
" *which even Europeans* would find it no eaſy matter
" *to imitate.* Sciences indeed they have none, becauſe
" they have no letters ; but in oratory, ſome of them,
" particularly the Indians *of the Five Nations,* are ſaid
" to be greatly our ſuperiors. It will be readily allow-
" ed, that the condition of a ſlave is not favourable to
" genius of any kind; and yet, *the negro ſlaves diſper-*
" *ſed over Europe,* have *often diſcovered ſymptoms of inge-*
" *nuity, notwithſtanding their unhappy circumſtances.*
" They *become excellent handicraftſmen, and practical*
" *muſicians,* and indeed learn every thing their maſters
" are at pains to teach them, perfidy and debauchery
" not excepted. That a negro ſlave, who can neither
" read nor write, nor ſpeak any European language,
" who is not permitted to do any thing but what his
" maſter'

their prejudices by tolerating amongſt
us a greater degree of *deſpotiſm* and *oppreſſion*

" maſter commands, and who has not a ſingle friend
" on earth, but is univerſally conſidered and treated as
" if he were of a ſpecies inferior to the human ;—that
" ſuch a creature ſhould ſo diſtinſtuiſh himſelf among
" Europeans, as to be talked of through the world for
" a man of genius, is ſurely no reaſonable expectation.
" To ſuppoſe him of an inferior ſpecies, becauſe he does
" not thus diſtinguiſh himſelf, is juſt as rational, as to
" ſuppoſe any private European of an inferior ſpecies,
" becauſe he has not raiſed himſelf to the condition of
" royalty.

" Had the Europeans been deſtitute of the arts of
" writing, and working in iron, they might have re-
" mained to this day as barbarous as the natives of
" Africa and America. Nor is the invention of theſe
" arts to be aſcribed to our ſuperior capacity. The ge-
" nius of the inventor is not always to be eſtimated ac-
" cording to the importance of the invention. Gun-
" powder, and the mariner's compaſs, have produced
" wonderful revolutions in human affairs, and yet were
" accidental diſcoveries. Such, probably, were the
" firſt eſſays in writing, and working in iron. Suppoſe
" them the effects of contrivance ; they were at leaſt
" contrived by a few individuals ; and if they required
" a ſu-

*preſſion* than was *ever permitted among the Jews,* or even among the ancient
Heathens!

" a ſuperiority of underſtanding, or of ſpecies in the in-
" ventors, thoſe inventors, and their deſcendents, are
" the only perſons who can lay claim to the honour of
" that ſuperiority.

" That every practice and ſentiment is barbarous
" which is not according to the uſages of modern Eu-
" rope, ſeems to be a fundamental maxim with many
" of our critics and philoſophers. Their remarks often
" put us in mind of the fable of the man and the lion.
" If negroes and Indians were diſpoſed to recriminate ;
" if a Lucian or a Voltaire from the coaſt of Guinea,
" or from *the Five Nations,* were to pay us a viſit ;
" what a picture of European manners might he preſent
" to his countrymen at his return ! Nor would carica-
" tura, or exaggeration, be neceſſary to render it hi-
" deous. *A plain hiſtorical account of ſome of our moſt*
" *faſhionable duelliſts, gamblers, and adulterers,* (to name
" no more) would exhibit *ſpecimens of brutiſh barbarity*
" *and ſottiſh infatuation,* ſuch as might vie with any
" that ever appeared in Kamſchatka, California, or the
" land of Hottentots.

" *It is eaſy to ſee with what views ſome modern au-*
" *thors throw out theſe hints to prove the natural inferiori-*
" *ty* of negroes. But let every friend to *humanity* pray,
" *that*

*Heathens!* for in one of our own *anti-christian* colonies, even the *murder* of a negro flave, when under *private* punifhment, *is tolerated* (fee the 329th act of Barbadoes) ; and by the fame diabolical act of affembly a man may " of *wantonnefs*, or of *bloody minded-* " *nefs*, or *cruel intention*" (it is exprefsly faid) " *wilfully kill* a negro, or *other flave of his own*," without any other penalty for it than a trifling fine of

F                          £15

" *that they may be difappointed.* Britons are famous for " generofity ; a virtue in which it is eafy for them to " excel both the Romans and the Greeks. *Let it never* " *be faid, that flavery* is countenanced by the bravest " and most generous people on earth ; by a people who " are animated with that heroic paffion, the love of " liberty, beyond all nations ancient or modern ; and " the fame of whofe toilfome, but unwearied, perfe- " verance, *in vindicating, at the expence of life and* " *fortune, the facred rights of mankind, will ftrike terror* " *into the hearts of fycophants and tyrants,* and excite " the admiration and gratitude of all good men, to " the lateft pofterity." Effay on Truth, P. 458, 459, 460, 461, 462, 463 and 464.

£15 fterling. (See remarks on this act
in my tract againft flavery in England,
(28) p. 66 and 67.) Many inftances
of Weft-India cruelty have fallen even
within my own knowledge, and I have
certain proofs of no lefs than three
married women being violentl torn
away from their lawful hufbands, (29)
even in London, by the order of their
pretenaed proprietors! Another remarkable inftance of tyranny, which
came

(28) A reprefentation of the injuftice and dangerous tend ncy of tolerating flavery in England. London, 1769.

(29) Nothing can be more prefumptuoufly contrary
to the laws of God, than thefe unnatural outrages!
" Have ye not read" (faid Chrift himfelf) " that he
" which made (them) at the beginning, made them
" male and female? and faid, for this caufe fhall a
" man leave father and mother, and fhall cleave to
" his wife: and they twain fhall be *one flefh*. Wherefore
" they are *no more twain*, but *one flefh*. What, there-
" fore, GOD HATH JOINED TOGETHER LET NO MAN
" PUT ASUNDER." Matth. xix. 4, 5 and 6.

came within my own *knowledge,* was
the advertizing a reward (in the Gazetteer
of the 1st June, 1772) for apprehend-
ing " *an East-India black boy about* 14
" *years of age, named Bob or Pompey :*"
he was further distinguished in the
advertizement by having " *round his*
" *neck a brass collar,* with a direction
" upon it to a house in Charlotte-street,
" Bloomsbury-square." Thus the *black
Indian Pompey* was manifestly treated
with as little ceremony as a *black name-
sake of the dog kind* could be. I inquired
after the author of this unlawful and
shameful advertizement ; and found,
that he was a merchant even in the
heart of the city of London, who shall
be nameless ; for I do not want to
expose *individuals,* but only their *crimes.*
Now if masters are capable of such
monstrous OPPRESSION, *even here in
England,* where their brutality renders
them

them liable to fevere penalties, how can
we reafonably reject the accounts of
TYRANNY *in America*, howfoever horrid and inhuman, where the abominable
plantation laws will permit a capricious
or paffionate mafter, with impunity, to
deprive his wretched flave even of life.

I am frequently told, neverthelefs, by
interefted perfons from the Weft-Indies,
how well the flaves are ufed; and that
they are much happier than *our own
poor at home.* But though I am willing
to believe that *fome few* worthy Weft-
Indians treat their flaves with humanity, yet it is, certainly, far from being
*the general cafe*; and the mifery of our
*own poor* will not be any excufe for *the
oppreffion of the poor* elfewhere! When
any of our own countrymen *at home*
are miferably *poor*, it is not always clear
whether themfelves, or others, are to
be

be blamed : all we can know for certain is, that it is the indifpenfable duty
of *every man* to *relieve them* according
to his ability ; and that the neglecting
an opportunity of doing fo, is as great
an offence before God as if we had
denied affiftance to *Chrift himfelf* in the
fame wretched condition ; for fo it is
exprefsly laid down in Scripture, (30)
through

(30) " Then fhall the king fay unto them on his right
" hand,—Come, ye bleffed of my Father, inherit the
" kingdom prepared for you from the foundation of the
" world ; For I was an hungred, and ye gave me meat :
" I was thirfty, and ye gave me drink : I was a *ftranger*,
" and ye took me in : naked, and ye clothed me : I was
" fick, and ye vifited me : I was in prifon, and ye came
" unto me. Then fhall the righteous anfwer him, faying,
" Lord, when faw we thee an hungred, and fed (*thee*)?
" or thirfty, and gave (*thee*) drink ? When faw we thee
" a *ftranger*, and took (*thee*) in, or naked, and clothed
" (*thee*) ? Or when faw we thee fick, or in prifon, and
" came unto thee ? And the king fhall anfwer, and
" fay unto them, Verily I fay unto you, inafmuch as ye
" have done (*it*) unto one of the leaft of thefe my bre-
" thren,

through the mercy of God towards *the poor :* but it is obvious to whom the mifery of *a flave* is to be attributed : for *the guilty poffeffor* will certainly be anfwerable to God for it ; and every man, who endeavours to palliate and fcreen fuch *oppreffion*, is undoubtedly *a partaker of the guilt*. The *flave-holder* deceives himfelf if hé thinks he can really *be a* CHRISTIAN, *and yet hold*

" thren, ye have done (*it*) unto me ! Then fhall he fay
" alfo unto them on the left hand, Depart from me, *ye*
" *curfed into everlafting fire*, prepared for the devil and
" his angels : For I was an hungred, and ye gave me no
" meat ; I was thirfty, and ye gave me no drink : I was
" a *ftranger*, and ye took me not in : naked, and ye
" clothed me not : fick, and in prifon, and ye vifited
" me not. Then fhall they alfo anfwer him, faying,
" Lord, when faw we thee an hungred, or a thirft, or a
" *ftranger*, or naked, or fick, or in prifon, and did not
" minifter unto thee ? Then fhall he anfwer them, fay-
" ing, Verily I fay unto you, *inafmuch as ye did* (*it*) *not*
" *to one of the leaft of thefe, ye did* (*it*) *not to me*. And
" thefe fhall go away into *everlafting punifhment :* but the
" righteous into *life eternal*." Matth. xxv. 34—46.

*hold such property.* Can he be said *to love his neighbour as himself?* (31) Does he behave to others as he would they should to him? " Ye have heard " that it hath been said, *Thou shalt* " *love thy neighbour,* and hate thine " enemy ; *but I say unto you* (said our " Lord himself) *love your enemies,* &c. " That ye may be the children of your " Father which is in Heaven : for he " maketh his sun to rise *on the evil,* and " on the good, and sendeth rain *on the* " *just and on the unjust;*" (Matth. v. 44, 45) so that *Heathens* are by no means excluded from the benevolence *of Christians.*

Thus Christ has enlarged the antient Jewish doctrine of *loving our neighbours*

*as*

---

(31) I have examined this point more at large in a tract on " *The Law of Liberty,*" which is intended also for publication.

*as ourselves*; and has also taught us, by the parable of the good Samaritan, that *all mankind*, even our *professed enemies* (such as were the Samaritans to the Jews) must necessarily be esteemed our *neighbours* whenever they stand in need of our charitable assistance; so that the *same benevolence* which was due from the *Jew to his brethren of the house of Israel* is indispensably due, *under the Gospel*, to OUR BRETHREN OF THE UNIVERSE, howsoever opposite in religious or political opinions; for this is the apparent intention of the parable.

No nation therefore whatever, can now be lawfully excluded as *strangers*, according to that uncharitable sense of the word *stranger*, in which the Jews were apt to distinguish all other nations from themselves; and, since *all men* are now to be esteemed " *brethren and neighbours*"

" *neighbours*" under the Gofpel, none of
the Levitical laws relating to the bondage of *ftrangers* are in the leaft applicable to juftify flavery *among Chriftians*;
though the fame laws bind *Chriftians* as
well as *Jews* with refpect to all the lef-
fons of *benevolence* to *ftrangers,* which
are every where interfperfed therein ; becaufe thefe are *moral doctrines* which
never change, for they perfectly corre-
fpond with " *the everlafting Gofpel* "(Rev.
xiv. 6.) As for inftance, " Thou fhalt *not*
" *opprefs a Stranger,* for ye know the heart
" of a *Stranger,* feeing ye were *ftrangers*
" in the land of Egypt." Exod. xxiii. 9.
This is an appeal to the *feelings* and experience of the Jews who had themfelves endured a *heavy bondage,* fo that
it clearly correfponds with the " *royal*
*law* " or " *law of liberty* " in the Gofpel.
" *Thou*

" *Thou shalt love thy neighbour as thyself.*"
Gal. v. 14. or as our Lord himself has
more fully expressed it. " *All things*
" *whatsoever ye would that men should*
" *do to you, do ye even so to them: for*
" THIS IS THE LAW AND THE PRO-
" PHETS. " Matth. vii. 12.


Again, "If a *stranger* sojourn with thee
" in your land, ye shall not vex or (oppress
" him) (*but*) the *stranger* that dwelleth
" with you, shall be unto you as one born
" among you, and thou SHALT LOVE
" HIM " (viz. *the stranger*)" AS THYSELF;
" for *ye were* STRANGERS in the land of
" Egypt. *I am the Lord your God.*" (Levit.
xix. 33.) Let every slaveholder consider
the importance of this command and
the unchangeable dignity of him who gave
it. "I AM THE LORD YOUR GOD" !--for
the

" the LORD YOUR GOD is *God* of *Gods*,
" and *Lord* of *Lords*, a *great* God, a *migh-*
" *ty*, and a *terrible*, which regardeth not
" perfons" (not the Mafters more than
any flaves) " nor taketh reward. He doth
" execute the judgment of the fatherlefs
" and widow, and LOVETH THE STRAN-
" GER, in giving him food and raiment.
" LOVE YE *therefore the ftranger* : for ye
" were *ftrangers* in the land of Egypt."
Deut. x. 17, 18, 19. And how can a
man be faid to *love* the *ftranger*, and
much lefs to *love him as himfelf* (fee the
exprefs command above) who prefumes
to vex and opprefs him with a perpetual involuntary bondage? Is this
obedience to tnat great rule of the Gofpel, which Chrift has given us as the
*fum of the law and the prophets?* Would
the American flaveholders relifh that contemptuous and cruel ufage with which
they opprefs their poor negroes ; and
that

that the *African* (31) *ſtrangers* ſhould do
even ſo to themſelves without the leaſt
perſonal provocation or fault on their part,
viz.

(31) The preſent deplorable ſtate of the *African
ſtrangers in general,* ought to warn us of ſimilar judgments againſt the inhabitants of theſe kingdoms ! My
own Grandfather *near a century ago* (wanting only
three years, viz in · 1679) warned our great national
counſel of God's vengeance *by this very example,*

" *That* AFRICA (ſays he) which is not now more
" fruitful of monſters, than it was once of excellent-
" ly wiſe and learned men ; that AFRICA which for-
" merly afforded us our Clemens, our Origen, our Ter-
" tullian, our Cyprian, our Auguſtine, and many other
" extraordinary lights in the church of God ; that FA-
" MOUS AFRICA, *in whoſe ſoil Chriſtianity did thrive*
" *ſo prodigiouſly, and could boaſt of ſo many flouriſhing*
" *churches, alas is now a wilderneſs. The wild boars*
" *have broken into the vineyard and eaten it up, and it*
" *brings forth nothing but briars and thorns :* to uſe the
" words of the prophet. And *who knows but* GOD *may*
" *ſuddenly make* THIS CHURCH AND NATION, THIS OUR
" ENGLAND, which, Jeſhurun like, is *waxed fat and*
" *grown proud,* and *has kicked againſt God,* SUCH
" ANOTHER EXAMPLE OF THE VENGEANCE OF THIS
" KIND ? "—See arch bp. Sharp's Sermons ſecond vol.
1ſt Serm. which was preached before the houſe of
Commons, April 11. 1679. (Page 22)

viz. to be branded with a hot iron, in order to be known and ranked as the cattle and private property of their oppreffors ? Like the cattle alfo to be ignominoufly compelled by the whip of a driver to labour hard " *without wages*" or recompence ? If the African merchants and American flaveholders can demonftrate that they would not think themfelves injured by fuch treatment from others, they may perhaps be free from the horrid guilt of *unchriftian oppreffion* and *uncharitable-nefs*, which muft otherwife inevitably be imputed to them, becaufe their actions will not bear the teft of that excellent rule of the Gofpel abovementioned, which Chrift has laid down as the meafure of our actions—" *All things whatfoever* " *ye would that men fhould do to you, do ye* " *even fo to them, for this is the law and the* " *prophets*." .Math vii. 12. I muft therefore

fore once more repeat, what I have before advanced, that the permiſſion formerly granted to the Jews of holding
*heathens and ſtrangers* in ſlavery is virtually repealed, or rather ſuperſeded by
the Goſpel, notwithſtanding the contrary
aſſertion of the African merchant, that
Chriſt " *did not repeal that of ſlaves*"

The *African merchant* has alſo re-
publiſhed the letters of his fellow advocate *Mercator*, who profeſſes in the
ſame manner to draw his authority
"*from Sacred hiſtory*"--" To the ſedate,
" to the reaſonable, to the Chriſtian read-
" ers (ſays he) I ſhall more fully ſet forth
" the *lawfulneſs of the ſlave trade* from the
" expreſs allowance of it in Holy writ :
(ibid appendix : B. iv,) but the very firſt
inſinuation concerning the origin of ſlavery
which follows this ſpecious addreſs to the
ſedate &c. is founded on TWO *falſe aſſertions*
*even*

*even in* ONE fentence, and therefore I cannot efteem him worthy of any further
notice than that of pointing out thefe
proofs of his little regard to truth ; " As
" to its origin (fays he) it may poffibly be
" derived from that fentence exprefled
" againft Canaan (*from whom the Africans,*
" fays he, *are defcended*) by his father No-
" ah at the hour of his death. (32) Curfed
" be Canaan, a fervant of fervants fhall he be
" to his brethren." But though the author
afterwards allows that " both the origin
" of flavery and the colour of the Africans
" are incapable of *pofitive proof,*" yet the
futility of his infinuation concerning the
*defcent*

---

(32) It was not " *at the honr of his death,*" but " *when he*
" *awoke from his wine* " after he had tafted too freely the
fruits of the vineyard, which he planted when he began
to be a hufbandman ; the time therefore was probably
very foon after the flood, and not *at the hour of his
death,* as mifreprefented by Mercator, for he lived after
the flood 350 years, Genefis ix. 28.

*defcent of the Africans* is not like the
other two circumftances " incapable of
" pofitive proof." For the *Africans* are
not *defcended from Canaan*, if we except the Carthaginians (a colony from
the fea coaft of *the land of Canaan*) who
were a free people, and at one time ri-
valled, even the Roman common wealth,
in power. The *Africans* are principally
defcended from the three other fons of
*Ham*, viz. *Cufh*, *Mifraim*, and *Phut* ; and
to prove this more at large I have fubjoined to this tract a letter which I received (in anfwer to mine on the fame
fubject) from a learned gentleman who
has moft carefully ftudied the antiquities
of the line of *Ham* : the infinuation therefore concerning the "*fentence expreffed
" againft Canaan*" can by no means juftify
the *African flave trade*, fo that *Mercator*
feems indeed to write like a *mere trader*,
for the fake of his iniquitous *Traffic*,

more

[ 49 ]

more than for the fake of *truth*, notwithftanding his profeffions of regard
for the Holy Scriptures.

If we carefully examine the Scriptures we fhall find, that flavery and oppreffion were ever abominable in the
fight of God; for though the Jews were
permitted by the law of Mofes (on account of the *hardnefs of their hearts*) to
keep flaves, as I have remarked in my
anfwer to the *Reverend Mr. Thompfon*
on this fubject (which is fubjoined,) yet
there was no inherent right of fervice
to be implied from this permiffion, becaufe whenever the flave could efcape
he was efteemed *free*; and it was *abfolutely unlawful* for any man (who believed the word of God) *to deliver him
up again to his mafter* (fee Deut.
xxiii. 15, 16.) whereas in our colonies, (which in acts of OPPRESSION
may

may too juftly be efteemed *antichriftian*)
the flave who *runs away* is " *deemed*
" *rebellious,*" and a reward of £ 50 is
offered to thofe who SHALL KILL *or*
" *bring in alive any rebellious flave*" (fee
the 66th act of the laws of Jamaica.) By
an act of Virginia (4 Ann, ch. 49 § 37
P. 227.) after proclamation is iffued
againft flaves that " *run away and lie*
" *out*" it is " LAWFUL for *any perfon*
" *whatfoever to* KILL a*nd* DESTROY
" SUCH SLAVES *by fuch ways and means*
" *as he, fhe, or they* SHALL THINK
" FIT, *without accufation or impeach-*
" *ment of any crime for the fame,*" &c.
See the remarks on thefe, and fuch
other *diabolical acts* of plantation affemblies in pages 63 to 73, of my reprefentation of the injuftice and dangerous tendency of tolerating flavery in
England. Printed in 1769.

By another act of Virginia, ( 12
Geo.

Geo. 1. chap. 4, § 8. P 368.) if a poor
fellow is taken up as *a runaway* and
committed to prifon, the goaler may
let him out to hire, in order to pay the
fees, even though he is not claimed,
" *and his mafter or owner* (fays the act)
" *cannot be known* ;" and in a following
claufe the goaler is ordered to " *caufe a*
" *ftrong* IRON COLLAR TO BE PUT ON
" THE NECK *of fuch negroe or runaway,*
" *with the letters* (P. G.) *ftamped thereon* ;"
a moft abominable affront to human nature ! our fpiritual enemy muft have
had a notorious influence with the
plantation law makers to procure an act
fo contradictory to the laws of God, (33)
and

(33) Even white fervants, *Englifh, Scotch, and
Irifh* are frequently taken up by the *fheriff* and *goalers*
without any warrant, or previous judgment whatever, merely " on *fufpicion of being fervants* ;" and
they are then *advertifed* to be *delivered up* to their tyrannical

and in particular to that (laſt cited)
from Deutrenomy, viz. " Thou ſhalt
" not

rannical maſters ; but though there is great injuſtice
and oppreſſion in taking up theſe poor people merely
" on ſuſpicion *of being ſervants,*" yet it does not appear
to be ſo flagrant a breach of God's command beforementioned, as the delivering up the poor runaway *negroes,* who are foreigners, and ſtrangers, and conſequently
leſs capable of obtaining redreſs when they are really
injured : the white ſervants are generally underſtood
to be bound to their maſters only for a ſhort limited
time, either with their own conſent by private contraᴄt,
or as felons who are baniſhed their mother country
after a fair trial *by jury* (which excludes any ſuſpicion
of injuſtice) and are ſold for a certain term to pay the
expences of their paſſage, &c. whereby the right of ſervice claimed from them by the maſter is more in the
nature of a *pecuniary debt* than of abſolute ſlavery, ſo
that the white runaway ſervant may perhaps, *as a debtor,*
be delivered up to his maſter without any direᴄt breach
of the law of God beforementioned ; provided there is
no apprehenſion or probability of his being treated with
cruelty on his return ; or that the maſter would be liable to exaᴄt more ſervice than is due ; in which caſe
the law ought to afford proteᴄtion and redreſs ; but no
pretences of this kind can juſtify the *delivering up* a
a negroe *ſtranger !* The poor negroes are claimed *for
life,*

" not deliver unto his master the ser-
" vant which is escaped from his master
" unto

*life*, as an *absolute property*, though (to compare their case with white servants) they never offended any member of our community either at home or abroad to justify such a severe punishment under *British Government*; neither are they capable of entering into such a *legal contract* for service, as might justify a master's claim to it, being absolutely incapacitated by *unlawful duress*, to *enter into any contract* as long as they are detained by force or fear in the *British dominions* (for which *injustice* to *strangers* the *British dominions* must sooner or later receive a severe *retribution*) and therefore *the delivering up to his master a negroe servant* " THAT HAS ESCAPED FROM HIS MASTER," and has since regained his natural liberty, must necessarily be esteemed a shameful and notorious breach of God's law. *Nevertheless our publick prints inform us even of an English man of war* and another vessel being lately sent from Grenada to the Spanish main, " to claim some " slaves that had made their escape from the Islands," (see Gazetteer June 30, 1773) the writer of the paragraph also expresses great disappointment on account of the issue of this unwarrantable and disgraceful embassy : " *instead of meeting with that justice and* " *civility which* (says he) *they had a right to expect, the* " *Governors at both places, we are told, treated them with* " *the*

" unto thee ; He fhall dwell with thee,
" among you. in that place which he
" fhall choofe" (that is manifeftly as a
free man ) " in one of thy gates *where*
" *it liketh him beft* ; *thou fhalt not* opprefs
" him". Deut. xxiii. 15, 16. This is
clearly a *moral law*, which muft be ever
binding as the will of *God*; becaufe the
benevolent *intention* of it is *apparent*,
and muft ever remain the fame : for
which

" *the greateft haughtinefs and contempt and refufed to give*
" *them the fmalleft fatisfaction* :" but alas the *very expectation* of better treatment (upon an errand fo unlawful in itfelf, and fo difgraceful to his Majefty's naval
fervice) is a proof of the moft deplorable degeneracy
and ignorance ! Even the cruel Spaniards are more
civilized and fhew more mercy to their flaves at prefent
than the Englifh, of which their new regulations for
the abolifhing of flavery afford ample proof, though the
RETRIBUTION for their former Tyranny has lately fallen heavily on them according to the laft accounts from
*Chiloe* and *Chili*, which ought to be confidered as merciful warnings to the reft of the world againft tyranny
and flavery !

which reafon I conclude that AN AC-
TION of TROVER *cannot lye for a flave ;*
and that no man can lawfully be profe-
cuted for protecting a negroe, or any
other flave whatever, that has " *efcaped*
" *from his mafter*" becaufe that would
be punifhing a man for doing *his indifpenfable duty* according *to the laws of
God :* and if any law, cuftom or precedent fhould be alledged to the contrary
it muft neceffarily be rejected as *null and
void*; becaufe it is a maxim of the common law of England, that " *the inferior*
" *law muft give place to the fuperior,*
" *man's laws to God's laws*". (attorney
general Noy's maxims P. 19) And the
learned author of the *Doctor* and *Stu-
dent* afferts, that even *Statute law* ought
to be accounted *null and void*, if *it is fet
forth contrary to the laws of God.*
" ETIAM SI ALIQUOD STATUTUM
" ESSE EDITUM, CONTRA EOS NUL-
" LIUS

" LIUS VIGORIS *in legibus Angliæ cenfe-*
" *ri debet, &c"*--- chap, vi.

The degree of fervitude, which the
Ifraelites were permitted to exact of
*their brethren,* was mild and equitable,
when compared with the fervitude
which (to our confufion be it faid) is
common among Chriftians ? I have already quoted from Leviticus a fpecimen
of the limitation to the fervitude of
BRETHREN ; but the Jews were not
only reftrained *from oppreffing their*
BRETHREN, but were alfo bound by the
law *to affift them generoufly and bounti-*
*fully* according to every man's ability,
when they difmiffed them from their
fervice ; which is a duty too feldom
practiced among Chriftians ! (fee Deutrenomy xv. 12.) " *If thy brother an*
" *Hebrew man, or an Hebrew woman, be*
" *fold unto thee, and ferve thee fix years ;*
" *then*

[ 57 ]

" *then in the* SEVENTH YEAR *thou*
" *shalt let him* GO FREE *from thee.* (34)
" *And when thou sendest him* out FREE
" *from thee, thou shalt* NOT LET HIM GO
" AWAY EMPTY : *Thou shalt furnish him*
" LIBERALLY *out of thy flock, and out of*
" *thy floor, and out of thy wine press:*
" (of that) *wherewith the Lord thy God*
" *hath blessed thee, thou shalt give unto him.*
" *And thou shalt remember that* THOU
" WAST A BONDMAN *in the land of E-*
" *gypt,* AND THE LORD THY GOD RE-
" DEEMED THEE : THEREFORE *I com-*
" *mand thee this thing to day.*" These are
the very utmost *limits of servitude* that
we might venture to exact of our brethren *even if we were Jews !* and how much
more are we bound to observe every thing
that is merciful in the law whilst we profess *Christianity?* What then must we think
of ourselves if we compare these Jewish

I limitations

(34) See also Exodus xxi. 2.

limitations with our Plantation laws!
*A bountiful recompence* for the fervice is
*plainly enjoined,* whereas the whole fubftance perhaps, of the moft wealthy
*Englifh* or *Scotch* flaveholders would not
fuffice to pay *what is due, in ftrict juftice,*
to thofe who have *laboured in his fervice,*
if the reward is to be proportioned to
their fufferings : but it fhall one day be
required of them --" *Your gold and filver*
" *is cankered; and the ruft of them fhall be*
" *a witnefs againft you, and fhall* EAT
" YOUR FLESH AS IT WERE FIRE : *Ye*
" *have heaped treafure together for the*
" *laft days.* BEHOLD THE HIRE OF
" THE LABOURERS *which have rea-*
" *ped down your fields, which is of you*
" *kept back by fraud,* CRIETH : *and* THE
" CRIES *of them* WHICH HAVE REAPED
" *are eutered into the ears of the Lord*
" *of Sabaoth"* (*or of* ARMIES) James. v.
3 and 4.

The

[ 59 ]

The *slaveholder* perhaps will say, that this text is not applicable to him, since he cannot be said to have " *kept back by* " *fraud*" *the hire of his labourers*, becaufe he never made any agreement with them for *wages*, having bought their *bodies* of the *slave dealer*, and thereby made them his *own private property* ; so that he has *a right* (he will say) *to all their labour without wages.* But this is a vain excufe for his *oppreffion*, becaufe it is not fo much *the previous agreement* as the LA-BOUR which renders *wages due* : for " THE LABOURER *is worthy of* HIS " HIRE" (Luke x. 7.) and the fin which " CRIETH *in the ears of the Lord of Sa-* " *baoth*" is the *ufing* a poor man's LABOUR " WITHOUT WAGES ;" fo that whether there is an *agreement for wages*, or *no a-greement*, yet, if THE LABOUR *is perfor-med*, the *wages are due* ; and thofe, who keep them back, may be said to *build their houfe in unrighteoufnefs:* as the prophet
Jeremiah

[ 60 ]

Jeremiah has declared in the ftrongeft terms (Jer. xxii. 13.) " *Wo unto him* " *that buildeth his houfe by unrighteouf-* " *nefs, and his chambers by wrong;* (*that*) " USETH HIS NEIGHBOUR'S SERVICE " WITHOUT WAGES, AND GIVETH " HIM NOT FOR HIS WORK."

And the holy Job, even before the law, declared his deteftation of UNRE-WARDED SERVICE. " *If my land* (faid he) " *cry againft me, or that the furrows like-* " *wife thereof complain:* IF I HAVE EAT-" EN THE FRUITS THEREOF WITHOUT " MONEY, *or have caufed the owners there-* " *of to lofe there life:* (35) *let thiftles* " *grow*

(35) Which was too much the cafe in the late Englifh acquifition of " *the fine cream part of the Ifland*" of St. Vincent's.—See authentic papers relative to the expedition againft the Charibbs. Page 24.

*" grow inſtead of wheat, and cockle in-*
*" ſtead of barley !* Job. xxxi. 38.---40

The wiſe ſon of Sirach has alſo added his teſtimony to the ſame doctrine
*" He that defraudeth the* LABOURER *of*
*" his hire is a bloodſheder.* Ecclefiafticus
xxxiv. 22. The ſlaveholder will perhaps endeavour to evade theſe texts alſo,
by alledging, that though, indeed, he
*" uſeth his neighbour's ſervice* WITHOUT
*"* WAGES, yet he cannot be ſaid to
*" give him nothing for his work,"* becauſe
he is at the expence of providing him
with food and cloathing (36) and therefore this ſevere text is not applicable to
him. But let ſuch a one remember (if
he calls himſelf a *Chriſtian*) that *Chris-*
*tian* maſters are abſolutely bound to have
ſome regard to *the intereſt* of their ſervants, as well as to their own *intereſt.*
*" Maſters*

_____

(36) Oſnabrug trowſers, and ſometimes alſo a Cap

" *Masters, give unto your* SERVANTS
" *that which is* JUST AND EQUAL, *know-*
" *ing that* YE ALSO *have a* MASTER *in*
" *heaven.*" Colloſ. iv. 1.

But *ſlaveholders* in general, have no
idea of what is " JUST AND EQUAL"
to be given *to ſervants* according to the
Scriptures !

It is not a mere ſupport in food and
neceſſaries, as a maſter feeds his horſe or
his aſs to enable the creature to perform
his labour: but as *man* is ſuperior to *brutes,*
a further reward is " *juſt and equal.*" to
be given to the human *ſervant.* I have
already ſufficiently proved that *every man*
under the Goſpel is to be conſidered as
our *neighbour* AND *brother,* and conſequently, whatever was " *juſt and equal*"
" to be given by a Jew, to his neighbour,
or *Hebrew brother* under the Old Teſtament,

ment, the fame muft, neceffarily, be confidered as "*juft and equal,*" and *abfolutely due* from *Chriftians* to men of *all nations* without diftinction, whom we are bound to treat *as brethren* under the Gofpel *in whatever capacity they ferve us.* Let the American *flaveholder* therefore remember, that *even according to the Jewifh law,* (if he argues upon it *as a* CHRISTIAN *ought to do*) he is abfolutely indebted to each of his flaves *for every days labour* BEYOND *the firft fix years* OF HIS SERVITUDE. " *In the* SEVENTH " *year* (faid the Lord by Mofes,) *thou* " *fhalt let him* GO FREE *from thee. And* " *when thou fendeft him out* FREE *from thee,* " *thou* SHALT NOT LET HIM GO AWAY " EMPTY . *Thou fhalt furnifh him* LI- " BERALLY *out of thy* FLOCK, &c. " *wherewith the Lord thy God hath blefs-* " *ed thee, thou fhalt give unto him*" &c.

If

If this was the indifpenfable duty *even of Jews!* how much more is it " JUST AND EQUAL to be obferved by *Chriftians* ? The fame command, when applied to the *American planter,* will include a proper ftock of plants for cultivation, as Sugar-Canes, Tobacco, Indigo, &c. as well as cattle and ftores, to enable a poor man to maintain himfelf and family upon a fmall farm, or lot of fpare ground, lett, for a certain limited time, on reafonable terms; and renewable on equitable conditions ; which are the only true means of reducing *the price of labour,* and *provifions.* Let not the planter *grudge* to part with his *fervant* when he has *ferved* a reafonable time in proportion to *his price,* (agreeable for, inftance, to the regulations adopted by the *Spaniards* which I have already recommended to the *Englifh* planters See Appendix 5.) for the word of God forbids any fuch bafe reluctance. " *It fhall not* " SEEM

" HARD

" SEEM HARD UNTO THEE *when thou*
"*ſendeſt* HIM AWAY FREE *from thee; for*
" *he hath been worth a double hired ſer-*
" *vant* (to thee) *in ſerving thee ſix years :*
" *and the Lord thy God ſhall bleſs thee in*
" *all that thou doeſt.*" Deut. xv. 18

The ſlaveholder perhaps will alledge
that, though the Jews were bound to
ſhew this benevolence to their *brethren
of Iſrael,* yet the ſame laws do not bind
the American planter, becauſe his ſlaves
are for the moſt part *heathens* or (as ſome
of the negroes are) *Mahometans,* and
therefore he is not bound to conſider
them as his *brethren;* being rather juſtified by the law, which permitted the
Jews to keep *heathen ſlaves,* and " *the*
" *children of the ſtrangers,*" in perpetual
bondage &c. They ſhall be your *bondmen
for ever*--ſee Leviticus xxv. 44, 45, and
46.--But I have already guarded againſt
**this**

this objection, in the former part of this tract; and it must clearly appear, by the several points since mentioned, that *as Chriſtians,* we muſt not preſume to look upon any man whatever in the ſame light that the *Iſraelites* once did upon " *the children of the ſtrangers,*" whether they be *black* or *white,* *Heathens* or *Mahometans.*

If a *Heathen,* or a *Mahometan,* happens to fall into our hands, ſhall we confirm his prejudices by *oppreſſion,* inſtead of endeavouring to inſtruct him as a *brother?* Surely the blood of ſuch a poor infidel muſt reſt on the guilty head of that *nominal* Chriſtian, who neglects the opportunity of adding to the number of *his brethren* in the Faith! And therefore, let that man, who endeavours to deprive others of their juſt privileges as *brethren,* take heed leſt he ſhould thereby unhappily occaſion his *own rejection*

in

in the end, when that dreadful doom,
which the uncharitable muſt expect
will certainly be pronounced!—For
then " *the* KING" (the King of King's)
" *ſhall anſwer, and ſay unto them,—*
" *Verily I ſay unto you,—In as much as*
" *ye have done* (it) *unto one of the leaſt*
" *of theſe* MY BRETHREN," (for that
glorious KING will eſteem even the
meaneſt SLAVES AS HIS BRETHREN, if
they believe in him,) "*ye have done* (it)
" *unto* ME ! DEPART FROM ME YE
" CURS D *into everlaſting Fire, pre-*
" *pared for the Devil and his Angels.*"
" (Matt. xxv. 40, 41.) *I know you not !*
" (xxv. 12.)—*I never knew you ;—De-*
" *part from me ye that work iniquity !*"
(Matt. vii. 23.)


Soli Deo Gloria et Gratia.



F I N I S

# APPENDIX

## ( N°. I. )

An ESSAY on

# SLAVERY,

Proving from SCRIPTURE its Inconsistency
with HUMANITY and RELIGION;

## By GRANVILLE SHARP.

" With an introductory PREFACE," (*by a Gentleman
of the Law, in West Jersey*) " containing the Sentiments of the Monthly Reviewers on a Tract,
by the Rev. T. Thompson, *in Favour* of the *Slave
Trade*."

*The Lord also will be a Refuge for the Oppressed—
a Refuge in Time of Trouble,* Psalm. ix- 9.

# Preface by the American Editor.

THE following Essay, though wrote,
' as the Author signifies, in haste,
' is thought to have such merit as
' to deserve a publication.—The copy was
' sent to one of the Writer's particular
' friends, whether for his own peculiar sa-
' tisfaction, or the press, is uncertain; but
' as the subject is *Liberty*, so it is expected
' the *Freedom* which is here taken, cannot
' justly give him offence, or be unaccepta-
' ble to the public.'

' IT was designed to confute a piece wrote
' by Thomas Thompson, M. A. some time
' fellow of C. C. C. entitled,' " The Afri-
" can trade for Negro Slaves shewn to be
" confistent with principles of humanity,
" and with the laws of revealed religion."
' Printed at Canterbury.'

' IN order to shew that the Essay Writer
' has not misrepresented the text, nor is
' single in his observations upon it, the sen-
' timents of the Monthly Reviewers on that
' pamphlet in May, 1772, are here insert-
' ed.'

" We must acknowledge," say they, " that
" the branch of trade here under considera-
" tion,

" tion, is a fpecies of traffic which we have
" never been able to reconcile with the dic-
" tates of humanity, and much lefs with
" thofe of religion. The principal argu-
" ment in its behalf feems to be, the *necef-*
" *fity* of fuch a refcource, in order to carry
" on the works. in our plantations, which,
" we are told, it is otherwife impoffible to
" perform. But this, though the urgency
" of the cafe may be very great, is not by
" any means fufficient to juftify the prac-
" tice. There is a farther confideration
" which has a plaufible appearance, and
" may be thought to carry fome weight;
" it is, that the merchant only purchafes
" thofe who were flaves before, and poffi-
" bly may, rather than otherwife, render
" their fituation more tolerable. But it is
" well known, that the lot of our Slaves,
" when moft favourably confidered, is very
" hard and miferable; befides which, fuch
" a trade is taking the advantage of the ig-
" norance and brutality of unenlightened na-
" tions, who are encouraged to war with
" each other for this very purpofe, and, it
" is to be feared, are fometimes tempted to
" feize thofe of their own tribes or families
" that they may obtain the hoped for ad-
" vantage : and it is owned, with regard to
" our merchants, that, upon occafion, they
" obferve the like practices, which are
                              " thought

" thought to be allowable, becaufe they
" are done by way of reprifal for theft
" or damage committed by the natives. We
" were pleafed, however, to meet with a
" pamphlet on the other fide of the quef-
" tion ; and we entered upon its perufal
" with the hopes of finding fomewhat ad-
" vanced which might afford us fatisfaction
" on this difficult point. The writer ap-
" pears to be a fenfible man, and capable
" of difcuffing the argument ; but the li-
" mits to which he is confined, rendered
" his performance rather fuperficial. The
" plea he produces from the Jewifh law is
" not, in our view of the matter, at all
" conclufive. The people of Ifrael were
" under a *theocracy*, in which the Supreme
" Being was in a peculiar fenfe their King,
" and might therefore iffue forth fome or-
" ders for them, which it would not be
" warrantable for another people, who were
" in different circumftances, to obferve.
" Such, for inftance, was the command
" given concerning the extirpation of the
" Canaanites, whom, the fovereign Arbiter
" of life and death might, if he had pleafed,
" have deftroyed by plague or famine, or
" other of thofe means which we term na-
" tural caufes, and by which a wife Provi-
" dence fulfils its own purpofes. But it
" would be unreafonable to infer from the
                              manner

" manner in which the Ifraelites dealt with
" the people of Canaan, that any other na-
" tions have a right to purfue the fame me-
" thod.    Neither can we imagine that St.
" Paul's exhortation to fervants or flaves,
" upon their converfion, to continue in the
" ftate in which chriftianity found them,
" affords any argument favourable to the
" practice here pleaded for.    It is no more
" than faying,   that Chriftianity did not
" particularly enter into the regulations of
" civil fociety at that time ; that it taught
" perfons to be contented and  diligent in
" their ftations : but certainly it did not
" forbid them, in a proper and lawful way,
" if it was in  their power, to render their
" circumftances more  comfortable.    Upon
" the whole, we muft own, that this little
" treatife is not convincing to us, though, as
" different  perfons are differently affected
" by the fame confiderations, it may prove
" more fatisfactory to others."
    ' In  another place they obferve,' " fince
" we are *all brethren,*  and God has given to
" *all* men a natural right to *Liberty*, we al-
" low of no *Slavery* among us, unlefs a per-
" fon forfeits his freedom by his crimes."
    ' That  Slavery is not confiftent with the
' Englifh conftitution,  nor admiffable  in
' Great Britain,  appears evidently by the
' late folemn determination, in the court of
                                    ' King's

' King's Bench at Weſtminſter, in the caſe
' of James Somerſet, the Negro; and why
' it ſhould be revived and continued in the
' colonies, peopled by the deſcendents of
' Britain, and bleſſed with ſentiments as
' truly noble and free as any of their fellow
' ſubjects in the mother country, is not eaſi-
' ly conceived, nor can the diſtinction be
' well founded.'

   ' IF " natural rights, ſuch as *life* and *Li-*
" *berty,* receive no additional ſtrength from
" municipal laws, nor any *human legiſlature*
" has *power* to abridge or *deſtroy them,* un-
" leſs the owner commits ſome act that a-
" mounts to a forfeiture;" *(a)* ' If " the
" natural *Liberty of mankind* conſiſts proper-
" ly in a power of acting as one thinks fit,
" without any reſtraint or controul unleſs
" by the *law of nature*; being a *right inhe-*
" *rent in us by birth,* and one of the *Gifts of*
" *God to man* at his creation, when he en-
" dued him with the faculty of *free will:*"
*(b)* ' If an *act* of Parliament is *controulable*
' *by the laws of God and nature*; *(c)* and *in*
' *its conſequences* may be *rendered void for*
' abſurdity, or a *manifeſt contradiction to*
' *common reaſon:* *(d)* If " Chriſtianity is a
" part of the law of England;" *(e)* and
                     " Chriſt

<hr>

*(a)* 1 Blackſtone's Commentaries, 54.  *(b)* Dit.
125.  *(c)* 4 Bacon's Abridg. 639.  *(d)* 1 Black.
Com. 91.  *(e)* Stra. Reports, 1113.

'Chrift exprefsly commands, " Whatfoever
" ye would that men fhould do to you, do
" ye even fo to them,' ' at the fame time
' declaring,' " for this is the law and the
" law and the prophets," (f) ' And if
' our forefathers, who emigrated from Eng-
' land hither, brought with them all the
' rights, liberties, and privileges of the
' Britifh conftitution (which hath of late
' years been often afferted and repeatedly
' contended for by Americans) why is it
' that the poor footy African meets with fo
' different a meafure of juftice in England
' and America, as to be *adjudged free* in
' the one, and in the other held in the moft
' *abject Slavery ?*

'  We are exprefsly reftrained from mak-
' ing laws, " repugnant to," and directed
' to fafhion them, " as nearly as may be,
" agreeable to, the laws of England."
' Hence, and becaufe of its total inconfif-
' tency with the principles of the conftitu-
' tion, neither in England or any of the
' Colonies, is there one law directly in fa-
' vour of, or enacting *Slavery*, but by a
' kind of fide-wind, admitting its exiftence,
' (though only founded on a barbarous
' cuftom, originated by foreigners) attempt
' its regulation. How far the point liti-
' gated in James Somerfet's *cafe*, would
bear

(a) Matt. vii. 12.

' bear a fober candid difcuffion before an
' impartial judicature in the Colonies  I
' cannot determine; but, for the credit of
' my country, fhould hope it would meet
' with a like decifion that it might appear
' and be known, that *Liberty* in America,
' is not a partial privilege, but extends to
' every individual in it.'

'  I MIGHT here, in the language of the
' famous JAMES OTIS, Efq; afk,  " Is it
" poffible for a man to have a natural right
" to make a Slave of himfelf or his pofteri-
" ty ? What man is or ever was born free,
" if every man is not? Can a father fuper-
" fede the laws of nature ? Is not every man
" born as free by nature as his father ? (*a*)
" There can be no prefcription old enough
" to fuperfede the law of nature, and the
" grant of God Almighty, who has given
" to every man a natural right to be free.
" (*b*)   The Colonifts are by the law of na-
" ture free born, as indeed all men are,
" white or black.   No better reafon can be
" given for the enflaving thofe of any co-
" lour, than fuch as Baron Montefquieu has
" humouroufly affigned, as the foundation
" of that cruel Slavery exercifed over the
" poor Ethiopeans;  which threatens one
" day to reduce both Europe and America
                b                    " to

(*a*)  1 American Tracts by Otis, 4.     (*b*) American Tracts b  Otis, 17.

" to the ignorance and barbarity of the
" darkeft ages. Does it follow that it is
" right to enflave a man becaufe he is black ?
" Will fhort curled hair like wool, inftead
" of chriftians hair, as it is called by thofe
" whofe hearts are hard as the nether mill-
" ftone, help the argument ? Can any lo-
" gical inference in favour of Slavery, be
" drawn from a flat nofe|| a long or a fhort
" face ? Nothing better can be faid in fa-
" vour of *a trade* that is the moft fhocking
" violation of the laws of nature; has a
" direct tendency to diminifh every idea of
" the ineftimable value of Liberty, and
" makes every dealer in it a tyrant, from
" the director of an African company, to
" the petty chapman in needles and pins,
" on the unhappy coaft." (*a*)

' To Thofe who think Slavery founded in
' Scripture, a careful and attentive perufal
' of the Sacred Writings would contribute
' more than any thing to eradicate the er-
' ror; they will not find even the name of
' *Slave* once mentioned therein, and applied
' to a fervitude to be continued from parent
' to child in perpetuity, with approbation.
' —The term ufed on the occafion in the
' facred text is *Servant*; and, upon a fair
' conftruction of thofe writings, there is no
' neceffity, nor can the fervice, confiftent
                       ' with

(*a*) American Tracts, 43, 44.

' with the whole tenor of the Scripture, be
' extended further than the generation fpo-
' ken of ; it was never intended to include
' the pofterity.

'THE miftaken proverb which prevailed
' in that early age, "The fathers had ea-
" ten four grapes, and the childrens teeth
" were fet on edge," was rectified by the
prophets Jeremiah and Ezekiel, who declared to the people, that " they fhould not
" have occafion to ufe that proverb any
" more ;—Behold all fouls are mine, as the
" foul of the father, fo the foul of the fon,
" the foul that finneth it fhall die ;—the fon
" fhall not bear the iniquity of the father,
" neither fhall the father bear the iniquity
" of the fon ;—the righteoufnefs of the
" righteous fhall be upon him, and the
" wickednefs of the wicked fhall be upon
" him. (a) ' And the apoftle Peter affures
' us, after the afcenfion of our Saviour, that
" God is no refpecter of perfons, but in
" every *nation* he that feareth him is ac-
" cepted of him." (b) ' It is alfo remark-
' able, that at that time, an *Ethiopian*, " a
" man of great authority," (c) was ad-
' mitted to the freedom of a Chriftian,
' whatever we may think of the colour now,
' as being unworthy of it.

b 2

' But

(a) Jer. xxxi. 29.    Ezek. xviii. 3, 4, and 20.
(b) Acts x. 34.    (c) Ditto, viii. 27.

' But admitting Slavery to be eftablifhed
' by Scripture, the command of the Sove-
' reign Ruler of the univerfe, whofe eye
' takes in all things, and who, for good
' reafons, beyond our comprehenfion, might
' juftly create a perpetual Slavery to effect
' his own purpofes, againft the enemies of
' his chofen people in that day, cannot be
' pleaded now againft any people on earth ;
' it is not even pretended to in juftification
' of Negro Slavery, nor can the fons of
' Ethiopia, with any degree of clearnefs, be
' proved to have defcended from any of
' thofe nations who fo came under the Di-
' vine difpleafure as to be brought into fer-
' vitude; if they are, and thofe denuncia-
' tions given in the Old Teftament were
' perpetual, and continue in force, muft we
' not look upon it meritorious to execute
' them fully upon all the offspring of that
' unhappy people upon whom they fell,
' without giving quarter to any ?

' Many who admit the indefenfibility
' of Slavery, confidering the fubject rather
' too fuperficially, declare it would be im-
' p litic to emancipate thofe we are poffeffed
' of; and fay, they generally behave ill
' wh n fet at liberty. I believe very few
' of the advocates for freedom think that
' all ought to be manumitted, nay, think
' it would be unjuft to turn out thofe who
                                    ' have

' have spent their prime of life, and now
' require a support; but many are in a
' fit capacity to do for themselves and the
' public; as to these let every master or
' mistress do their duty, and leave conse-
' quences to the Disposer of events, who,
' I believe, will always bless our actions in
' proportion to the purity of their spring.
' But many instances might be given of
' Negroes and Mulatoes, once in Slavery,
' who, after they have obtained their li-
' berty, (and sometimes even in a state of
' bondage) have given striking proofs of
' their integrity, ingenuity, industry, ten-
' derness and nobility of mind; of which,
' if the limits of this little Piece permit-
' ed, I could mention many examples; and
' why instances of this kind are not more fre-
' quent, we may very naturally impute to
' the smallness of the number tried with
' freedom, and the servility and meanness of
' their education whilst in Slavery. Let us
' never forget, that an equal if not a grea-
' ter proportion of our own colour behave
' worse with all the advantages of birth,
' education and circumstances; and we
' shall blush to oppose an equitable emanci-
' pation, by this or the like arguments.

" Liberty, the most manly and exalt-
" ing of the gifts of Heaven, consists in a
" free and generous exercise of all the hu-
　　　　　　　　　" man

" man faculties  as far as they are compati-
" ble with  the good of fociety to which we
" belong  ; and  the moft delicious part of
" the enjoyment of the ineftimable blefling
" lies  in  a confcioufnefs that  we are *free*.
" This happy perfuafion,  when it  meets
" with a noble  nature, raifes the foul,  and
" rectifies the heart ;  it gives dignity to  the
" countenance and animates every word and
" gefture ;  it elevates  the mind above the
" little arts of deceit,  makes it  benevolent,
" open, ingenuous and juft, and adds a new
" relifh to every better fentiment of huma-
" nity."  *(a)*  On  the contrary,  " Man is
" bereaved of half his virtues that day when
" he is caft into bondage."  *(b)*

' THE  end  of the chriftian difpenfation,
' with which we are at prefent favoured, ap-
' pears in  our Saviours words,'  " The fpi-
" rit  of the Lord is  upon me,  becaufe he
" hath anointed me to preach the  gofpel to
" the poor ; he hath fent me to heal the *bro-*
" *ken  hearted* ;  to  preach deliverance to the
" captives ; and recovery of *fight to the blind* ;
" to  fet at  *liberty them that are bruifed* ;  to
" preach the *acceptable year of the Lord*."  *(c)*

' THE Editor is united in opinion with the
' author of the Effay, that flavery is contra-
' ry to the laws of reafon, and the principles
                                          ' of

*(a)* Blackwell's Court of Auguftus.  *(b)* Homer.
                *(c)* Luke iv.  18.

‘ of revealed religion ; and believes it alike
‘ inimical and impolitick in every ſtate and
‘ country ; for as “ righteouſncſs exalteth a
“ nation, ſo ſin is a reproach to any people.”
‘ (a) Hence whatever violates the purity of
‘ equal juſtice, and the harmony of true li-
‘ berty, in time debaſes the mind, and ulti-
‘ mately draws down the diſpleaſure of that
‘ Almighty Being, who ‘‘ is of purer eyes
“ than to behold evil, and cannot look on ini-
“ quity .” (b) ‘ Yet he is far from cenſuring
‘ thoſe who are not under the ſame convic-
‘ tions, and hopes to be underſtood with cha-
‘ rity and tenderneſs to all. Every one does
‘ not ſee alike the ſame propoſitions, who
‘ may be equally friends to truth, as our
‘ education and opportunities of knowledge
‘ are various as our faces. He will candidly
‘ confeſs to any one who ſhall kindly point
‘ it out: any error which in this inquiry hath
‘ fell from his pen. There can be but one
‘ beatific point of rectitude, but many paths
‘ leading to it, in which perſons differing in
‘ modes and non-eſſentials, may walk with
‘ freedom to their own opinions ; we may
‘ much more innocently be under a miſtake,
‘ than continue in it after a hint given,
‘which occaſions our adverting thereto ; for
‘ it ſeems a duty to inveſtigate the way of
‘ truth

(a) Prov. xiv. 34. (b) Habakuk i, 13.

' truth and juftice with our utmoft ability.

' A much more extenfive and perfect view
' of the fubject under confideration, has of
' late prevailed than formerly ; and he be-
' lieves nothing is wanting but an impartial
' difinterefted attention to make ftill greater
' advances. Thus, by a gradual progreffion,
' he hopes the name of *Slavery* will be eradi-
' cated by the general voice of mankind in
' this land of *Liberty*.

' THE mode of manumitting negroes in
' New-Jerfey is fuch as appears terrific, and
' amounts almoft to a prohibition, becaufe of
' its incumbering confequences, which few
' prudent people chufe to leave their fa-
' milies liable to. It is much eafier in fe-
' veral other colonies. In Pennfylvania a
' recognizance entered into in THIRTY
' POUNDS to indemnify the townfhip, is a
' compleat difcharge. In Mariland, where
' Negroes are fo numerous, I am informed,
' the mafter or miftrefs may at pleafure
' give Liberty to their flaves without the
' leaft obligation, and be clear of any future
' burden. Both thefe are exceptionable,
' and may be improved. Proper diftinctions
' are neceffary ; for as the freedom of all
' gratis might be unjuft, not only to the
' publick but the Slave : fo any clog upon
' the owner who gives up his right at an
' age when he cannot have received much
' or any advantage from the labour of the
                              ' individual

‘ individual, would be unreafonable.   The
‘ wifdom of a legiflature earneftly difpofed
‘ to do good, will I hope be directed to fur-
‘ mount every little difficulty in pointing
‘ out a fcheme more equal and perfect, by
‘ fteering a middle courfe ; and proper care
‘ being kindly taken to affift and provide for
‘ the ufefulnefs of thofe deferving objects of
‘ benevolence, the approbation of Divine
‘ Providence will I doubt not, attend fuch
‘ laudable endeavours, and crown them with
‘ fuccefs.—That the legiflative body of each
‘ province in America may give due atten-
‘ tion to this important engaging fubject,
‘ and be bleffed to frame and eftablifh a
‘ plan worthy of the united jurifprudence,
‘ wifdom, and benevolence of the *Guardians*
‘ *of Liberty,* is the fincere wifh of’

THE  E D I T O R.

A N

A N

# ESSAY on SLAVERY,

Proving from Scripture its inconsistency, with Humanity and Religion,

*By* Granville Sharp.

A REVEREND author, Mr. Thomas Thompson, M. A. has late-
ly attempted to prove " that the Afri-
" can trade for Negroe Slaves is con-
" siftent with the principles of *humanity*
" and *revealed religion.*"

From Leviticus xxv. 39 to 46, he draws
his principle conclusion, viz. " that the
" buying and felling of Slaves *is not con-*
" *trary to the law of nature,* for (fays
" he)

" he) the *Jewish conſtitutions* were
" ſtrictly therewith conſiſtent *in all*
" *points* : and theſe are in certain caſes
" the rule by which is determined by
" *learned lawyers* and caſuiſts, what is,
" or is not, *contrary to nature.*" I have
not leiſure to follow this author me-
thodically, but will, neverthelefs, examine his ground *in a general way*, in
order to prevent any ill uſe that may be
made of it againſt the important queſtion
now depending before the judges. *(a)*

THE reverend Mr. Thompſon's *pre-
miſes are not true*, for the Jewiſh conſtitutions *were not "ſtrictly conſiſtent"*
with the *law of nature* in all points, as
he ſuppoſes, and conſequently his principal *concluſion* thereupon is erroneous.
Many things were formerly tolerated
among the Iſraelites, merely through
the

*(a)* Meaning I ſuppoſe, (ſays the American editor)
the caſe of Somerſet, which then depended.

the mercy and forbearance of God, in confideration of their extreme frailty and inability, at that time, to bear a more perfect fyftem of law. Other laws there are in the five books (befides the ceremonial laws now abrogated) which are merely *municipal*, being adapted to the peculiar polity of the Ifraelitifh commonwealth, on account of its fituation in the midft of the moft barbarous nations, whom the Hebrews were at all times but too much inclined to immitate.

THE univerfal *moral laws* and thofe of *natural equity* are, indeed, every where plentifully interfperfed among the *peculiar laws* abovementioned; but they may very eafily be diftinguifhed by every fincere Chriftian, who examines them with *a liberal mind,* becaufe the *benevolent purpofe* of the Divine Author

is

is *always apparent* in thofe laws which are to be *eternally binding* ; for " it is " *the reafon* of the law which confti- " tutes the *life of the law*," according to an allowed maxim of our own country, " Ratio Legis eft anima Legis," (Jenk. Cent. 45.) And with refpect to thefe *moral* and *equitable* laws, I will readily agree with the Reverend Mr. Thomp- fon, that they are the beft rule by which " learned judges and cafuifts can deter- " mine what is, or is not, *contrary to* " *nature*."

But I will now give a few examples of laws, which are in *themfelves contra- ry to nature or natural equity*, in order to fhew that Mr. Thompfon's *premifes* are totally falfe :

The Ifraelites were exprefsly *permitted by the law of Mofes* to give a bill of di-

vorce

vorce to their wives whenever they
pleafed, and to marry *other women*; and
the women who were put away, were
alfo exprefsly permitted, by the Mofaic
law, *to marry again*, during the lives of
their former hufbands.

ALL which practices were manifeftly contrary to *the law of nature* in its
purity, though not perhaps to *the nature
of our corrupt affections and defires*; for
Chrift himfelf declared, that " *from the*
" *beginning it was not fo*,"Matt. xix 8, 9.
and at the fame time our Lord informed the Jews, that " Mofes, becaufe
" of *the hardnefs of their hearts*, fuffered
" them to put away their wives."

NEITHER was it *according to the law
of nature*, that the Jews were *permitted*
in their behaviour and dealings, to
make a partial diftinction between their
*brethren*

*brethren* of the houfe of Ifrael, and
ftrangers. This national partiality was
not, indeed, either commanded or recommended in their law—but it was
clearly *permitted* or *tolerated*, and probably, for the fame reafon as the laft
mentioned inftance —" thou *ſhalt not*
" *lend* upon ufury to *thy brother*," &c.—
" unto *a ſtranger* thou mayeft *lend upon*
" *uſury* &c. Deut. xxiii. 19.—Again---
" of *a foreigner* thou *mayeſt exact* ;"
(that is, whatfoever *has been lent*, as appears by the preceding verfes) but that
which is, " thine, *with thy brother*,
" thine hand ſhall releafe," Deut. xv. 3

Now all thefe laws were " *contrary
to the law of nature*" or " *natural equity*," (whatever Mr. Thompfon, may
think) and were certainly, annulled or
rather *ſuperſeded*, as it were, by the
more perfect doctrines of *univerſal benevolence* taught by Chrift himfelf, who
" came

*" came not to deſtroy, but to fulfill the law."*

In the law of Moſes we alſo read,
" Thou ſhalt not avenge or bear grudge
" againſt *the children of thy people but*
" *thou ſhalt love thy neighbour as thy-*
" *ſelf,"* Leviticus xix. 18.

The Jews, accordingly, thought
themſelves ſufficiently juſtified, if they
confined this glorious perfection of charity, viz. *the loving others as themſelves,*
to the perſons mentioned in the ſame
verſe, viz. " *the children of their own*
" *people ;"* for they had no idea that ſo
much love could poſſibly be due to any
other ſort of *neighbours* or *brethren.* But
Chriſt taught them by the parable of
*the good Samaritan,* that *all ſtrangers
whatever* even thoſe who are declared
enemies, (as were the Samaritans to the
Jews) are to be eſteemed our *neighbours*

*bours* or *brethren*, whenever they ſtand in need of our charitable aſſiſtance.

" THE Jewiſh inſtitution" indeed, as Mr. Thompſon remarks " permited the " uſe of *bondſervants*," but did not per-mit the *bondage of brethren :* STRAN-GERS ONLY could be *lawfully* retain-ed as *bondmen*——" of the heathen," (or, more agreeable to the Hebrew words, מאת הגוים *of the nations*) " that " are round about you; of *them* ſhall ye " buy *bond* men and *bond* maids. More-" over of the children of *ſtrangers* that " do ſojourn among you, *of them ſhall* " *ye buy*," &c.----" *They* ſhall be your " *bondmen for ever.*" Levit, xxv 39 to 46.

THIS was the law, I muſt acknow-ledge, with reſpect to *a ſtranger* that was *purchaſed ;* but with reſpect to *a brother*

or Hebrew of the feed of Abraham, it was far otherwife, as the fame chapter teftifies ; (39th verfe) for, " if thy *bro-*
' *ther* that dwelleth by thee be waxen
" poor, and be *fold* unto thee ; thou *fhalt*
" *not compel him to ferve as a bondfervant:*
" but as an hired fervant, and as a fo-
" journer he fhall be with thee, and
" fhall ferve thee unto the year of ju-
" bilee. And *then fhall he depart from*
" *thee, both he and his children with him,*"
&c. This was the *utmoft fervitude* that a Hebrew could *lawfully* exact from a-ny of his *brethren* of the houfe of Ifrael, unlefs the fervant entered *voluntarily* into a perpetual fervitude : and, let me add, that it is alfo, the very *utmoft fervitude* that can *lawfully* be admitted *among chriftians:* becaufe we are bound as chriftians to efteem EVERY MAN *as our*
*-brother,* and *as our neighbour,* which I have already proved; fo that this confequence
which

which I have drawn, is abfolutely *un-avoidable*. The Jews indeed, who do not yet acknowlege the commands of Chrift, may perhaps ftill think them-felves *juftified* by the law of Mofes, in making partial diftinctions between *their brethren* of Ifrael, *and other men*? but it would *be inexcufable* in chriftians to do fo! and therefore I conclude, that we certainly have no right to exceed the *limits of fervitude,* which the Jews were bound to obferve, whenever their poor *brethren* were fold to them : and I ap-prehend that we muft not venture *even to go fo far,* becaufe the laws of *brother-ly love* are infinitely enlarged, and ex-tended by the gofpel of peace, which proclaims " *good will towards men,*" without diftinction ; and becaufe we cannot be faid to " *love our neighbours* " *as ourfelves* ;" or to *do to others as we would they fhould do unto us*"---whilft we

retain

retain them againſt their *will,* in a deſ-
picable ſervitude as *ſlaves,* and *private
property,* or *mere chattels!*

THE glorious ſyſtem of the goſpel
deſtroys all *narrow, national partiality;*
and makes *us citizens of the world,* by
obliging us to profeſs *univerſal benevolence :* but more eſpecially are we bound,
as chriſtians, to commiſerate and aſſiſt
to the utmoſt of our power all perſons
in *diſtreſs,* or *captivity;* whatever " the
" *worſhipful* committee of the compa-
" ny of merchants trading to *Africa,*"
may think of it, or their advocate, the
reverend Mr. Thompſon.

CHARITY, indeed, begins at home;
and we ought moſt certainly to give the
preference to our own countrymen,
whenever we can do ſo without injuſtice; but we may " *not do evil that*
" *good*

" *good may come* ;" (though our ſtateſ-
men, and their political deceivers may
think otherwiſe) we muſt not, for the
ſake of *Old England,* and its *African
trade,* or for the ſuppoſed advantage,
or imaginary neceſſities of our *American*
colonies, lay aſide our *chriſtian charity,*
which we owe to *all the reſt of mankind :*
becauſe, *whenever we do ſo,* we certainly deſerve to be conſidered in no better
light than as an overgrown *ſociety of
robbers,* a *mere banditti,* who, perhaps, may *love one another,* but at the
ſame time are at enmity with *all the reſt
of the world.* Is this *according to the
law of nature ?*------For ſhame Mr.
Thompſon !

I HAVE much more to communi-
cate, but no more time to write :---if I
had, I could draw from the ſcriptures
the

the moſt alarming examples of God's ſevere judgments upon the Jews, for tyrannizing over *their brethren*, and, *expreſsly*, for exceeding the *limits* of *ſervitude* juſt now mentioned. *(a)* I muſt find time however to adopt one obſervation even from the reverend Mr. Thompſon, (p. 11.) viz. " This ſubject will " grow more ſerious upon our hands, " when we conſider the *buying and ſell-* " *ing Negroes*, not as a clandeſtine or " piratical buſineſs, but as an *open pub-* " *lic trade*, *encouraged* and promoted by " acts of parliament; for ſo, if being " *contrary to religion, it muſt be deemed* A " NATIONAL SIN; *b*) and as ſuch may " have

*(a)* This I have ſince accompliſhed in a tract, intituled, " THE LAW OF RETRIBUTION, &c.

*(b)* If this juſt remark by Mr. *Thompſon*, be compared with the above mentioned tract on *the Law of Retribution*, (wherein the uſual courſe of *God*'s judgements

" have a confequence that *would be*
" *always to be dreaded.*" May God give
us grace to repent of this abominable
" NATIONAL SIN," before it is too late!

If I have vindicated the law of Mofes, much eafier can I vindicate the benevolent apoftle Paul, from Mr. Thompfon's infinuations, with refpect to flavery; for he *did not* entreat *Philemon* to
take back his fervant *Onefimus*, " in his
" former capacity," as Mr. *Thompfon*
has afferted, in order to render bondage " *confiftent with the principles of re-*
" *vealed religion,*"---but St. *Paul* faid
*exprefly*, " *not now as a fervant, but,*
" *above*

ments againft NATIONS, is fairly demonftrated by a
variety of unqueftionable examples in the fcriptures,)
it will appear that nothing but *a thorough reformation*
with refpect to the faid " NATIONAL SIN," can afford
us the leaft room *even to hope* that THIS NATION, may
efcape the tremendous effects of G O D S TEMPORAL
VENGEANCE now dreadfully hanging over us!

" *above a servant*, a *brother beloved*," *(a)* &c.  So that Mr. *Thompson* has notoriously wrested St. *Paul*'s words.

In the other texts where St. *Paul* recommends submission to *Servants*, for conscience-sake, he at the same time enjoins the master to entertain such a measure of *brotherly love* towards his servants, as must be entirely subversive of the *African* trade, and *West-Indian* slavery.

*(a)* This single circumstance one would think a sufficient bar to the inferences drawn from this epistle, in favour of slavery, by the reverend Mr. *Thompson*, and others ; and yet even the learned Archbishop *Theophylact* seemed inclined to admit the same supposed *right of the master*. In the preface to his commentary on this epistle, where he gives a short account of the use and purport of it, and of the doctrines which may be deduced from it, (he says) Τριτον, ὁτι ὁ χρη προφασει ευλαβειας δυλυς αποσπαν των δεσποτων μη βυλομενων. *Thirdly. That it is not fit, through pretence of piety, to draw away servants from masters, that are unwilling to part*

flavery. And though St. *Paul*, recommends chriftian patience under fervitude, yet, at the fame time, he plainly infinuates, that it is inconfiftent with
e       chriftianity,

*part with them.*" But though the apoftle declared,
indeed, to *Philemon* the mafter, (v. 14.) " *without
thy mind, would I do nothing ;*" &c. yet this by no
means proves *the right of the mafter*, but only that the
apoftle, in love and courtefy to *Philemon*, defired, that
" *the benefit*," which he required of him, " *fhould
not be as it were of neceffity, but willingly,*" (ver. 14.)
for the apoftle's *right* to have retained *Onefimus*, even
*without the mafter's confent*, is fufficiently implied in *a*
preceding verfe, (viz. 8.) " *though I might be
much bold in Chrift, to enjoin,* (or command) " *thee
that which is convenient. Yet,* (faid the apoftle,) "*for*
LOVE's SAKE, *I rather befeech.*" &c. And a further
reafon for his not *commanding*, is alfo declared, viz.
that he depended on the willing obedience of *Philemon*. " *Having confidence* (faid he) *in thy obedience, I
wrote unto thee, knowing that thou wilt alfo do more than
I fay.*" And yet that which he really did *fay*, or require in behalf of *Onefimus*, was as ftrong a recom-
mendation

chriſtianity, and the dignity of Chriſt's kingdom, that a *chriſtian brother* ſhould be

mendation to *favour* and *ſuperior kindneſs* as could be expreſſed. He required him to receive *Oneſimus*, "*not now as a ſervant, but above a ſervant, as a* BROTHER *beloved*," &c. (16 verſe.) that "*if he hath wronged thee, or* OWETH OUGHT," (ἡ οφειλει, in which expreſſion even the ſuppoſed *debt of ſervice* may be included,) "*put that on my account*," (ſaid the apoſtle, ver. 18.) which muſt be a complete diſcharge of all the maſter's temporal demands on *Oneſimus*; and therefore it is a ſtrange perverſion of the apoſtle's meaning to cite this epiſtle, *in favour of ſlavery*, when the whole tenor of it is in behalf of the *ſlave!* But there is ſtill a further obſervation neceſſary to be made, which puts the matter out of diſpute.

*Theophylact*, himſelf, allows that *Oneſimus* (at the very time he was ſent back,) was *a miniſter of the goſpel*, or a *miniſter of preaching* (Τ8 κηρυγματος, ‡) which is an office

‡ αλλα παλιν αποςελει προς υπηρεσιαν τ8 κηρυγματος, 8 κ᷉ αυτος εργατης εςι. But that he ſhould ſend him back again, to the *ſervice* of *preaching*, of which he is *a labourer*, (or miniſ-ter.) Comment on the 1ſt. verſe, page 863. *edit. London,* 1636.

be a *Slave*. " Can'ft thou be made
" free ?" (fays he to the chriftian fervants)
" *choofe it rather*, for he that is *called*
" of the Lord, *being a fervant*, is the
" *freeman* of the Lord ; and, in like

e 2         " manner,

office of the facred miniftry, not beneath the higheft
order in the church, for it was the principal employment even of the apoftle himfelf.

And this opinion of *Theophylact*, is corroborated by
a variety of circumftances. By the epiftle to the *Co-
loffians*, it appears that *Onefimus* was joined with *Tychicus*, (therein declared to be a *minifter*,) ‖ in an *ecclefiaftical*

‖ ' *All my ftate fhall* TYCHICUS *declare* unto you, *(who is) a be-
'loved brother,* A FAITHFUL MINISTER AND FELLOW SERVANT
'IN THE LORD ; *whom I have fent unto you for the fame purpofe, that
'he might* KNOW YOUR ESTATE, AND COMFORT YOUR HEARTS
*with* ONESIMUS, *a faithful and beloved brother*," *(by which it is
apparent that *Onefimus* was joined in the fame fervices, " to KNOW
THEIR ESTATES AND COMFORT THEIR HEARTS," an office
that would have very ill become him, had he been fent back to
his mafter as a SLAVE, or as Mr. *Thompfon* fays ' IN HIS FORMER
'CAPACITY !*)'* " *who is one of you*. *They (*that is *Tychicus* and *Onefimus*, jointly) *fhall make known unto you all things which* (are done*)
here*." *Colofs.* iv. 7. 9.

" manner, he that is called, *being free,*
" is the *servant of Christ,*"—" *Ye are*
" *bought with a price;* BE NOT THERE-
" FORE THE SERVANTS OF MEN."
The apoſtle, indeed, had juſt before
recom-

*tical commiſſion* from the apoſtle to the church of the
*Coloſſians,* at the very time that he was ſent back to
*Philemon;* § and it would ſurely have ill become the
apoſtle to ſend back *Oneſimus,* then a *miniſter of the goſpel,*
to ſerve his maſter *Philemon, in his former capacity,*
(that is as a SLAVE) which is the doctrine preſumed in
page 18, of the reverend Mr. *Thompſon*'s tract; Mr.
*Thompſon,* as a clergyman, ought to have conſidered,
that this would not have been for the credit of the
*goſpel miniſtry.* But *Oneſimus* was not only a *miniſter,* and
*preacher,* but afterwards even a *biſhop,* which will by
no means ſuit with Mr. *Thompſon*'s doctrine. The
learned biſhop *Fell,* teſtified from the authority of *the
ancients,* that this *Oneſimus* was a biſhop. " *Oneſimus*"
ſays

§ Ludov. Capellus, remarks that theſe epiſtles, (viz. to *the Coloſ-
ſans* and to *Philemon)* were wrote, (and conſequently ſent) at the ſame
time, ard after aſſigning ſeveral reaſons for his opinion, concludes
as followe, " *Ex iis itaque, (*ſays he*) liquere puto utramque Epiſto-
lam ſimul codem tempore fuiſſe ſcriptam.*" Hiſt. Apoſt. illuſt. page
79. ed *Genevæ,* 1634.

recommended to his difciples to *abide in the fame calling,* wherein they were called, and, " *being fervants, not to care for it :*" That is, not to grieve on account of *their temporal* ftate ; (for if, inftead of thus enjoining *fubmiffion,* he had abfolutely declared *the iniquity of* SLAVERY, tho' *eftablifhed* and *authorized* by the laws of *temporal* governments, he would have occafioned more

tumult

(fays he in his commentary on Colloff. iv, 5 ) "*fervant to Philemon, a chief man in Coloffe. The antients fay that he fucceeded Timothy, in the* BISHOPRICK *of Ephefus.*" And the great archbifhop *Ufher,* makes exprefs mention of *Onefimus* in that *bifhoprick,* from tne authority both of *Eufebius* and *Ignatius,* (fee his little tract de Epifcoporum et Metropolitanorum Origine, p. 9. ed. Lond. 1687.) So that though *Paul* mentions to *Philemon* the receiving ONESIMUS FOR EVER (*that thou fhouldeft receive him* FOR EVER." ver. 15 ) yet it would be moft unreafonable to conceive that the apoftle meant that he fhould receive him FOR EVER AS A SLAVE! The feveral circumftances I have mentioned, demonftrate the contrary.

*tumult* than *reformation* among the multitude of SLAVES, more ftriving for *temporal* than *fpiritual* happinefs ; yet it plainly appears, by the infinuations, which immediately follow, that he thought it derogatory to the honour of chriftianity, that men, *who " are " bought,"* with the ineftimable *price of Chrift's* blood, fhould be efteemed *fervants* ; that is, *the Slaves,* and private property of other men ; and had chriftianity been eftablifhed by *temporal* authority, in thofe countries where *Paul* preached, as it is at prefent in thefe kingdoms, we need not doubt but that he would have *urged,* nay, compelled the mafters, *as he did Phile-mon,* by the moft prefling arguments, to treat their quondam flaves, " NOT " NOW AS SERVANTS, BUT ABOVE " SERVANTS----AS BRETHREN BE- " LOVED."

A N

A N

# E  L  E  G  Y

On the miſerable STATE of an AFRICAN
SLAVE, by the celebrated and ingenious WILLIAM SHENSTONE, Eſq;

—SEE the poor native quit the Lybian ſhores,
 Ah ! not in love's delightful fetters bound !
No radiant ſmile his dying peace reſtores,
 Nor love, nor fame, nor friendſhip heals his wound.

Let vacant bards diſplay their boaſted woes,
 Shall I the mockery of grief diſplay ?
No, let the muſe his piercing pangs diſcloſe,
 Who bleeds and weeps his ſum of life away !

On the wild beach in mournful guiſe he ſtood,
 Ere the ſhril boatſwain gave the hated ſign ;
He dropt a tear unſeen into the flood ;
 He ſtole one ſecret moment, to repine.

Yet the mufe liften'd to the plaints he made;
  Such moving plaints as nature could infpire;
To me the mufe his tender plea conve 'd,
  But fmooth'd, and fuited to the founding lyre.

" Why am I ravifh'd from my native ftrand?
  What favage race protects this impious gain?
Shall foreign plagues infeſt this teeming land,
  And more than fea-born monfters plough the main?

Here the dire locufts horrid fwarms prevail;
  Here the blue afps with livid poifon fwell;
Here the dry dipfa wriths his finuous mail;
  O can we not here, fecure from envy, dwell:

When the grim lion urg'd his cruel chace,
  When the ftern panther fought his midnight prey,
What fate referv'd me for this chriftian race?
  O race more polifh'd, more fevere than they!

Ye prouling wolves purfue my lateft cries!
  Thou hungry tyger, leave thy reeking den!
Ye fandy waftes in rapid eddies rife!
  O tear me from the whips and fcorns of men!

Yet in their face fuperior beauty glows;
  Are fmiles the mein of rapine and of wrong?
Yet from their lip the voice of mercy flows,
  And ev'n religion dwells upon their tongue.

Of blifsful haunts they tell, and brighter climes,
  Where gentle minds convey'd by death repair,
But ftain'd with blood, and crimfon'd o'er with crimes
  Say, fhall they merit what they paint fo fair?

No, carelefs, hopelefs of thofe fertile plains,
  Rich by our toils, and by our forrows gay,
They ply our labours, and enhance our pains,
  And feign thefe diftant regions to repay.

For

For them our tufky elephant expires;
　For them we drain the mine's embowel'd gold;
Where rove the brutal nations wild defires?—
Our limbs are purchas'd, and our life is fold!

Yet fhores there are, bleft fhores for us remain,
　And favour'd ifles with golden fruitage crown'd,
Where tufted flow'rets paint the verdant plain.
　Where ev'ry breeze fhall med'cine ev'ry wound.

There the ftern tyrant that embitters life
　Shall vainly fuppliant, fpread his afking hand;
There fhall we view the billow's raging ftrife,
　Aid the kind breaft, and waft his boat to land."

APPEN-

# APPENDIX

## ( No. 2. )

Extract of a Letter from a Gentleman in *Maryland,* to his Friend in *London.*

' BUT whether I fhall go thither or
' return home, I am yet undeter-
' mined; indeed, no where fhall I ftay
' long from England, for I had much ra-
' ther enjoy the bare neceffaries of life
' there, than the moft affluent circumftan-
' ces in this country of moft wretched Sla-
' very; which alone would render the life
' of any humane man moft miferable.
' There are four things under the Sun,
' which I equally abhor and abominate,
' viz. *Slavery* (under which I comprehend
' all cruelty, oppreffion and injuftice) and
' *licentioufnefs, pride* and *impudence,* all
' which abound here in a monftrous de-
' gree.
' The punifhments of the poor negroes
' and convicts, are beyond all conception,
' being entirely fubject to the will of their
' favage

' favage and brutal mafters, they are often
' punifhed for not doing more than ftrength
' and nature will admit of, and fometimes
' becaufe they can't on every occafion fall
' in with their wanton and capricious hu-
' mours.  One common punifhment, is to
' flea their backs with cow hides, or other
' inftruments of barbarity, and then pour
' on hot rum, fuperinduced with brine
' or pickle, rub'd in with a corn hufk, in
' the fcorching heat of the Sun.  For cer-
' tain, if your judges were fenfible of the
' fhocking treatment of the convicts here,
' they would hang every one of them, as
' an infinitely lefs punifhment, and tranf-
' port only thofe, whofe crimes deferve the
' fevereft death.  Better be hanged *feven*
' hundred times, than ferve *feven* years
' here! and there is no redrefs, for magif-
' trates and all are equally interefted and
' criminal.  If I had a child, I had rather
' fee him the humbleft fcavenger in the
' ftreets of *London*, than the loftieft ty-
' rant in *America*, with a thoufand flaves
' at his beck.'——

APPEN-

❦❦❦❦❦❦❦❦❦❦❦❦

# A P P E N D I X,

---
## ( N°. 3. )
---

A Letter from *Granville Sharp*, to *Jacob Bryant*, Efq; concerning the Defcent of the Negroes.

### S I R,

' I Have conceived a very high opinion
' of your abilities, by perufing your
' learned account of *Egypt, and the Shep-*
' *herd Kings*, &c. and as you feem to have
' ftudied, very particularly, the hiftory of
' the *Cufeans* and antient *Arabians*, you
' can (I apprehend) eafily refolve fome
' doubts, relating thereto, which occurred
' to me on reading your book.

' I HAD always fuppofed that black men
' in general were defcended from *Cufh*, be-
' caufe a diftinction in colour from the reft
' of mankind, feems to have been particu-
' larly attributed to his defcendants, *the Cu-*
' *fhim*, even to a proverb.' " *Can the Cufhi*
" (commonly rendered Ethiopian) *change his*
" *Skin,*" &c. (Jeremiah, xiii. 23.) and
' therefore

' therefore I concluded that all negroes,
' as well *Eaſt Indian* as *African*, are en-
' titled to the general name of *Cuſhim*,
' as being, probably, deſcended from dif-
' ferent branches of the ſame ſtock, be-
' cauſe the proverb is equally applicable to
' both, with reſpect to their complection,
' tho' in many reſpects they are very dif-
' ferent. But in p. 254, of your learned
' work, where you are ſpeaking of the *Cu-*
' *ſeans* in general, you ſay, that they are
" to be found within the tropics, almoſt
" as low as the Gold coaſt," &c. as if you
' apprehended, that the negroes on the
' Gold coaſt, and below it, *were not de-*
' *ſcended from Cuſh.*

' Now, Sir, I ſhall think myſelf greatly
' obliged if you will be pleaſed to inform
' me, whether you really have any particu-
' lar reaſon to apprehend that the negroes
' on the coaſt of *Guinea* (from whence our
' plantations are moſt commonly ſupplied)
' are deſcended from any other ſtock ? Or
' whether their deſcent can at all be traced ?

' I am far from having any particular
' eſteem for the negroes, but as I think
' myſelf *obliged* to conſider them as *Men,*
' I am certainly *obliged*, alſo, to uſe my beſt
' endeavours to prevent their being treated
' *as beaſts*, by our unchriſtian countrymen,
' who deny them the privileges of *human*
' *Nature*; and, in order to excuſe their
                                        ' own

' own *brutality*, will fcarcely allow that
' negroes are *human Beings*.

   ' THE tracing their defcent, therefore,
' is a point of fome confequence to the
' fubject, in which I am now engaged for
' their defence.'  *  *  *  *

 

I am,

SIR,

Your moft obedient,

*Old Jewry,*
*19th Oct.* 1772.       humble Servant,

GRANVILLE SHARP.

JACOB BRYANT, Efq;

# APPENDIX

## ( No. 4. )

Mr. *Bryant*'s Anſwer to the foregoing
Letter.

*Cypenham, 20th Octr.* 1772.

S I R,

' I MOST ſincerely wiſh you ſucceſs in
' your laudable purpoſe : and am **very**
' glad to find in theſe baſe times, that there
' is a perſon, who will ſtand up in defence
' of human nature ; and not ſuffer it **to be**
' limited to a ſet of features and complexion.
' There is nothing, I believe, in my wri-
' tings, that can affect any argument,
' which you may think proper to urge in
' favour of thoſe, whom you would patro-
' nize. But to take away all embarraſ-
' ment, and uncertainty, I will give you
' my opinion upon the ſubject, which you
' have ſtated to me in your letter, in
' reſpect to the origin of the Nigritæ or
' Negroes. You ſeem to think, that all,
' who are of that very deep tint, which is
                                    ' obſervable

' obſervable in the natives upon the coaſt
' of Guinea, are the offspring of *Chus*:
' and all black men in general are of the
' fame origin.  To this I take the liberty
' to anſwer, that all the natives of *Africa*
' are more or leſs ſwart: and even among
' the negroes there are a great variety of
' tints, from a light copper colour to the
' darkeſt black.  All the inhabitants of
' this vaſt continent are aſſuredly the ſons of
' *Ham*: but not equally deſcended from
' *Chus*.  For though his poſterity was very
' dark, yet many of the collateral branches
' were of as deep a die: and *Africa* was
' peopled from *Ham*, by more families
' than one.  It was poſſeſſed by ſome of
' them, as there is good grounds to ſur-
' miſe, before the *Cuſhites* came into *Egypt*.
' We learn from ſcripture, that *Ham* had
' four ſons, *Chus, Mizraim, Phut* and *Ca-*
' *naan*, Gen. x. v. 6. *Canaan* occupied
' *Paleſtine*, and the country called by his
' his name: *Mizraim Egypt*: But *Phut*
' paſſed deep into *Africa*, and, I believe,
' moſt of the nations in that part of the
' world are deſcended from him: at leaſt
' more than from any other perſon.
' *Joſephus* ſays, " *that Phut was the foun-*
" *der of the nations in Libya,* * *and the*
                                    " *people*

---

* See Joſephus, Antq. lib. 1 c. 7,

" *people were from him called,* (Φυτοι)
" *Phuti.*"  By *Libya* he underſtands, as the
' *Greeks* did, *Africa* in general : for the
' particular country, called *Libya* proper,
' was peopled by the *Lubim,* or *Lehabim,*
' one of the branches from *Mizraim,* Λαβιειμ
' 3ξ ου Λιβυες.  Chron. Paſchale, p. 29.

    ' THE ſons of *Phut,* ſettled in *Maurita-*
' *nia,* where was a country called *Phuſia,*
' and a river of the like denomination.
" Mauritaniæ Fluvius uſque ad præſens
" tempus *Phut* dicitur, omniſque circa
" eum regio *Phutenſis.* (Hierons. Tradit.
" Hebrææ.) —— Amnem, quem vocant
" *Fut* :" (Pliny, lib. 5. c. i.)—Some of this
' family ſettled above Egypt, near Æthi-
' opia, and were ſtiled Troglodytæ.   Φουδ
' εξ ου Τρωγλοδυται   Syncellus, p. 47.
' Many of them paſſed inland, and peopled
' the *Mediterranean* country.  In proceſs of
' time, (after their expulſion from *Egypt,)*
' the ſons of *Chus* made ſettlements upon
' the ſea coaſt of *Africa,* and came into
' *Mauritania.*   Hence we find traces of
' them alſo in the names of places, ſuch as
' *Churis, Chuſares,* upon the coaſt : and a
' river *Cuſa,* and a city *Cotta,* together
' with a promontory *Cotis* in *Mauritania,*
' all denominated from *Chus;* who at dif-
' ferent times and by different people was
' called *Chus, Cuth, Coſh* and *Cotis.*   The
' river *Cuſa* is mentioned by *Pliny,* lib. 5

                                   ' c    I

‘ c. 1, and by *Ptolomey*. Many ages after
‘ thefe fettlements, there was another ir-
‘ ruption of the *Cufhites* into thefe parts,
‘ under the name of *Saracens* * and *Moors* ;
‘ who over ran *Africa*, to the very extre-
‘ mities of mount *Atlas*.  They paffed
‘ over, and conquered *Spain* to the north :
‘ and they extended themfelves fouthward,
‘ as I faid in my treatife, to the rivers *Sene-*
‘ *gal* and *Gambia*, and as low as the *Gold*
‘ *Coaft*.  I mentioned this, becaufe I do
‘ not think, that they proceeded much far-
‘ ther :  moft of the nations to the fouth
‘ being, as I imagine, of the race of *Phut*.
‘ The very country upon the river *Gambia*
‘ on one fide, is at this day called *Phuta*, of
‘ of which *Bluet*, in his hiftory of *Juba Ben*
‘ *Solomon*, gives an account.

‘ It is not poffible to difcriminate at this
‘ æra of time the feveral cafts among the
‘ black nations, but I fhould think, that
‘ we may be pretty certain, that they were
‘ not all *Cufhim*, or *Cufeans*.  The Negroes
‘ are woolly headed; and fo were fome of
‘ the *Æthiopes* or *Cufhim*: but nothing can
‘ be inferred from this : for many of the
‘ latter had long hair, as we learn from *He-*
‘ *rodotus*, lib. 7. c. 70. ιθυτριχες.  We
‘ find

* *Query.*—Whether the *Saracens* may not rather be
faid to be of the line of *Shem*, as being defcended
from *Abraham* ?—Though indeed, both the mother
and the wife of *Ifhmael*, were *Egyptians*.

‘ find from *Marcellinus*, that the *Egyp-*
‘ *tians* were *Crispi*, and had a tendency to
‘ woolly hair : fo that this circumftance can-
‘ not always be looked upon as a family
‘ charaƈteriftic.

‘ THIS, Sir, is my opinion concerning
‘ the people in queftion, which I fubmit to
‘ your confideration, merely as matter of
‘ opinion : for I cannot pretend to fpeak
‘ with certainty.  It makes very little dif-
‘ ference in refpeƈt to tne good caufe,
‘ which your humanity prompts you to ef-
‘ poufe, whether the Nigritæ are *Phutians*,
‘ or *Cufhites.* They are certainly the fons
‘ of *Ham :* and, what is more to the pur-
‘ pofe, they are the workmanfhip of God,
‘ formed in his image witn a living Soul ;
‘ as well as ourfelves.  Confequently they
‘ deferve better treatment, than they have
‘ generally experienced from thofe, who
‘ look upon themfelves, as more enlighten-
‘ ed, and poffeffed of a greater degree of
‘ humanity.  I join with you fincerely in
‘ detefting the cruel traffic : and am, with
‘ great truth,   S I R,

Your moft obedient,
and moft humble Servant,
J A C O B  B R Y A N T.

‘ P. S. You are pleafed to obferve, *that*
‘ *a diftinƈtion in colour from the reft of man-*
‘ *kind*

'*kind* seems to have been *particularly attri-*
'*buted to the descendants of the Cushim.* They
'certainly were very dark : but so were all
'the sons of *Ham.* And it is difficult to
'say, who were the darkest, as it was a
'circumstance depending upon the situation
'of the people spoken of, and upon many
'occult causes. The same family in differ-
'ent parts varied from itself, as I have shewn
'from *Herodotus.* The sacred writers speak
'of the *Cushi*'s complexion particularly, be-
'cause they were most acquainted with it,
'as being very near *Shem.* There were se-
'veral regions, called *Cushan* or *Æthiopia,*
'one of which was upon the confines of
'*Judæa,* near *Amalec* and *Edom* ; but still
'nearer to *Midian.* Hence the prophet
'*Habbakuh* says in a vision,—" *I saw the*
'" *tents of* Cushan *in affliction, and the cur-*
'" *tains of* Midian *did tremble.*" C. iii. v. 7.
'These were the *Araba Cushitæ*; with
'whom the *Israelites* were most acquainted.
'Of the sons of *Phut,* and of the *Ludim,*
'*Lehabim,* and other descendants of *Ham,*
'in *Africa,* they had probably little or no
'cognizance, excepting only the *Mizraim,*
'and the *Æthiopians* immediately above
'them to the south of *Syene.* With these
'they were acquainted. Should it be in
'my power to give you any farther satisfac-
'tion, I shall be very proud of your com-
'mands. * * * * * *

THE

' THE whole of what you mention, that
' all Moors, Negroes, and black perſons are
' from one common ſtock is moſt aſſuredly
' true, if you make the head of that family
' *Ham*, inſtead of *Chus*. One remove higher
' makes every thing ſtrictly conſonant to
' the truth.'

APPEN-

# A P P E N D I X,

## ( No. 5. )

The Regulations lately adopted by the *Spaniards*, at the *Havanna*, and some other Places, for the gradual *enfranchisement of Slaves*, are to the following Effect.

'     S foon as a flave is landed, his
'  **A**  name, price, &c. are regiftered in
' a public regifter ; and the mafter is oblig-
' ed, by law, to allow him *one working day*,
' in every week, to himfelf, *befides Sundays* ;
' fo that, if the flave chufes to work for his
' mafter on that day, he receives the *wages*
' *of a freeman* for it ; and whatever he gains
' by his labour, on that day, is fo fecured to
' him by law, that the mafter cannot de-
' prive him of it. This is certainly a con-
' fiderable ftep towards the abolifhing *abfo-*
' *lute flavery.* As foon as the flave is able
' to purchafe *another working day*, the maf-
' ter is obliged to fell it to him at a propor-
' tionable price, *viz.* one fifth part of his
'                                                    ' original

' original coft ; and fo, likewife, the re-
' maining four days, at the fame rate, as
' foon as the flave is able to redeem them;
' after which *he is abfolutely free*: This is
' fuch encouragement to induftry, that even
' the moft indolent are tempted to exert
' themfelves. Men, who have thus work-
' ed out their freedom, are enured to the
' labour of the country, and are certainly
' the moft ufeful fubjects that a colony can
' acquire. Regulations might be formed
' upon the fame plan to encourage the in-
' duftry of flaves *that are already imported*
' *into the colonies*, which would teach them
' how to maintain themfelves, and be *as*
' *ufeful*, as well as *lefs* expenfive to the plan-
' ter. They would by fuch means become
' members of fociety, and have an intereft
' in the welfare of the community ; which
' would add greatly to the ftrength and fe-
' curity of each colony : whereas, at pre-
' fent, many of the plantations are in *conti-*
' *nual danger of being cut off by their flaves,*
' a fate which they but *too juftly deferve.*'

APPEN-

# APPENDIX,

## ( No. 6. )

### Extract of a Letter from the Author, to a Gentleman at *Philadelphia*.

' —— and furely there needs no argu-
' ment to demonftrate the weaknefs and dan-
' ger of the more fouthern colonies, from *the*
' *immenfe multitude of flaves*, that are forci-
' bly detained therein !

' THE congrefs have acted nobly in for-
' bidding the iniquitous importation of *more*
' *flaves*; but the bufinefs is but half done,
' 'till they have agreed upon fome equitable
' and fafe means of *gradually enfranchifing*
' thofe which remain.  No time fhould be
' loft in forwarding this equitable meafure ;
' —and, to fecure the affections of the ne-
' groes, affurances fhould be immediately
' given of fuch friendly intentions towards
' them, left any attack fhould, in the mean
' while, be made in thofe quarters, which
might

' might encourage *an insurrection*. I tremble
' for the probable consequences of such an
' event! for though *domestic slavery*, (which
' I detest from my heart) would thereby be
' abolished, yet that effect would be wrought
' at the expence of *public Liberty*; and the
' *tyranny* and injustice of private individuals
' would seem, perhaps, to be too severely
' punished by that horrid carnage and im-
' placability, which usually attend the con-
' flicts between masters and slaves !

' LET *private interest* therefore give place
' to *justice* and *right*, which will most effec-
' tually administer to the public safety.

' LET it be remembered that many of
' the negroes are natives of the colonies,
' and consequently have *a natural right* to a
' *free existence* therein, as well as the Land-
' holders themselves. I shall not presume
' to *advise* the mode of effecting this im-
' portant and necessary enfranchisement,
' but will only offer a few hints in order to
' promote the consideration and determina-
' tion of those who are best able to judge
' of the matter.

' SUPPOSE the value of every slave now in
' the colonies, was to be fairly estimated, by
' juries appointed for that purpose, and the
' value to be entered, under their inspection,
' (as a pecuniary *debt* due from each negroe
' to his master,) in a public register for each
' district. Suppose also that the landholders,
' who

'who do not occupy all their grounds, were
'advifed to divide what lands they can fpare
'into *compact little farms*, with a fmall wooden
'cottage to each, which fhould be allotted
'to thofe negroes only, who are natives of
'the colony, or elfe have been fo long in it,
'that their difpofitions are fufficiently known,
'whether or not they may fafely be entruft-
'ed with their liberty. Let fuch negroes hold
'thefe fmall portions of land by leafes, for
'a certain term of years; and at equitable
'rents, to be paid in fuch portions of *the*
'*produce* from time to time, as fhall be
'thought moft reafonable, leaving the ten-
'ants a moderate gain, (befides their necef-
'fary fubfiftence) to encourage induftry, and
'yet fo as to yield the landlords a due profit
'from each portion of their eftates, befides
'an adequate allowance to reimburfe (within
'the limited time) not only the regiftered
'price of their quondam flaves, but alfo
'whatever fums they may have advanced to-
'wards the expence of *building*, of *implements*,
'of *live ftock*, of *feed*, &c. &c. the amount
'of which ought to be added to the firft
'debt and regiftered, in like manner, before
'the leafes are executed. By thefe means the
'landlords will lofe nothing of their wealth,
'and yet the moft ufeful and worthieft of the
'negroes will acquire a *natural intereft* in
'the welfare and fafety of the community,
'which will infure their affiftance againft
                                         'any

'any hoftile attempt of the reft. Other
'negroes, that are not capable of managing
'and fhifting for themfelves, nor are fit to be
'trufted, all at once, with liberty, might be
'delivered over to the care and protection of
'a county committee, in order to avoid the
'baneful effects of *private property in men*;
'and might, by the faid committee, be let
'out, as *hired fervants*, to fuch perfons as
'would undertake the charge of them, to
'be paid (alfo *in produce*) towards the dif-
'charge of the regiftered debt for each
'man's original price ; and the labourer
'himfelf in the mean while to be allow-
'ed one day in a week (befide the Sun-
'day) for his own profit, or be paid
'for it according to the mode of the
'*Spanifh regulations*, (which I before tranf-
'mitted) that he may have an opportuni-
'ty to acquire a little property of his own,
'which will *prepare his mind*, as well as
'his circumftances *for freedom*, by enabling
'him, as a member of the community to
'fhift for himfelf at the time of his dif-
'charge. By fome fuch regulations, as
'thefe, flavery might be changed into a
'condition, more nearly refembling that of
'*hired fervants*, as no mafter would be the
'*abfolute proprietor* of thofe he employs,
'and yet all reafonable advantages arifing
'from their labour, would remain ; which
'muft occafion a reciprocal improvement
'in the morality and humanity both of maf-
'ters

‘ ters and servants; and in process of time,
‘ instead of *wretched slaves*, a new and use-
‘ ful order of men, at present unknown in
‘ America, (where every *freeman* cultivates
‘ his own ground only) would be established
‘ amongst you; I mean a hardy body of
‘ *free peasants*, serving either as *trusty ten-*
‘ *ants* or *farmers*, to improve the estates of
‘ landed gentlemen, or else as *laborious cot-*
‘ *tagers*, who might be employed with in-
‘ finite advantage to the neighbourhood,
‘ wherever established, especially if they
‘ were encouraged by an allotment of a
‘ small patch of land for a potatoe ground
‘ or garden, with a right of pasture for a
‘ little live stock upon some common field
‘ in the neighbourhood of their little cot-
‘ tages.—Landholders by this means would
‘ have their estates better peopled and im-
‘ proved, and yet avoid the guilt and dan-
‘ ger of oppression.   In the mean while, the
‘ hours of labour should be uniformly regu-
‘ lated, to prevent the oppression of avari-
‘ cious exactors, and the danger of discon-
‘ tent:   and schools should be opened in
‘ every district, to give the poor labourers
‘ and their children, some general ideas of
‘ morality and religious knowledge, which
‘ constitute the most effectual *bond of peace.*
‘ These regulations I mention only by way
‘ of hint :  you have the same earnest regard
                                    ‘ for

' for the cauſe of *general liberty*, and *the*
' *natural rights of mankind* that I have,
' and much greater abilities to defend them,
' and to propoſe a more perfect ſyſtem than
' what is here ſuggeſted.   Let me therefore
' intreat you to conſider this matter, and to
' forward, as ſoon as poſſible, ſome ſcheme
' of general enfranchiſement, becauſe Ame-
' rican liberty cannot be firmly eſtabliſhed
' 'till this is done.


' I am with great eſteem,


'Dear S I R,


' Your affectionate friend


' and humble ſervant.'

London,
18 July, 1775:

'GRANVILLE SHARP.'


A P P E N-

# A P P E N D I X,

---

( No. 7. )

---

Extract from Mr. *Morgan*'s Book, intituled, ' *A Plan for the Abolition of*
' *Slavery, in the West Indies.*'

—Page 12.——' Nothing can be more
' oppofite to every idea of juftice and mo-
' rality than the prefent practice of buying
' flaves, to cultivate the Weft Indian iflands
' and the fouthern provinces on the conti-
' nent of America; nor can any thing, I
' *think, be eventually more fatal* — * * *

Page 13.——' Yet fomething, out of
' worldly prudence. ought to be done;—for,
' as this evil has been violently introduced,
' contrary to the natural courfe of things
' and the conftitution of the world, it will
' one day find a remedy even in its excefs.
' Matters will be fatally brought to a crifis,
' and nature will vindicate her own laws,
' and

' and reftore the credit of her equal and
' juft adminiftration, to the lafting punifh-
' ment of thofe who abufed it.   THIS WILL
' BE WHEN THE BLACKS OF THE SOUTH-
' THERN COLONIES ON THE CONTINENT
' OF AMERICA SHALL BE NUMEROUS
' ENOUGH TO THROW OFF AT ONCE THE
' YOKE OF TYRANNY TO REVENGE THEIR
' WRONGS IN THE BLOOD OF THEIR OP-
' PRESSORS, AND CARRY TERROR AND
' DESTRUCTION TO THE MORE NORTHERN
' SETTLEMENTS.   Such a revolution can-
' not take place in the iflands until this
' period, on account of the want of intel-
' ligence and communication between the
' flaves of one ifland and another, and of
' the eafy communication and mutual af-
' fiftance of whites.   But an infurrection on
' the continent, once communicated, will
' be an incitement in the iflands, and a fig-
' nal for a general and (but that every
' Englifhman is alike concerned, and the
' planter not peculiarly criminal) A MERIT-
' ED CARNAGE.

    ' Nothing can be conceived MORE DE-
' STRUCTIVE, MORE INSATIATE, THAN
' THE WARS WHICH WILL FOLLOW THIS
' EVENT ; they will be every where marked
' with THE MOST HORRIBLE CRUELTIES,
' and THE MOST FURIOUS REVENGE.   The
' diftinction of *black* and *white*, which we
                                        ' have

' have fo unreafonably made the marks of
' *freedom* and *flavery*, will then become
' the obvious colours of mutual hoftility and
' revenge; and it feems likely that thefe
' wars MAY END TO THE DISADVANTAGE
' OF THE WHITES; becaufe the blacks, as will
' be prefently obferved, will increafe fafter,
' and becaufe their nature feems better able
' to bear the feverity of cold, than the
' whites can that of heat.'—*&c.*

APPEN-

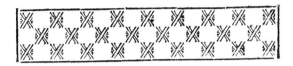

# A P P E N D I X,

## ( No 8. )

A Copy of what " *is faid* to be the " fubftance of Lord *Mansfield's* fpeech " in the cafe of *Somerfet* and *Knowles :*"

ON Monday the 22d June, in Trinity term, 1772, the court of *King's Bench*, proceeded to give judgement in the Cafe of *Somerfet* and *Knowles*, upon the return of the Habeas Corpus. LORD MANS-FIELD firft ftated the return; and then fpoke to the following purport, which is taken from the fecond edition of a Tract, printed in 1773, intituled, " *Confidera-*" *tions on the Negroe Caufe, fo called, ad-*" *dreffed to the right honourable lord* Mans-" field, *lord chief juftice of the court of* " *King's Bench, by* SAMUEL ESTWICK, " *A. M. Affiftant Agent for the ifland of* " Barbadoes." page vii. *viz.*

    ' WE pay due attention to the opinion ' of Sir *Philip Yorke* and Mr. *Talbot*, in ' the year 1729, by which they pledged ' themfelves to the Britifh planters for the
                       ' legal

' legal confequences of bringing Negroe-flaves
' into this kingdom, or their being baptiz-
' ed ; which opinion was repeated and re-
' cognized by lord Hardwicke, fitting as
' chancellor, on the 19th of October, 1749,
' to the following effect : he faid,' " that
" trover would lay for a negroe-flave : that a
" notion prevailed, that if a flave came into
" England, or became a Chriftian, he there-
" by became emancipated ; but there was no
" foundation in law for fuch a notion : that
" when he and Lord Talbot were attorney
" and folicitor general, this notion of a flave
" becoming free by being baptized per-
" vailed fo ftrongly, that the planters induf-
" trioufly prevented their becoming chrif-
" tians : upon which their opinion was taken ;
" *and upon their beft confideration they were*
" *both clearly of opinion,* that a flave did not
" in the leaft alter his fituation or ftate to-
" wards his mafter or *owner,* either by be-
" ing chriftened, or coming to England :
" that though the ftatute of Charles II. had
" abolifhed" (*homage* ‡ ) " tenure fo far,
" that no man could be a *Villein regardant* ;
" yet if he would acknowledge himfelf a
" *Villein* engroffed in any court of record, he
                                        ' knew

---

(‡) See a part of my lord *Mansfield's* fpeech printed
in the Appendix, (p. 11.) of " *a Treatife upon the*
" *Trade from* Great Britain *to* Africa, *by an African*
" *merchant,*" wherein this word " *homage*" is inferted.

" knew of no way by which he could be en-
" titled to his freedom, without the confent
" of his mafter." ' We feel the force of
' the inconveniences and confequences that
' will follow the decifion of this queftion :
' yet all of us are fo clearly of one opinion
' upon the *only* queftion before us, that we
' think we ought to give judgment without
' adjourning the matter to be argued before
' all the judges, as ufual in the habeas cor-
' pus, and as we at firft intimated an inten-
' tion of doing in this cafe.  The only quef-
' tion then is, *Is the caufe returned fufficient*
' *for the remanding him ?  If not*, he muft be
' difcharged.  The caufe returned is, the
' *flave* abfented himfelf and departed from
' his mafter's fervice, and refufed to return
' and ferve him during his ftay in *England* ;
' whereupon, by his mafter's orders, he was
' put on board the fhip by force, and there
' detained in fecure cuftody, to be carried
' out of the kingdom and fold.  So high
' an act of dominion muft derive its autho-
' rity, if any fuch it has, from the law of
' the kingdom *where* executed.  A foreig-
' ner cannot be imprifoned *here* on the au-
' thority of any law exifting in his own coun-
' try.  The power of a mafter over his fer-
' vant is different in all countries, more or
' lefs limited or extenfive , the exercife of
' of it therefore muft always be regulated
                                    ' by

' by the laws of the place where exercifed.
' The ftate of flavery is of fuch a nature,
' that it is incapable of being now intro-
' duced by courts of juftice upon mere rea-
' foning, or inferences from any principles
' natural or political; it muft take its rife
' from *pofitive law*; the origin of it can in
' no country or age be traced back to any
' other fource. Immemorial ufage preferves
' the memory of *pofitive law* long after all
' traces of the occafion, reafon, authority,
' and time of its introduction, are loft, and
' in A CASE SO ODIOUS AS THE CONDITION
' OF SLAVES MUST BE TAKEN STRICTLY.
' (*Tracing the fubject to natural princi-*
' *ples, the claim of flavery never can be fup-*
' *ported.*) (‡) THE POWER CLAIMED BY
' THIS RETURN WAS NEVER IN USE
' HERE: (or *acknowledged by the law.*) No
' mafter ever was allowed here to take a
' flave by force to be fold abroad becaufe he
' had deferted from his fervice, or for any
' other reafon whatever; WE CANNOT SAY,
' *the caufe fet forth by this return* IS ALLOW-

I 2                                      ' ED

(‡) Thefe additions in Italics between hooks before
and after the words " THE POWER CLAIMED BY
THIS RETURN WAS NEVER IN USE HERE," are
taken from the notes of a very ingenious and able
counfellor, who was prefent when the judgement
was given.—The reft of his notes fufficiently agree
in fubftance with what Mr. *Eftwick* has printed.

' ED OR APPROVED OF BY THE LAWS OF
' THIS KINGDOM, and therefore the man
' muſt be diſcharged '

Upon this Mr. *Eſtwick* has been pleaſed
to obſerve as follows, ' *I muſt confeſs* (ſays he)
' *I have been greatly puzzled in endeavouring*
' *to reconcile this judgement with this ſtate of*
' *it, and with my comprehenſion,*' &c. But the
writer quoted by the *African merchant* before
mentioned, is not ſo modeſt in his cenſure
of this judgement, nor ſo honeſt in his *re-*
*cital* of it, as Mr *Eſtwick,* for he partially
conceals the moſt material part of the learned judge's ſpeech, becauſe it happens to
make againſt his own wicked cauſe ; and
tells us by way of excuſe for ſo notorious
and partial an omiſſion—that " *the remain-*
' *der of the ſpeech is too vague to come into*
' *conſideration,*' &c. (p. 12.) Another anonymous writer (author of a pamphlet, intitled
' CANDID REFLECTIONS *upon* THE JUDGE-
' MENT *lately awarded by the Court of King's*
' *Bench, in Weſtminſter Hall, on what is com-*
' *monly* called the NEGROE CAUSE, *by a Plan-*
' *ter,*' ) after comparing this JUDGEMENT
of the King's Bench, with the opinions of the
judges *Holt* and *Powel,* and thoſe of the
attorney and ſolicitor general, *York* and *Tal-*
*bot,* &c. is pleaſed to *reflect* thereupon as
follows. " *A point,* (ſays he) *upon which*
" *theſe great Oracles of the law have publiſhed*
                                        " *ſuch*

" such opposite sentiments, seems as far as ever
" from being established upon the solid ground of
" absolute PRECISION. The planters of course
" have been left (says he) as much puzzled
" by this DELPHIC AMBIGUITY, as the sages
" themselves appear to have been, in forming
" their judgements upon the subject. The mat-
" ter having been CONFOUNDED in this
" GRAND UNCERTAINTY," &c. (p. 57.)
But these heavy charges of the want of
" PRECISION," of " DELPHIC AMBIGUITY,"
and of being " CONFOUNDED in GRAND UN-
"CERTAINTY," &c. are so far from being
" CANDID REFLECTIONS," (as this author
would have us believe them,) that even *his
own evidence* on the preceeding page, clearly proves the falsehood and injustice of his
censures ; for he has there given us the
EFFECT of that late judgment of the court
of King's Bench, in THE CLEAREST TERMS,
without the least *doubt* or *difficulty* ; so that
the *delphic ambiguity*, of which he *immediately after* complains, must be (even according to his own evidence,) a mere *calumny*!

After reciting the opinion of lord chief
justice *Holt*, he immediately adds as follows.

" Lord chief justice *mansfield* (says he)
" adds to this effect.

" That the laws of *Great Britain* do not
" authorize a master to *reclaim* his fugi-
" tive SLAVE, *confine* or *transport* him out of
" the kingdom. In other words;" (says
he)

he) " that a negroe flave, coming from the
" colonies into *Great Britain* becomes, *ipfo*
" *facto*, FREE."

Thus, notwithftanding the *un-candid reflections* of this author about DELPHIC AM-
BIGUITY, yet even *he himself* has without
*doubt* or *difficulty*, declared THE *certain* and
*unavoidable* EFFECT of the judgement delivered by Lord *Mansfield!* That this author (notwithftanding his prejudices, and
unjuft cenfures about ambiguity) has really ftated the *certain* and *unavoidable* EFFECT
of the faid judgment, will appear by the
following remarks upon it.

# A P P E N D I X.

## ( No. 9. )

Remarks on the Judgment of the Court of *King*'s *Bench*, in the Cafe of *Stewart* and *Somerfet*. By *Granville Sharp*.

THIS judgment will not appear doubtful and inexplicit, (as fome have too haftily efteemed it) if the whole be taken together, and THE EFFECT of it be duly confidered.

LORD *Mansfield* pronounced the fentiments or judgment *of the whole bench,* and therefore if any thing was wrong, the blame ought not to reft on him alone ; neverthelefs, if we fairly examine what was faid, we fhall find no room for blame or cavil, His lordfhip faid, " WE *pay due* ' *attention* to the opinion of Sir *Philip* ' *York* and Mr. *Talbot,* in the year 1729,'

Now

Now the purport of that opinion was, that the mafter ' *may legally compel* his flave ' *to return to the plantations.*'

LORD *Mansfield* modeftly declined giving a direct contradiction, in exprefs words, to the opinion of two fuch very eminent and learned lawyers; but chofe rather to condemn it, tacitly, by *the effect* of the judgment, which he was about to pronounce ; and therefore he merely recited the opinion without the leaft comment; and proceeded to the determination of the court upon the cafe before them ; which is clear and incontrovertible with refpect to the main point of the queftion, viz. the power claimed by the mafter, of carrying away his flave by force.

' *The power claimed by this return,* (faid the ' chief juftice) *was never in ufe here, or ac-* ' *knowledged by the law.*' Now it was certainly the duty of the court to give judgment according to *the known laws,* and not to be influenced by *any opinion* whatfoever.

THEY acknowledged, indeed, the having " *paid due attention*" to the faid opinion ; but as their determination was diametrically oppofite to the affertions in that opinion, it is manifeft, that the court *did not think it grounded in law,* according to which alone they were bound to determine. The conclufion of lord *Mansfield*'s fpeech contains
more

more fubftantial and unanfwerable reafons
for the judgment he was about to give, than
the generality of his hearers, perhaps, were
aware of ; for he very ingenioufly expreffed
in the fmall compafs of two fhort fentences,
that the mafters claim was contrary to
three principal foundations of the *Englifh*
law, viz. NATURE, USE, (or *Cuftom*,) and
the WRITTEN LAW; which laft allo includes
two other foundations, viz. MAXIMS and
STATUTES. With refpect to the firft, he faid
— " *traceing the fubject to* NATURAL *princi-*
" *ples, the claim of* SLAVERY *never can be*
" *fupported.*" With refpect to the fecond, he
faid, —" *the power claimed by this return, was*
" *never in* USE *here*," and thirdly, that it was
" never *acknowledged by* THE LAW."

THESE feem to have been *the reafons* of
the determination ; and confequently the
court was obliged *by the common law*
(which always favours LIBERTY ‖ to difcharge the man from the *unnatural* and *un-
precedented* claims of his mafter, which was
accordingly don , fo that the true meaning
of this determination is rendered clear and
incontrovertible, as well by *the effect of it,*
as by the unanfwerable *reafons* above mentioned.

THAT

‖ ' *Law favoureth life,* LIBERTY, *and* DOWER.'
' *Law regards the* PERSON *above his poffeffions,* - LIFE
' and LIBERTY, *moft*,' &c. (Principia Legis et Æquit.
P. 56.
' LIBERTAS *eft res ineftimablis.*' (Jenk. Cent. 52.)

THAT there is nothing *doubtful* or *inexplicit* in this *judgement*, delivered by lord *Mansfield*, will further appear by the following report of a cafe in the PREROGATIVE COURT, wherein this very determination on *Somerfet's* cafe, is exprefsly cited, and the EFFECT of it clearly and fully declared by a learned judge of that court.    And the propriety of the faid judgment has very lately been ftill further confirmed by a decree alfo in THE HIGH COURT OF ADMIRALTY, after a very learned and folemn debate concerning the *legality,* or, *illegality of flavery in England,* wherein the merits of the queftion on both fides was fully examined and difcuffed.    A fhort ftate of the Cafe, together with the fubftance of the decree will be found in Appendix, No. 11.    The offence expreffed in this latter Cafe was fo flagrantly wicked in all its circumftances, and upon the whole, was fo notorious a contempt of the laws and conftitution of this kingdom, as well as of *natural right* and common honefty, that all perfons, who have any regard for juftice, muft be moved with indignation againft the authors of the mifchief, and muft wifh to fee them corrected by fome *adequate* and *exemplary punifhment,* inftead of a decifion againft them for the mere *recovery of wages.* In order therefore to prevent any unjuft prejudice of well meaning people, againft the manner of proceeding in this cafe for redrefs, it is neceffary

ceſſary to remark, that the negroe did not 'apply for redreſs of theſe injuries,' till more than two years after they were committed, whereby he was deprived of the ſatisfaction to which THE HABEAS CORPUS ACT would otherwiſe have entitled him 'IN ANY OF HIS MAJESTY'S COURTS OF RECORD,' viz.---
'to recover his treble coſts, beſides damages,
'which damages ſo to be given, (ſays the act)
'ſhall not be leſs than FIVE HUNDRED POUNDS,' that is five hundred pounds from each offendor,—frm every individual concerned (and theſe ſeem, in the preſent caſe, to have been more than 4 or 5) that had either been 'advising, aiding, or 'aſſiſting,' in ſo flagrant a breach of the peace; and they would likewiſe have been ſubject to all the 'pains, penalties, forfeitures, loſſes or diſſabilities ordained in THE STATUTE of PROVISION and PRÆMUNIRE! See my 'Repreſentation of the 'injuſtice, and dangerous tendency of tole-'rating Slavery in England,' printed in 1769, pages 25 to 29.


GRANVILLE SHARP.


APPEN.

# A P P E N D I X,

---

( No. 10. )

---

# C A S E,

*Prerogative Court,* May 11th, 1773.
CAY and CRICHTON.

——A. B. deceafed, *in* 1769, among other effects, left behind him a *negroe fervant.* CRICHTON, the executor, was called upon by CAY, to give in an *inventory* of the deceafed's *goods and chattels,* which he accordingly did, but omitted the *negroe.*

*This omiffion* was made a ground of exception to the inventory, as being, therefore, not *perfect.*

UPON argument, it was faid by the council on behalf of *Crichton,* that by a very late cafe in the King's Bench, of *Knowles*
*and*

*(a) and Somerset,* negroes were declared *to be free in England,* and consequently, they could not be the subjects of *property,* or be considered as any part of a personal estate.

It was answered, that the case above-mentioned was determined only in 1772; that A. B. died in 1769, at which time negroes were in some respects, considered as property, and therefore that he ought to have been included in the account,

The judge (Dr. *Hay,*) said that this court had no right to try any question relating to freedom and slavery; but as *Negroes* had been *declared free* by the court which had the proper jurisdiction, that determination referred to them, as well at the preceeding time, as at the present, and therefore directed, that article, in which the *negroe* was mentioned, to be struck out of the *exceptive allegation.*

---

(a) *Knowles* was the master of the ship who detained *Somerset,* by order of Mr. *Stewart,* who claimed the latter as his *property.*

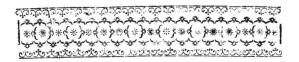

# A P P E N D I X,

---

( No. II. )

---

High Court of Admiralty, before Sir **Geo.**
Hay, *Knt. L.L.D.* June, 29, 1776.

# C A S E.

*ROGERS*, alias *RIGGES* against *JONES*

| | |
|---|---|
| Dr. *Wynne* | Dr. *Harris* |
| Dr. *Bever* | Dr. *Calvert* |
| Proctor *Torriano.* | Proctor *Holman.* |

'GEORGE ROGERS alias RIGGES,
'a negro about nineteen years of age, had
'been a servant to several gentlemen in
'*England*, and in the summer of 1766,
'being

' being then out of place, became ac-
' quainted with *John Latter* and *John*
' *Seffins*, who contracted with *Arthur Jones*
' for the sale of him; an assignment,
' was accordingly drawn for that purpose,
' and signed by *John Latter*, by which
' *Rogers* was transferred to Messrs. *Mason*
' and *Jones*, as a slave. for the sum of
' twelve guineas.

'  SOME time in August, 1766, after the
' sale above mentioned, *Rogers*, under some
' false pretences, was carried on board the
' ship *Britannia*, then lying at *Deptford*, of
' which Messrs. *Mason* and *Jones* were owners,
' was there detained against his will, and that
' he might not escape, was carried down into
' the sail room, by order of the chief mate,
' and the gratings were put upon him.   In
' this confinement he was kept, till the ship
' set sail, when he was released, and suffer-
' ed to go about upon deck; but not being
' entered in the ship's books as a mariner,
' nor having any particular office, or wages
' assigned to him, he was set to work about
' the ship's duty in general  till he was ap-
' pointed as an assistant to the cook, which
' office he executed sometimes as assistant,
' and sometimes as principal cook, during
' the whole voyage.   The ship first sailed to
' the coast of *Africa*, on the SLAVE TRADE,
                                      and

‘ and from thence to *Porto Rico*, where he
‘ was offered to fale, by the captain of
‘ the *Britannia*, as a prime flave ; but
‘ *Rogers* having found an opportunity
‘ of relating his ftory to the *Spanifh*
‘ merchants, they refufed to purchafe
‘ him ; he therefore returned with the
‘ fhip, in which he ftill acted in his
‘ former capacity of affiftant cook ; and
‘ upon their arrival in the port of *Lon-*
‘ *don*, in *May* 1/68, when the other ma-
‘ riners were paid and difcharged, he
‘ was ftill detained on board againft his
‘ will.

‘ Here he continued for fome time, till
‘ he contrived to give the officers the flip,
‘ and by the affiftance and advice of fome
‘ friends, went to *Doctors Commons*, and ap-
‘ plied to Mr. *Faulckner*, a proctor, to put
‘ him in a way of recovering his wages, or
‘ fome other recompence for his labour.
‘ Mr. *Faulckner* accordingly wrote to
‘ *Arthur Jones*, one of the owners, for
‘ that purpofe ; and *Rogers* being ap-
‘ pointed likewife to meet *Jones* at the
‘ proctor’s office, was waiting at a pub-
‘ lic houfe, in *Doctors Commons*, till fent
‘ for ; when *Jones*, *Seffins*, and another
‘ man, came into the houfe, forced *Ro-*

‘ gers

' *gers* into a coach, conveyed him back,
' and forced him on board another ship,
' where he was chained to the main-
' mast, till he was released by the deputy-
' marshal of the High Court of Admiralty,
' with the assistance of Mr. *Shea*, one of his
' old masters, and some other friends, who
' had obtained a warrant to take him out of
' his confinement.

   ' Several reasons prevented his ap-
' plying for redress of these injuries,
' till the beginning of the year 1774,
' when Mr. *Torriano* was employed to
' commence an action against *Arthur*
' *Jones*, as one of the owners, for the
' purpose of recovering the usual wages,
' or some other recompence in lieu there-
' of.

   ' After the usual proceedings. the
' cause was brought for hearing on June,
' 29, 1776; when the facts being all
' clearly proved as above stated, the prin-
' cipal question was,——*How far the plea*
' *of SLAVERY, set up by the defendant,*
' *could be admitted in bar of the demand of*
' *wages ?*

   ' It was insisted on by the counsel on be-
' half of *Rogers*, that the kind of slavery,
' here spoken of, never had any existence
' under the laws of *England*; and in support
' of that, referred to the well known Case
              ' of

' of *Knowles* and *Somerset*, before lord
' *Mansfield*; and likewise to a late one
' in the PREROGATIVE COURT, of *Cay* and
' *Crichton*.

' THE counsel for the detendant argu-
' ed, that, till the case of *Somerset*, the
' law of *England* admitted slavery; and
' in support of this, they quoted the au-
' thority of Lord Chief Justice *Hale*; and,
' in particular, the opinions of the Lords
' *Talbot* and *Hardwick*.'

THE Decree of the Court thereupon was,
in substance, as follows.

' *THERE are two principal points in*
' *this cause*; (said the Judge)
' 1st. *Whether such a service is proved (as*
' *stated in the summary Petition) as to enti-*
' *tle the plaintiff to the wages demanded? and*
' 2dly. *Whether the plea of slavery shall be*
' *a sufficient bar to the claim?*
' *With regard to the* FIRST, *it appears by*
' *the fullest evidence, that the plaintiff had serv-*
' *ed on board the ship, either in the capacity*
' *of assistant to the cook, or as cook himself,*
' *during the greatest part of the voyage, and*
' *consequently was entitled to some recompence*
' *for his services; but not being entered as a*
' *mariner in the ship's books, nor having any*
' *stipulated*

' *ſtipulated wages aſſigned him*, *it being proba-*
' *ble that the owners meant to ſell him again in*
' *the Weſt Indies*, *he cannot be allowed any ſpe-*
' *cific ſum under the name of* WAGES; *but as*
' *he certainly performed the duty to which he*
' *was aſſigned, without any objection to his be-*
' *haviour in it, the maritime law clearly gives*
' *him a* QUANTUM MERUIT. *The cook's*
' *wages appear to have been* £1. 5s. 6d. *per*
' *Month, which is more than* Rogers, *moſt*
' *probably, cou.d fairly deſe ve. But upon in-*
' *ſpection of the mariners contract, it appears*
' *that there were ſeveral negroe boys in the*
' *ſame ſhip, in the quality of apprentices, who*
' *were allowed from* 10s. *to* 17s. *and* 6d. *per*
' *month ;*' he ſignifi d his opinion therefore,
*that* Rogers *might fairly deſerve* 15s. *per*
*month,* which he accordingly decreed him,
from the time of his being firſt carried on
board

  ' *With regard to the* SECOND *point, it was*
' *urged (ſaid the judge) that the plaintiff was*
' *a* SLAVE, *and conſequently was not entitled to*
' *any reward for his ſervice at all*

  ' *The practice of buying and ſelling ſlaves*
' (the learned judge remarked) *was cer-*
' *tainly very common in* England, *before*
' *the caſe of* SOMERSET, *in the Court of*
' *King's Bench,* 1772, *but however it might*
' *have been the law of the Royal Ex-*
                          ' *change*

' *change.*' he hoped, ' *it never was the law of*
' *England.*

' *The* OPINIONS *of lord* Hardwicke, *and*
' *lord* Talbot, *when Attorney and Solicitor-*
' *general, have been quoted in support of this*
' *practice, and have formerly given too much*
' *countenance to it, though they seemed origi-*
' *nally to have been only applied to the diffe-*
' *rence created by baptism.*'

' *But by a late determination of one of the*
' *ablest judges that ever presided in this king-*
' *dom, these opinions have been held to be mis-*
' *taken and unsound; and there can be no fur-*
' *ther doubt, that the claim of* SLAVERY *is not*
' *maintainable by the laws of* England.

' *The law therefore was the same before the*
' *time of the above opinions, as since; and, con-*
' *sequently, refers to all sales whatsoever of*
' *this nature; which are every one illegal: and*
' *therefore the pretended sale in the present*
' *case, in* 1766, *was an absolute nullity; and*
' *when the allegation, stating the sale, was*
' *admitted on behalf of the owners, had* Rogers
' *appeared, under protest, upon this point of*
' *law, it would have been received in bar of*
' *the plea!*

' *The owners seem to have acted upon a*
' *mistaken notion of their right; but as the*
' *claim of slavery is clearly against the law of*
' *this country, and as it appeared that* Rogers
'                                          ' *had*

'  *had always acted in some useful capacity dur-*
'  *ing the whole time of his having been on*
'  *board,*' the judge said, he thought ' *him*
'  *entitled to a* QUANTUM MERUIT *for his*
'  *service,*'——which he accordingly fixed as
above; and condemned the owners in costs;
which were immediately taxed to the amount
of £81. 11s. 0d.

APPEN-

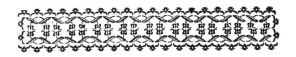

# A P P E N D I X,

## ( No. 12. )

From the General Evening Poſt, No.
6033. *June* 13th, 1772.

*To the Editor of the* General Evening Poſt.

### S I R,

AS the great cauſe depending between
Mr. *Stuart*, and *Somerſet*, the negro,
is at preſent one of the principal topics of
general converſation, by inferting the following you will afford a feaſonable and rational entertainment to your readers. I am
your's, &c.

*Extract of a letter from a perſon in* Maryland, *to his friend in* Philadelphia.

‘ I am ſo happy as to think as you do,
‘ with regard to trading in man, or keep-
‘ ing

' ing him a flave.  The cuftom is wicked
' and iniquitous,  neither  confiftent with
' reafon,  or the laws  of God or man.
' Poor unhappy flaves,  particularly thofe
' forced from their places of nativity, are
' moft certainly deplorable objects of com-
' miferation.  I never bought more than
' two during twenty years refidence here.
' One proved to be the fon of an African
' Prince; he was a moft comely youth : hav-
' ing obferved his uncommon good parts,
' I fent him to fchool, and ufed him like
' a free man during his ftay with me.  The
' directors of the African Company having
' enquired, and offered a reward for him,
' I by a public act prefented the poor crea-
' ture with his freedom, gave him an order
' for the reward aforefaid, and fent him to
' London ; from whence the following year
' he remitted me the fame fum he coft me,
' and fundry rich goods to the amount of
' three hundred pounds and upwards, and
' therewith a letter in his own native lan-
' guage, tranflated by Dr. Defaguillier, of
' Cambridge.

   ' The next I purchafed was an unhap-
' py  lad,  kidnapped from his free pa-
' rents  at  the  taking  of  Guadaloupe.
' During his ftay with me he decayed or
' pined fo much, and expreffed fo fenfible
' a forrow of cruel feparation from his
                                    ' aged

' aged parents, relations, and countrymen,
' that actuated by the unerring good provi-
' dence which directs us in all our good deeds,
' I likewise set this poor creature free, and
' sent him to his native place. Providence
' again would not excuse my being further
' rewarded, for performing this my duty
' as a Christian. The truly honest father,
' from the produce of his plantations, has
' made me presents to the amount of fifty
' pounds sterling, with direction to draw
' upon him for the full cost of the poor
' youth, which I do never intend, being
' more than paid by presents.

' I write this to convince you that the in-
' habitants of Africa are not such senseless
' brutish creatures as thoughtless authors
' represent them to be: they undoubtedly
' are capable of receiving instruction, and
' far out-do Christians in many commend-
' able virtues. Poor creatures! their great-
' est unhappiness is being acquainted with
' *Christians.* ‡

‡ The worthy and benevolent writer must mean
such *Christians* only as those, who carry out with them
nothing of that most amiable profession of religion
but *the name*, to the ' *ship-wrack*,' of their own souls,
and to the disgrace of their native country, if that also
is called *Christian!*

The

' The following is a letter from the
' Negro Prince, some time after he
' arrived at *London*, to his master
' in *Maryland*. Translated by Dr.
' *Defaguillier*, of *Cambridge*, 1743.

*From the great city, 3d moon after my release.*

' O my kind merciful master, my good
' white brother, too good, a very good son of
' a good woman, and of a very good old
' man, created good old people by the GREAT
' SPIRIT, who made my country, thy poor
' (I should say heretofore poor) most grate-
' ful black prisoner, now rendered rich by
' thy goodness and mercy, is now most
' dead, most drunk, most mad with joy!
' Why is he so? because he is going to his
' good warm country, to his good old mo-
' ther, to his good old father, to his little
' sister and his brother. In my good warm
' country all things are good, except the
' white people who live there, and come in
' flying houses to take away poor black priso-
' ners from their mothers, their fathers, their
' sisters and brothers, to kill them with hun-
' ger and filth, in the cellars of their flying-
' houses, wherein if they do not die fast
                                    ' enough,

' enough, and poor prifoners talk for bread
' and water, and want to feel the wind,
' and to fee THE GREAT SPIRIT, to com-
' plain to him, to tell him all, or to fee the
' trees of his good warm country once
' more for the laft time, the King of the
' white people [*probably the negro meant*
' *the captain*] orders the officer called Jack,
' to kill many of the black prifoners, with
' whips, with ropes, knives, axes and falt.
' The governor of thy flying-houfe has
' been to fhew that which is to carry me and
' him to my good warm country; I am
' glad, very glad indeed! He goes there
' with wine. Should he be fick, (and white
' people feldom efcape being fo there,) be-
' caufe of thee my kind merciful mafter,
' and good white brother, and becaufe he
' has been good to me, and is a very good
' white man too, I will nurfe him myfelf,
' my mother, my father, my little fifter,
' and my brother, fhall be his brother, his
' mother, his father, and his fifter too;
' he fhall have one large heap of ele-
' phants teeth and gold, for thee my kind
' merciful mafter, and kind brother, and
' one for himfelf alfo (but fmaller.) He at
' prefent is my father, I eat at his houfe,
' and lie there too upon the bed thou pre-
' fented me with. His woman is my mo-
                                      ' ther,

' ther, and kindly nurfes me, being very
' fick of the fea and fire made of black
' ftones.   I have received a great quantity
' of gold, befides what thou did prefent
' me with by means of thy hand writing,
' to the people who are to fend me to my
' country, fome part whereof I have given
' to the governor of thy fwimming-houfe,
' to be fent to thee; had I an houfeful
' fhould fend the whole with equal plea-
' fure; however, thou fhalt fee hereafter,
' that black people are not beafts, and do
' know how to be grateful.   After thou my
' kind merciful mafter and good white bro-
' ther left me in thy fwiming-houfe, we,
' thy white people, and we thy grateful black
' prifoners, were by the GREAT SPIRIT, who
' was angry with us, fent by the wind into
' an immenfe great river, where we had like
' to have been drowned, and where we could
' fee neither fun nor moon, for fix days and
' nights.   I was dying during one whole
' moon, the governor was my father, and
' gave me thofe good things thou prefented
' me with on my bed, he lodged me in the
' little room thy carpenter built for me.
' Thou gave me more cloaths than 1 could
' carry, yet I was very cold; nothing avail-
' ed with poor black prifoner, till at laft hav-
' ing THE GREAT SPIRIT to fend me fafe to
' thy houfe on fhore, I thought I was carried
                                        ' there,

' there, [*this appears to have been a dream*]
' where thou my good white brother did use
' me with wonted goodness, spake to THE
' GREAT SPIRIT, and TO HIS SON, that I
' might keep so during the voyage and af-
' terwards, which they have done for thy
' sake ; they will always do me good because
' of thee my good white brother ; therefore
' my kind merciful master, do not forget thy
' poor black prisoner. When thou dost speak
' to THE GREAT SPIRIT and TO HIS SON, I
' do know he will hear thee, I shall never
' be sick more, for which I shall be thank-
' ful.   Pray speak for my good old mother,
' my good father, my little sister, and my
' brother ; I wish they may be healthy, to
' many very many moons, as many as the
' hairs on thy head ; I love them all much, yet
' I think not so much as I do thee, I could die
' in my country for thee, could I do thee any
' kindness. Indeed THE GREAT SPIRIT well
' knows I mean no lie, shall always speak to
' him for thy good, believe me my good
' white brother, thy poor black prisoner is
' not a liar.

>        *Dgiagola, son of Dgiagola, Prince*
>        *of Foat, ‖ Africa.*

‖ The country, here called FOAT, is probably named (the sound being nearly the same) from PHUT, the
third son of *Ham;* concerning whom, and his de-
                                        scendants

ſcendants in the interior part of *Africa*, particular
mention is made in Mr. *Bryant's* letter, on the deſcent
of the negroes. See Appendix, No. 4. pages 48 to 52:
or perhaps it may mean ' *the very country upon the ri-*
' *ver Gambia on one ſide*,' which (as Mr *Bryant* informs us from *Bluet* ) ' *is at this day called* PHUTA.'
See p. 50.

# I N D E X

## O F

## Texts referred to in the foregoing Work.

### G E N E S I S.

| Chap. | Verses. | Pages. |
|---|---|---|
| ix. | 28. | 47 n. |
| x. | 5, 6. | App. 48. |

### E X O D U S.

| | | |
|---|---|---|
| xxi. | 2. | 57 n. |
| | 5, 6. | 15. |
| xxiii. | 9. | 7, 41. |
| xxxiv. | 11, 12. | 4 n. |

### L E V I T I C U S.

| | | |
|---|---|---|
| xviii. | | 4, 12. |
| xix. | 18. | App. 24. |
| | 33, 34. | 6, 9, 42. |
| xxv. | 44 to 46. | 3, 26, 65. |
| | 39 to 43. | 16. |
| | 39 to 46. | App. 18, 25. |

### N U M B E R S.

| | | |
|---|---|---|
| xxxi. | 17. | 11 n. |
| xxxiii. | 55, 56. | 12 n. |

D E U-

## DEUTERONOMY.

| Chap. | Verſes. | Pages. |
|---|---|---|
| vii. | 1. | 8. |
| | 2. | 11 n. |
| | 16. | 5, 11 n. |
| | 23, 24. | 5 n. |
| ix. | 5. | 12 n. |
| x. | 17 to 19. | 6, 43. |
| xv. | 3. | App. 23. |
| | 12. | 56. |
| | 12 to 14. | 63. |
| | 15. | 7. |
| | 18. | 65. |
| xx. | 16. | 10 n. |
| xxiii. | 15, 16. | 49, 54. |
| | 19. | App. 23. |
| xxv. | 19. | 11. |

## II CHRONICLES.

| xiv. | 9. | 22 n. |
|---|---|---|
| xvi. | 8. | 22. |

## JOB.

| xxxi | 38 to 40. | 60, 61. |
|---|---|---|

## PSALMS.

| lxviii. | 31. | 22, 24. |
|---|---|---|

## PROVERBS.

| xiv. | 34. | App. 15. |
|---|---|---|

## JEREMIAH.

| xiii. | 23. | App. 44. |
|---|---|---|
| xxii. | 13. | 60. |
| xxxi. | 29. | App. 11. |

## EZEKIEL.

| xviii. | 3, 4, 20. | App. 11. |
|---|---|---|

AMOS.

## A M O S.

| Chap. | Verſes. | Pages. |
|---|---|---|
| viii. | 7, 8. | 15 n. |

## H A B A K K U K.

| i. | 13. | App. 15. |
|---|---|---|
| iii. | 7. | App. 52. |

## E C C L E S I A S T I C U S.

| xxxiv. | 22. | 61. |
|---|---|---|

## M A T T H E W.

| v. | 44, 45. | 39. |
|---|---|---|
| vii. | 12. | 42, 45. |
| | | App. 8. |
| | 23. | 67. |
| xix. | 8, 9. | App. 22. |
| xxiv. | 30. | 21. |
| xxv. | 34 to 46. | 37, 38. |
| | 40. | 21, 67. |
| | 12. | 67. |
| xxviii. | 19. | 18. |

## L U K E.

| iv. | 18. | App. 14. |
|---|---|---|
| x. | 7. | 59. |

## A C T S.

| viii. | 27, 28. | 24. |
|---|---|---|
| | 27. | App. 11. |
| x. | 34. | App. 11. |

## R O M A N S.

| viii. | 17. | 20. |
|---|---|---|

## I C O R I N T H I A N S.

| iii. | 16, 17. | 19. |
|---|---|---|
| vi. | 19, 20. | 19. |
| vii. | 22, 23. | App. 35, 36. |

GALA-

[ 98 ]

### GALATIANS.

| Chap. | Verses. | Pages. |
|---|---|---|
| iv. | 5, 6, 7. | 19. |
| v. | 14. | 42. |

### EPHESIANS.

| iii. | 6. | 19. |

### COLOSSIANS.

| iv. | 1. | 62. |
| | 7, 9. | App. 35. |

### I THESSALONIANS.

| iii. | 13. | 21. |

### PHILEMON.

The Intention of the whole Epistle considered as far as it relates to Onesimus. } App. 31 to 38.

### JAMES.

| v. | 3, 4. | 58. |

### II PETER.

| i. | 3, 4. | 20. |

### JUDE.

| xiv. | 15. | 21. |

### REVELATIONS.

| i. | 7. | 21. |
| xiv. | 6. | 41. |

**INDEX.**

---

# INDEX.

## A.

ADMIRALTY, report of a Determination against *Slavery* in the Admiralty Court before Sir George Hay, in the Cafe of *Rogers*, alias *Rigges*, againſt *Jones*, *App.* 75. 79.

Africa, the Gofpel of Chriſt received there earlier than in Europe, 21. The antiquity and purity of the church of Habaſſinia, 23. Early councils aſſembled there, 24. Lamentable apoſtafy of the African church, the caufe of the prefent barbarous ignorance which now prevails there, 26. This Example cited by Abp. Sharp as a Warning to Britain, 44, *note*. All the inhabitants' of, aſſuredly the defcendants of Ham, *App.* 48.

African Merchant, the juſtification of ſlavery from the Mofaic law, by a writer under that name, examined, 3. Prince, letter from, to his maſter in Maryland, *App.* 90.

Africans, their defcent inquired into, 48. See *Negroes*.

America, a propofal for the gradual enfranchiſement of negro ſlaves there, *App.* 57.

Ariſtotle, his argument in juſtification of ſlavery refuted, 27, *note*.

Barbadoes,

## B.

Barbadoes, the killing of negroes there, only punished by a fine, 33.

Beattie, Dr. his examination of Ariftotle on the fubject of flavery, and of Mr. Hume on the mental inferiority of negroes, 27, *note.*

Benevolence, univerfal, the diftinguifhing characteriftic of Chriftianity, *App.* 28.

Bifhops, numerous Affemblies of them in the Ecclefiaftical Synods of Africa, 24, 25.

Blackwell, Dr. his definition of liberty, *App.* 13.

Bond-fervants among the Ifraelites, who might legally be made fo, 3. The law of, repealed by the Gofpel, 46.

Brethren, all mankind connected under the idea of, by our Chriftian obligations, 40. It is inconfiftent with Chriftianity that any of them fhould be flaves, *App.* 33.

Bryant, Mr. his letter to the Author concerning the defcent of the negroes, *App.* 47.

## C.

Canaan, falfely reputed the Father of the African negroes, 47, 48.

*Candid Reflections* upon the Judgement lately awarded by the Court of King's Bench, &c. on the Negroe Caufe. The Author of a Book fo entitled, convicted of *uncandid Reflections*, *App.* 69 to 71.

Cave, Dr. his Account of the great Ecclefiaftical Synods in Africa cited, 24, 25.

Cay and Crichton, report of the cafe of, in the Prerogative Court, *App.* 77.

Charity, Chriftian, is not to be partial in its objects, *App.* 28.

Chriftianity,

Chriſtianity, the benevolent ſpirit of, totally in‑
conſiſtent with the tyrannical claims of ſlave‑
holding, 17. Negroes, as well as the reſt of
mankind, included under the Goſpel diſpenſation,
19. Connects all the human race under the idea
of brethren, 40. None of the Levitical laws can
juſtify ſlavery under, 41.

Chuſim, the uſual Name for *Negroes* in the Old Teſta‑
ment, 22. See alſo Letters on the Deſcent of the
Negroes, *App.* 44 47.

Congreſs, American, their prohibition of the impor‑
tation of ſlaves, ſhould be followed by the gradual
emancipation of thoſe now in the country, *App.*
56.

Councils, Chriſtian, a liſt of thoſe held in Africa
during the third and fourth centuries, 24.

### D.

Dgiagola, Prince of *Foat*, releaſed from Slavery by
his Maſter in Maryland, *App.* 88. His grateful
Letter for that favour tranſlated by Dr. Deſaguillier,
*App.* 90.

Deſaguillier, ſee above.

### E.

Elegy on the miſerable ſtate of an African ſlave, by
Mr. Shenſtone, *App.* 39.

Emancipation of ſlaves, in the Colonies, a com‑
parative view of the different modes of, *App.* 16.
This work remains to be done by the American
Congreſs, *App.* 56.

Eſtwick, Mr. his report of the late Judgement in the
Court of King's Bench by Lord Mansfield, in
the Caſe of *Somerſet* and *Knowles*, *App.* 65. His
own Remarks thereupon, *App.* 69. Anſwered by
other Remarks on that Judgement, *App.* 72.
Ethiopians,

Ethiopians, received the Christian faith before the Europeans, 21. Their descent traced, 22, *note.*

## F.

*Foot,* a Region in Africa, probably the same that is called *Phuta* from *Phut* the Son of Ham, *App.* 93.

## H.

Habaffinia, Church of, remains a Monument of Christianity among the Sons of Ham, 23.

Habeas Corpus Act. Severity thereof against those who attempt to carry away any person by force out of this Kingdom, *App.* 76.

Ham, the common father of all the inhabitants of Africa, *App* 48.

Havanna, regulations adopted by the Spaniards there, for the gradual enfranchisement of negroes, *App.* 54.

Hay, Sir George. See Admiralty and Prerogative Court.

Heathen, under the Mosaic law, who were implied by that term, 3. Were devoted to destruction for their abominable vices, 4. Distinguished from *strangers,* 5. The bondage they were doomed to, not to be extended to strangers at large, 9. Are by no means excluded from the benevolence of Christians, 39.

Hume, Mr. His opinion of the mental inferiority of Negroes, controverted by Dr. Beattie, 28, *note.*

## I.

Jews, were by the Mosaic law permitted to make bond servants or slaves of the Heathen, 3. And
2     why,

why, 4. Were commanded to treat ſtrangers kindly, 6. Over whom their legal power of bondage extended, 8. Their national privileges not to be claimed by any other people, 10. The limitations under which they might hold their brethren in bondage, 14. Such bond brethren were to be generouſly aſſiſted on diſmiſſion, 56. Their conſtitutions not ſtrictly conſiſtent with the law of nature as aſſerted by Mr. Thompſon, *App.* 19. Inſtances of contrariety, *App.* 21.

Infidelity of the preſent age, ſo many proofs of our growing apoſtaſy from the Chriſtian Religion, 26, *note*.

### K.

King's Bench, report of a Determination in that Court before Lord Mansfield *againſt Slavery*, in the Caſe of *Somerſet* and *Knowles*, or *Stewart*, *App.* 65. Remarks on that Determination, ditto 69. A Defence of, ditto, ditto, 72.

### L.

Labourer always worthy of his hire, 59.

Law of England, both common and ſtatute, not to contradict the laws of God, 55.

Letter, from an African prince to his maſter in Maryland, *App.* 90.

Liberty, the univerſality of, aſſerted by Mr. Otis, *App.* 9. Definition of, *App.* 13.

Lutholf, his account of the antiquity and purity of the church of Habaſſinia cited, 23, *note*.

### M.

Mansfield, Lord, the ſubſtance of his ſpeech in the caſe of Somerſet and Knowles, *App.* 65. Remarks on it, *App.* 69. See King's Bench Court.

Maryland,

Maryland, account of the cruel treatment of the he-
groes and convict flaves there. *App.* 42.

Mafon and Jones, *App.* 80.

Mauritania, how firft peopled, *App.* 49.

Mercator, the pleas in behalf of .flavery by the
writer under this title, refuted, 47.

Monthly Review, confiderations on negroe flavery
extracted from, 3.

Morgan, Mr. extract from his **Plan** for the abolition
of flavery in the Weft Indies, *App.* 62.

Mofaic law, how far, and on what account, flavery
was tolerated under it, 3. The benevolent treatment of ftrangers ftrongly inculcated by, 6. Will
not juftify flavery under the Chriftian difpenfation, 41. Is fuperfeded by it, 46. Not ftrictly
confiftent with the law of nature, as afferted by
Mr. Thompfon, *App.* 19. Inftances of contrariety,
*App.* 21.

## N.

Negroes, the enflaving of, not to be juftified from
the Mofaic law, 8. Are branded by their mafters
with hot irons, 15, *note.* Are equally intitled to
the promifes of God in the Gofpel, with the reft
of mankind, 19. Received the Chriftian faith
before the Europeans, 21. Dr. Beattie's defence
of, againft the infinuations of Mr. Hume, 28, *note.*
Their murder compounded for by money in Barbadoes, 33. One advertifed for in London, and
defcribed by a brafs collar like a dog, 35. Are
not treated according to the Chriftian law of doing
as we would be done by, 43. Are treated like
cattle, 45. Not defcended from Canaan, 47,
48. alfo *App.* 12. Rewards offered by our Colony
laws for killing them when they run away, 50.
Their different treatment in England and America
inconfiftent with reafon, law, and religion, *App.*

7. Ought to be emancipated, *App.* 12. Examination into the moft prudent means of emancipation, *App.* 16. Their cruel treatment in Maryland, *App.* 42. Queries refpecting the defcent of them, *App.* 44. Reply to. *App.* 47. Regulations adopted by the Spaniards for the enfranchifement of, *App.* 54. A Propofal for the gradual enfranchifement of the Britifh American flaves, *App.* 57. May thus be converted into free peafants, *App.* 60. Natural tendency of our retaining them in flavery, *App.* 62. Remarks on the judgement of the Court of King's Bench in the cafe of Somerfet, *App.* 72.

Neighbours, all mankind intitled to be efteemed fo, under the Chriftian difpenfation, 40.

### O.

Onefimus, in what fenfe he was recommended back to his former mafter Philemon by St. Paul, *App.* 31. Was then a minifter of the Gofpel, *App.* 34, *note.* Became bifhop of Ephefus, *App.* 37, *note.*
Otis, Mr. afferts the univerfality of liberty, *App.* 9.

### P.

Paleftine, the feven nations of, the only *ftrangers* whom the Jews were permitted to hold in abfolute flavery, 8.
Paul, St. his Exhortation to Slaves to continue in the State in which they were called, affords no Argument for flavery, *App.* 6. Is vindicated from Mr. Thompfon's charge of juftifying flavery, *App.* 31.
Philemon. St. Paul's Epiftle to him confidered, *App.* 31—38. See Onefimus.

Planters,

Planters, American, their pleas for flavery invali-
dated, 59.

Prerogative Court, report of a Determination
in that Court before Dr. Hay againft *Slavery*, in
the Cafe of Cay and *Crichton*, *App.* 75. 77.

Propofal by the Author for the gradual enfranchifement of negroe flaves in America, *App.* 57.


### R.

Reports of Determinations in the feveral Courts of
Law againft *Slavery*, viz King's Bench, *App.* 65.
Admiralty Court, ditto 79. Prerogative Court,
ditto 77.

Retribution, Law of, referred to, *App* 30.

Rogers, alias Rigges, againft Jones, report of the
cafe of, in the high court of Admiralty, *App.*
79.


### S.

Saracens, query relating to their defcent, *App.* 50,
*note.*

Servants, fugitive, how treated in the Britifh Colonies, 50, 51. Comparifon between their cafe and
that of negroe flaves, 52, *note.*

Sharp, Abp. his warning to England by the example
of God's Judgements againft the Africans, 44, *note.*

Shenftone, Mr. his elegy on the miferable ftate of an
African flave, *App.* 39.

Slavery, is not to be juftified by any of the Levi-
tical laws under the Chriftian difpenfation. 41.
Confiderations on, from the Monthly Review,
*App.* 3. No pofitive law in favour of, either in
England or America, *App.* 8.

Slaves, who might legally be made fo by the Ifraelites, 3. Are branded with hot irons in the
Britifh

British plantations, 15, *note*. The killing of them compounded for by act of assembly at Barbadoes, 33. One advertised for and described by a brass collar like a dog, 35. The holders of, cannot be real christians, 38. How treated on running away, by our American laws, 50. Examination into the most prudent means of emancipating, *App.* 16.

*Somerset* and *Knowles*, Case of, see King's Bench.

Spaniards, regulations adopted by, for the gradual enfranchisement of negroes, *App* 54.

Strangers, benevolence toward, strongly enjoined by the Mosaic law, 6. 41. The parable of the good Samaritan teaches Christians to consider all men as neighbours, *App.* 24.

## T.

Theophylact, Abp. his plea for slavery on the authority of St. Paul, refuted, *App.* 32, *note*.

Thompson, Rev. Mr. examination of his defence of the negroe slave trade, *App.* 18.

## W.

Wages, always due for labour, 59. Are decreed by the high court of Admiralty to a negroe slave, *App.* 83.

F I N I S.

# THE

# L A W

## OF

# PASSIVE OBEDIENCE,

## OR

*Chriſtian Submiſſion to Perſonal Injuries:*

Wherein is ſhewn, that the ſeveral texts of ſcripture,
which command the entire ſubmiſſion of *ſervants* or
*ſlaves* to their *maſters*, cannot authorize the latter *to
exact an involuntary ſervitude*, nor, in the leaſt degree,
juſtify the claims of modern *Slaveholders*.

*By* GRANVILLE SHARP.

' SERVANTS, *obey in all things* (your) *maſters, accord*
' *ing to the fleſh* ; *not with eye ſervice, as men pleaſers, but*
' *in ſingleneſs of heart, fearing God :*' &c. Coloſſ. iii. 22.

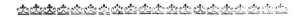

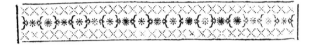

# T H E
# LAW of PASSIVE OBEDIENCE,
## O R
## CHRISTIAN SUBMISSION to PERSONAL INJURIES.

THE illegality of flavery among Chriftians is a point which I have long laboured to demonftrate, as being deftructive of morality, and confequently dangerous both to body and foul. There are neverthelefs fome particular Texts in the New Teftament, which, in the opinion even of feveral well meaning and difinterefted perfons, feem to afford fome proof of the toleration of flavery among the primitive Chriftians; and, from thence, they are

induced

induced to conceive, *that Chriſtianity doth not oblige its profeſſors to renounce the practice of ſlaveholding.*

A learned and reverend correſpondent of mine ſeems to have adopted this notion, and has ſignified his opinion nearly to the ſame effect, in a private letter to me on this ſubject, to which I have not yet ventured to ſend him a reply, though it is a conſiderable time ſince I received his letter; but, to ſay the truth, the queſtion in which I had never before apprehended any difficulty, was rendered very ſerious and important, upon my hands, by my friend's declaration; and I thought myſelf bound to give it the ſtricteſt examination, becauſe I conceived (as I do ſtill) that the honour of the Holy Scriptures, which of all other things, I have moſt at heart, was concerned in the determination of the point in queſtion; and yet I know, that my

friend

friend is full as zealous for the honour
of the Scriptures as myfelf, and much
more learned in them, being very eminent in that moft effential branch of
knowledge.

I believe alfo that he is perfectly difinterefted, and of undoubted *Chriftian
benevolence.* The objection has therefore
acquired an accumulated weight from
the authority and worth of the perfon
who made it ; and confequently, it demanded more circumfpection and reading, to anfwer it in any reafonable time,
than my fhort broken intervals of leifure
(the only time that I was then mafter
of) would permit me to beftow upon it;
and as fo muchtime has already elapfed,
the anfwer which I originally intended
for my friend's private perufal, fhall now
be addreffed to all well meaning perfons
in general, who may have had the fame
motives for admitting in any degree the
legality

[ 6 ]

legality of flavery; and that there are
many fuch (even among thofe that are
concerned in the practice of flaveholding) the example of my difinterefted
friend's opinion, and common charity,
oblige me to fuppofe. I fhall therefore
confider my friend's opinion as the common excufe of our American and Weft
Indian brethren for tolerating flavery a-
among them.

‘ *I do not think* (fays he) *that Chrif-*
‘ *tianity releafed flaves from the obligation*
‘ *they were under according to the cuftom*
‘ *and law of the Countries, where it was*
‘ *propagated.*’

This objection **to my** general doctrine
*is* expreffed in the moft *guarded* terms;
—fo *guarded,* that it obliges me to acknowledge, that the obfervation is, in
fome refpects, ftrictly *true.* My prefent attempt is not to confute, but
rather

rather to demonſtrate wherein this *truth* conſiſts, which will afterwards enable me to point out ſuch a due limitation of the doctrine, as will render it entirely conſiſtent with the hypotheſis, which I have ſo long laboured to maintain, viz. *the abſolute illegality of ſlavery among Chriſtians,*

In conformity to my worthy friend's declaration I muſt firſt obſerve, that the diſciples of Chriſt (whoſe *Kingdom,* he himſelf declared,—' *is not of* THIS ' WORLD.' John xviii. 36.) had no *expreſs* commiſſion to alter *the* TEMPO-RAL CONDITION OF MEN, but only to prepare them for a BETTER WORLD by the general doctrines of *faith, hope, charity, peace and goodwill,* (or univerſal love and benevolence to all mankind) *ſubmiſſion to injuries, dependence upon God,* &c. &c. &c. which (though *general* doctrines) are amply and ſuffi-

ciently

ciently efficacious indeed, for the *particular* reformation of ALL CONDITIONS OF MEN, when *sincerity* is not wanting in the application of them; but the principal intention of the whole system is evidently to draw men from the the cares and anxieties of *this present life,* to a better hope in the *life to come,* which is Chrift's proper kingdom: Chriftian fervants therefore were of courfe inftructed to be *patient,* to be *humble* and *submissive* to their mafters, ‘ *not only to the good and gentle, but al-* ‘ *fo to the froward.*’ So that even *ill ufage* does not juftify *perverfenefs* of behaviour in chriftian flaves.

THE apoftle *Paul* alfo frequently infifts upon the abfolute neceffity of an unfeigned obedience in the behaviour of chriftian fervants to their mafters. ‘ *Let every man abide in the fame calling* ‘ *wherein he was called.*’ ‘ *Art thou* ‘ *called*

' *called being a servant ? care not for it;*"
&c. ɪ Cor. vii. 2ɪ. and again, ' *Ser-*
' *vants be obedient to them that are* (your)
' *masters according to the flesh, with fear*
' *and trembling, in singleness of your*
' *heart as unto Christ; not with eye service,*
' *as men pleasers, but as the servants of*
' *Christ, doing the Will of God from the*
' *heart ; with good will doing service, as to*
' *the Lord, and not to men : knowing that*
' *whatsoever good thing any man doeth, the*
' *same shall he receive of the Lord, whe-*
' *ther he be bond or free,*" Ephef. vi 5-8.
' Again, ' *Servants obey in all things*
' (your) *masters according to the flesh; not*
' *with eye service, as men pleasers but*
' *in singleness of heart fearing God : and*
' *whatever you do, do it heartily, as to*
' *the Lord, and not unto men* ' Colof. iii.
' 22, 23. The fame apoſtle inſtructs *Ti-*
' *mothy* to recommend obedience to fer-
' vants, ' *Let as many servants* ſays the
' apoſtle) *as are under the yoke, count*
                                    ' *their*

' *their own masters worthy of all honour,*
' *that* THE NAME OF GOD AND HIS
' DOCTRINE BE NOT BLASPHEMED.
' *And they that have believing masters, let*
' *them not despise* (them) BECAUSE THEY
' ARE BRETHREN; BUT RATHER DO
' (them) SERVICE, BECAUSE THEY
' ARE FAITHFUL AND BELOVED PAR-
' TAKERS OF THE BENEFIT. *These*
' *things teach and exhort: If any man*
' *teach otherwise, and consent not to whole-*
' *some words,* (even) *the words of our*
' *Lord Jesus Christ, and to the doctrine*
' *which is according to godliness; he is*
' *proud, knowing nothing, but doting*
' *about questions, and strifes of words,*
' *whereof cometh envy, strife, railings,*
' *evil-surmisings, perverse disputings of*
' *men of corrupt minds, and destitute of*
' *the truth, supposing that gain is godli-*
' *ness. From such withdraw thyself. But*
' *godliness with contentment is great gain.*
' *for we brought nothing into* (this) *world,*
' *and*

' *and it is certain we can carry nothing*
' *out. And having food and raiment, let*
' *us be therewith content.*' 1 Tim. vi.
' 1 to 8.—And again he infifts on the
' fame doctrine, ' (Exhort) *fervants,*
' *(*fays he*) to be obedient unto their own*
' *maſters,* (and) *to pleaſe* (them) *well in all*
' things, *not anſwering again, not pur-*
' *loining, but ſhewing all good fidelity;*
' *that they may* ADORN THE DOC-
' TRINE OF GOD OUR SAVIOUR IN
' ALL THINGS.' Titus ii. 9, 10.

THESE Texts are amply fufficient to
prove the truth of my learned friend's
affertion, fo far as it relates to THE
DUTY OF THE SLAVES THEMSELVES,
but this *abſolute ſubmiſſion* required of
Chriftian fervants, by no means implies
the *legality* of flaveholding ON THE
PART OF THEIR MASTERS, which
*he* feems to apprehend.

THE

THE flave violates no precepts of the gofpel by his abject condition, provided that the fame is *involuntary* (for if he can be made free, he is exprefsly commanded by the apoftle to *ufe it rather* §) but how the mafter who enforces *that involuntary fervitude*, can be faid to act confiftently with the hriftian profeffion, is a queftion of a very different nature, which I propofe to examine with all poffible ca e and impartiality, being no otherwife interefted in it, than as a Chriftian who efteems both mafters and flaves as brethren, and confequently, while he pities the unhappy *temporal condition* of the latter, is extremely anxious for the *eternal welfare* of the former.

I

§ *Art thou called* (being) *a fervant? care not for it;* BUT IF THOU MAYEST BE MADE FREE, USE IT RATHER *For he that is called in the lord* (being) *a fervant, is the lord's freeman, &c.* ' *ye are bought with a price,* 'BE NOT YE THE SERVANTS OF MEN.' 1 Cor. vii. 21-23.

I HAVE already admitted, that CHRIS-
TIANITY DOTH NOT RELEASE SLAVES,
' from the obligation they were under ac-
' cording to the custom and law of the
' countries where it was propagated,'
agreeable to my learned friend's asser-
tion, in favour of which I have produced a variety of texts: but as ' the
' reason of the law,' (according to a
maxim of the *English* law) 'is the life of
' the law,' we cannot with justice
draw any conclusion from thence, in favour of the master's claim, till we have
examined the principles, on which the
doctrine *of submission,* in these several
texts, is founded; and we shall find, upon a general view of the whole, that
the principal reason of enforcing the
doctrine was not so much because the
persons to whom it was addressed,
*were slaves,* as because they *were Chris-*
*tians,* and were to overcome EVIL
with

with GOOD, to the GLORY OF GOD *and* RELIGION.

THESE principles are clearly *expreſſed* in ſeveral of theſe very texts, and *implied* in all of them, viz. ' *That the name of God and his doctrine be not blaſphemed.*' (1 Tim. vi. 1.) and again, ' *that they* ' *may adorn the doctrine of God our Savi-* '*our* IN ALL THINGS.' (Titus ii. 10.) So that a zeal for the GLORY OF GOD, and of HIS RELIGION (the principles of the firſt great commandment) is the appa-rent ground and ſole purpoſe of the Chriſtian *ſlave's* SUBMISSION, which was therefore to be ' WITH SINGLE-' NESS OF HEART AS UNTO CHRIST.' ' *not with eye ſervice,* AS MEN PLEASERS, ' *but as* THE SERVANTS OF CHRIST, ' *doing the will of God from the heart* ; ' *with good will doing ſervice,* AS TO THE ' LORD, *and* NOT TO MEN : *knowing* ' *that whatſoever good thing any man doeth,* ' *the ſame ſhall* HE RECEIVE OF THE LORD,

'Lord, *whether he* be bond or free.'
Ephef. vi. 5-8. And again, the fame
apoſtle charges the ſervants among the
Coloſſians, to obey ' *not* as men plea-
' sers, *but in ſingleneſs of heart,* fear-
' ing God : *and whatſoever they do, to*
' *do it heartil , as* to the Lord, *and*
' not unto men.' Coloſſ. iii. 2.

Thus it is plain that the ſervice was
to be performed ' as to the lord,'
and ' not to men,' and therefore it
cannot be conſtrued as an acknowledgement of any *right,* or *property* really
veſted *in the maſter.* This will clearly
appear upon a cloſer examination of
ſome of theſe texts. In the firſt, for
inſtance, though the apoſtle *Peter*
enforces the neceſſity of the ſervants *ſubmiſſion* to their maſters, in
the ſtrongeſt manner, commanding
them to be ſubject ' *not only to*
' *the good and gentle, but* also to the
froward,' &c. (I. Pet. ii. 18.)
yet

yet he adds in the very next verfe.---
‘ *for this is thank worthy, if a man,* FOR
‘ CONSCIENCE TOWARDS GOD, *endure*
‘ *grief,* SUFFERING *wrongfully,*’——πασχων
αδικως, fo that, it is manifeft, the apoftle did not mean to *juſtify* the claim
of the mafters, becaufe he enjoined the fame fubmiffion to the fervants that fuffered *wrong fully,* as to
thofe who had good and gentle mafters :
and it would be highly injurious to the
*goſpel of peace,* to fuppofe it capable of
authorizing *wrong ful ſufferings,* or of
eſtabliſhing a *right* or power in any rank
of men whatever, to oppreſs others *unjuſtly,*
or αδικως ! And though the apoftle *Paul,*
alſo. ſo ſtrongly exhorts fervants to ſub-
mit to their mafters, and ‘ *to abide in*
‘ *the ſame calling wherein they were call-*
‘ *ed,*’ and ‘ *not to care for it.*’ ( 1 Corinthians, vii. 20, 21.) Yet at the fame
time he clearly inſtructs them, that it is
their duty to prefer a ftate of *freedom*
whenever they can fairly and honeftly
obtain

obtain it; '*but if thou mayest be made*
'*free* (says he) USE IT RATHER.' (V.21.)
And the reason, which he assigns for
this command, is as plainly delivered,
viz. *the equality of servants with their*
*masters in the sight of the Almighty,* 'For he
' *that is called in the Lord,* (being) *a* SER-
' *VANT* (says he) *is the Lord's* FREE-
' *MAN:* LIKEWISE, *also he that is call-*
' *ed* (being) FREE, *is Christ's* SERVANT.'
(verse 22 ) *Christ* having purchased all
men to be his *peculiar servants,* or rather *freemen.* '*Ye are bought with a*
'*price* says the apostle, in the 23d verse.)
' BE NOT YE THE SERVANTS OF MEN,'
which plainly implies, that it is inconsistent with the dignity of a Christian,
who is the *servant* or *freeman of* GOD,
to be held in an *unlimited* subjection, as
the bond *servant* or *slave of a* MAN;
and, consequently, that a toleration
of slavery, in places where Christianity
is established by law, is intirely illegal;
for

for tho' THE SLAVE commits no crime by submitting to the *involuntary service*, (which has been already demonstrated,) yet the CHRISTIAN MASTER is guilty of a sort of sacriledge, by appropriating to himself, as an *absolute property*, that body, which *peculiarly belongs to God by an inestimable purchase !* For if God said of the Jews, even under the old law, (Levit. xxv. 52.) ' THEY ' ARE MY SERVANTS, *which I* ' *brought forth out of the land of Egypt* ; " THEY SHALL NOT BE SOLD " AS BONDMEN.' ‡ How much more

‡ My learned friend, (mentioned in the beginning of this Tract) has remarked that ' *tho' God expressed* ' *himself concerning the Jews under the law in this* ' *manner.* " THEY ARE MY SERVANTS, WHICH I " BROUGHT FORTH OUT OF THE LAND OF EGYPT, " THEY SHALL NOT BE SOLD AS BONDMEN." &c. yet ' *This did not signify* (says he ) *that they were not to be* ' *slaves at all. They might be slaves for seven years, as is* ' *well known, notwithstanding they were God's redeemed ser-* ' *vants. Nay, they might remain slaves 'till the jubilee,* ' WITH

more ought Chriſtians to eſteem their *brethren*, as *the peculiar ſervants of* God on account of their being *freed* from the more *ſevere bondage* of our ſpiritual ene-

C 2

my,

' WITH THEIR OWN CONSENT, *at the expiration of that* ' *ſhort term of involuntary ſervitude. Theſe words indeed* ' *contained a declaration that none of the Iſraelites were* ' *to be ſlaves for ever like the Heathen. But what a ſlip-* ' *pery proof*, (ſays he) *of this exemtion with regard to* ' *Chriſtians ? How dangerous* (continued he,) *is it to* ' *build doƈtrines upon ſuch parallels and compariſons !'* But my worthy friend ſeems to forget that the kind of ſlavery which I oppoſe, is not that *limited temporary ſervitude*, which he deſcribes *as conſiſtent with the law*, for that differs very little from the condition of *hired ſervants*, in which light, the Hebrew maſters were *bound by the law*, to look upon their brethren, even though bought with their money as bond ſervants or ſlaves,' *If* ' *thy brother* (that dwelleth) *by thee be waxen poor*, and ' BE SOLD *unto thee* ; THOU SHATL NOT COMPEL HIM ' TO SERVE AS A BOND SERVANT: (but) AS AN HIRED ' SERVANT AND AS A SOJOURNER, *he ſhall be with thee*, ' and *ſhall ſerve thee unto the year of* Jubile. *And then* ' *ſhall he depart from thee*, (both) *he and his children with* ' *him*, &c. *For they are my ſervants*, (ſaid the Almighty) ' THEY SHALL NOT BE SOLD AS BOND-MEN.'

' THOU

my, (of which the *Egyptian bondage* was only a type) by the ineftimable price of Chrift's blood! and, furely, we may therefore fay, ' *they* are GOD's SER-VANTS,' whom Chrift hath redeemed with his own blood, as much as the Jews of old who were on that account exprefly *enfranchifed* from worldly bond-age, ' THEY ARE MY SERVANTS, THEY SHALL NOT BE SOLD AS ' BONDMEN ;' for this application of the text is entirely to the fame effect as the apoftle's expreffion to the Co-rinthians,-------' *Ye are bought with* ' *a price*, BE NOT YE THE SER-VANTS OF MEN.' (1. Cor. vii. 23.)

Dr.

' THOU SHALT NOT RULE OVER HIM WITH RI-' GOUR, *but fhalt fear thy God.*' Levit. xxv. 39, 43. Here is the very *text*, (with it's *context*) which I had quoted, to fhew the *illegality* of holding a *brother* If-raelite in abfolute flavery, and as I have elfewere fully demonftrated that men of all nations are to be confidered as *brethren* under the gofpel difpen-fation, fo my learned friend furely does great injuftice to the argument, when he calls it ' *a flip-* ' *pery*

Dr. *Whitby*, indeed suppofes that the words ' *ye are bought with a price,*' refer only to a pecuniary price given by the primitive Chriftians, *to buy their brethren out of flavery.*' But the authority of *Juftin Martyr* and *Tertullian*, which he cites, by no means proves his interpretation of the text, tho' it may fufficiently prove the primitive practice of *redeeming flaves*; which alfo furnifhes a new argument againft the legality of *flavery among Chriftians*, fo far

---

' *pery proof* of *this exemption with regard to Chrif-* ' *tians,*' and afferts that the text in queftion *does not fig-nify that they* (the Ifraelites) *were not to be flaves at all !* It clearly *fignifies* however, that whatfoever *right* a mafter might have acquired (even by an abfolute *pur-chafe*) over his Hebrew brother, yet that he was ftill required to treat him as an *hired fervant*, and to difcharge *him* and *his* at a *limited time :* and when we compare it with the parallel text in Deuteronomy, (xv. 12, 14.) we find the mafter is there ftrictly enjoined to reward the Bond-man LIBERALLY for his paft fervices, viz. ' *And when thou fendeft him out free from thee,* THOU ' SHALT FURNISH HIM LIBERALLY *out of thy* ' *flock, and out of thy floor, and out of thy wine prefs,*' &c. Surely when the true nature of fuch *limited fervitude*

is

far as the example of the *primitive Chriſtians* is concerned. But ſcripture is beſt interpreted by ſcripture, and therefore the moſt certain means of aſcertaining the true meaning of the words τιμης ηγορασθητε, ' *ye are bought with* ' *a price*,' is to have recourſe to the very ſame expreſſion (ηγορασθητε γαρ τιμης, the words being only tranſpoſed) in the preceding chapter, 20th verſe, where we ſhall find that it can refer to nothing leſs than the ineſtimable price of Chriſt's redemption, ' *What know ye not* (ſays ' the apoſtle) *that your* BODY *is the* TEM-

' PLE

---

is duly conſidered, it affords but ' *a ſlippery* proof,' (if I may uſe my friend's expreſſion) ' that *they were to* ' *be ſlaves at all*, at leaſt, ' *at all*,' in the ſenſe contended for by our American and Weſt India ſlaveholders (which is the only matter in diſpute at preſent) eſpecially as the condition of a *hired ſervant* is expreſsly mentioned, as the rank in which ſuch Bondmen were to be eſteemed. And therefore I truſt I may fairly retort the obſervation of my learned friend,---- ' *How dangerous is it to build doctrines*,' (that is in favour of abſolute ſlavery) ' *upon ſuch parallels and* ' *compariſons !*'

' PLE OF THE HOLY GHOST, (which
' is) *in you, which you have of God, and* YOU
' ARE NOT YOUR OWN? FOR YE ARE
' BOUGHT WITH A PRICE: *therefore glo-*
' *rify God* IN YOUR BODY, *and in your*
' *spirit,* WHICH ARE GOD'S,' (1 Cor. vi.
19, 20.) and, consequently, it is the duty of
a *Christian legislature* to vindicate THE
LORD'S FREEMEN *from* SLAVERY, as
all mankind are included in the same
*inestimable purchase,* for it is not only
their *souls* but even their *bodies, which
are God's;'* and therefore it is an abominable *sacriledge,* that those *bodies* which
are capable of being the ' *temple of*
' *the Holy Ghost,*' should be esteemed
the mere *chattels* and private property
of mercenary planters and merchants,
merely for the sake of a little worldly
gain!

BUT slaveholders may perhaps alledge that *believing masters* are mention-
**ed**

ed as ' *faithful and beloved,*' in one of
the texts, which I have cited, and are
alſo expreſsly accounted as ' *partakers
of the benefit,*' (ſee 1 Timothy, vi. 2.)
ſo that, from thence, they may perhaps
infer, that *ſlavekeeping* is not inconſiſtent with their Chriſtian profeſſion.

But theſe expreſſions are included
in that part of the apoſtles charge to
*Timothy,* which relates merely to the
inſtruction of ſervants, ſo that there is
no room to ſuppoſe, that any reference
was intended to the practice of the maſters by way of *juſtification.* The meaning therefore can amount to no more
than this, viz. that, as it is the duty of
ſervants to ' *count their own maſters,*'
(even thoſe that are *unbelievers*) ' *wor-*
' *thy of* ALL HONOUR ‡, THAT THE
NAME OF GOD AND HIS DOCTRINE
BE

‡ Apparently meaning, ' *all honour,*' which is not inconſiſtent with their duty to God.

'BE NOT BLASPHEMED,' fo the fame
reafon obliges them, more efpecially, **to**
count their *believing* mafters ' *worthy*
' of *all* (lawful) *honour*,' becaufe of
their *Chriſtian profeſſion*, which renders
them *accepted of God*. For common
charity obliges us, as Chriftians, to fuppofe that all men, who believe and hold
the fame profeffion as ourfelves, are
' *faithful aud beloved*,' as well as ' *par-*
' *takers of the benefit*' of Chrift's redemption, ‡ becaufe *Belief* is the true means
D                         of

---

‡ Chrift's redemption does not feem to be ' *the bene-*
*fit*' fpoken of in the text, though I have admitted this
implication to avoid controverfy. Dr. *Whitby*, fup-
pofes that *the benefit of the ſervice* is meant, and he con-
ftrues the fentence accordingly, ' *becauſe they who par-*
' *take of the* BENEFIT OF THE SERVICE, *are faithful and*
' *beloved*.' And Dr. *George Benfon*, alfo, renders it in
the fame fenfe, viz. ' *becauſe they who partake of* THE
'BENEFIT OF THEIR SERVICE, *are Chriſtians, and be-*
' *loved of God*.' And then he adds in a note, ' *This*
' (fays he) *I take to have been ſpoken of* THE MASTERS,
' who *received the* BENEFIT OF THE SERVICE *of their*
' *ſlaves. So the author of the Syriae verſion ſeems to have*
' *underſtood*

of leading and difpofing men to acquire
fuch happinefs; and though many
other necefſary Chriſtian qualities may
feem wanting in our *believing brethren*,
yet we muſt not prefume to condemn
them; God alone being their *Judge:*
and, for this reafon alfo, *Chriſtian fervants* muſt not condemn and defpife
their *believing maſters*, (though they know
themfelves *equal in dignity as brethren*, and
that it is, confequently, their maſters *duty*
to treat them *as brethren*,) but muſt
render them fervice the more willingly
on this *account*, having *brotherly love*
as an additional motive to *faithful fervice*. It is manifeſt, therefore, that
this text was intended to regulate the
conduct

‘ *underſtood the words*. The MS. *called Pet.* 2. read
‘ (εργασιας *labor*) *and Pet.* 3. *and Borner*, read ευσεβειας
‘ *piety*,’--for which he refers us to *Kuſter's* edition of Dr.
*Mill*,--‘*And finally* (fays he) *I would obfervethat* ενεργεσια
‘ *is never uſed, throughcut the New Teſtament, for the pri-*
‘ *vilege of having the goſpel or the unſpeakable* BENEFIT
‘ *of eternal life,*

conduct of *Chriſtian ſervants*, and not
that of *Chriſtian maſters*; for, with regard to the former, the doctrine is perfectly conſiſtent with the other texts,
that I have quoted; which is not the
caſe when it is applied to juſtify the
mere temporal claims of *maſters* or
*ſlaveholders*, becauſe there are many
clear and incontrovertible precepts
throughout the New Teſtament for re-
gulating the conduct of *Chriſtian maſters*, which exclude the *juſtification* of
any *ſuch claims* among Chriſtians, and
conſequently forbid any application
or interpretation of theſe particular texts
in favour of them: and beſides we
muſt always remember, that it is not
lawful to maintain an hypotheſis upon
the teſtimony *of any one ſingle text of
doubtful interpretation*, eſpecially when
the ſame does not clearly correſpond
with the reſt of the ſcriptures, and cannot bear the teſt ' *of the royal law*,' of
which

which more fhall be faid in my tract
' on *the Law of Liberty.*'

I mention this text of St. *Paul,* as
one of ' *doubtful interpretation,*' becaufe
commentators are divided concerning
the application of the very words on
which the imaginary juftification of the
flaveholder is fuppofed to be founded !
Many learned men (and Dr. *Hammond*
among the reft) have conftrued the
words — ' ὁτι πιϛοι ειϲιν και αγαπητοι,
ὁι της ευεργεϲιας αντιλαμϐανομενοι, ( 1 Tim.
vi. 2,) ‡ in a very different manner from
the common verfion, and applied them
*to the fervants,* which entirely deftroys
the prefumption in favour of the flave-
holder.

Neverthelefs I have contented myfelf
th the common rendering, being convinced

---

‡ Thefe words are tranflated by Dr. *Hammond,* as
follows, —— ' *becaufe they who help to do good, are*
' *faithful and beloved,*' and he ufes feveral arguments
to fhew that thefe epithets refer *to the fervants,* rather
than *to the mafters.*

vinced that no conclusions can fairly be
drawn from this text in favour of Slavery, even when the epithets " *faith-*
" *ful and beloved*," &c. are applied *to
the Masters*; because the signification
of them must necessarily be restrained
within the bounds of *gospel doctrine*;
and, therefore, we cannot conceive that
the apostle intended, by the application of these epithets, to justify any
practices which are inconsistent with *the
benevolence* enjoined in other parts of
the New Testament; for this would be
liable to produce a contrary effect from
that which the apostle expressly intended
by his injunction, viz. that " *the name
of God and his doctrine be not blasphemed.*"


Thus it appears, I hope, that the
principles, on which the doctrine of the
*servants submission* is founded, are clearly expressed; so that *Slaveholders* can
have no right to avail themselves of any
of

of thefe texts to *enforce an* ABSOLUTE
SUBMISSION ; for, though thefe feveral
texts clearly juftify *the Slave,* yet they
cannot juftify the Mafter, unlefs he can
fhew that the fame *principles, (or reafon
of the Law,)* on which they are founded,
hold good alfo on *his* fide of the queftion. (1) Can the Slaveholders and
African

(1) This is apparently the cafe in the other " *dif-*
" *ferent relations of life, mentioned in thefe contexts* ;" as in
*the relation* between *hufbands* and *their wives, parents*
and *their children,* but is far otherwife in the *relation* between *mafters and their fervants,* (unlefs free *hired fer-*
*vants* are to be underftood,) and therefore the objection of my learned friend, drawn from thence, cannot
be juft. He fays, " *If the connexion of perfons in the*
" *two former refpects be lawful, fo that hufbands had a*
" *right to the fubjection of their wives, and wives a*
" *right to the love of their hufbands ; parents had a right*
" *to the honour and obedience of their children, and chil-*
" *dren a right to maintenance and inftruction by their pa-*
" *rents : unnatural* (fays he) *is it to imagine the connection*
" *between Mafters and Slaves was looked upon by him as*
" *abfolutely unlawful, fo that the former had no right to*
" *rule the latter ! Indeed, he very clearly fignifies* (fays he)
" *that the right of dominion remained, when he oppofes*
" DOING WRONG to OBEYING IN ALL THINGS
" THEIR MASTERS ACCORDING TO THE FLESH,
" &c.

African traders alledge, for inftance, that they fhall " *adorn the doctrine of* " *God*

" &c. *as he does.* Coloff. iii. 25." " Ὁ δε αδικων " κομιεται ὁ ηδικησεν."

But my learned friend has entirely mifunderftood the purport and intention of my arguments on thefe feveral texts relating to *obedience* and *fubmiffion*. I have not attempted to prove, *by thefe particular expreffions of the apoftle*, that " *the connexion between Mafters and Slaves* " *was looked upon by him as abfolutely unlawful*, fo that " *the former had no right to rule the latter* ;" for this I have demonftrated, I truft, by OTHER AUTHORITIES *of Scripture* equally authentic, and much lefs liable to be mifunderftood My attempt to explain the texts in queftion extends no farther than to fhew that they do not really *juftify the uncharitable claims of the modern Slaveholders*, though they are frequently cited for that purpofe.

An attempt to fhew *that any particular doctrine is* NOT NECESSARILY IMPLIED *in a certain text or texts of* cripture, is a very different thing from an attempt to PROVE or AUTHENTICATE AN OPPOSITE DOCTRINE *by the fame text of Scripture!* For inftance, when my learned friend afferts, as above, that the apoftle to the Coloff- " fians, iii. 25. *very clearly fignifies that the right of do-* " *minion remained, when he oppofes* DOING WRONG *to* " OBEYING *in all things their Mafters*," &c. I do not pretend to build an *oppofite doctrine upon the very fame words*, but fhall only endeavour to fhew that this fup- pofed " *right of dominion*" is not neceffarily *implied* in the text which my friend has cited in fupport of it.

The

"*God our Saviour,*" (Titus ii. 10.) by
perfifting in their unnatural pretenficns
to

The fervants are indeed exprefsly and plainly exhorted to *obediei e* and *fubmiffion,* as well in this as in
all the other texts before recited, fo that a contrary
behaviour in them might certainly be efteemed a "*do-*
"*ing wrong*" on their part yet this by no means
implies "*a right of dominion*" vefted in the Mafter;
for that would prove too much; becaufe the like fubmiffion is elfewhere equally enjoined to thofe who are
exprefsly faid to "*endure grief,* SUFFERING WRONG-
" FULLY." (πασχων αδικως,) and we cannot fuppofe
(as I have before obferved) that the *fubmiffion enjoined*
implies a *right* in the Mafter to exercife fuch a *dominion*
as that of *oppreffing others* UNJUSTLY, or *αδικως*; for
that could not poffibly tend to promote the declared
purpofes of the apoftle's exhortations, viz. "*that the*
*name of God and his doctrine be not blafphemed,*" (1 Tim. vi.)
and again, "*that they may adorn the doctrine of God in*
"*all* THINGS," (Titus ii. 9.) Thefe purpofes, however, are fully anfwered in the advice given by the
fame apoftle to all the other *different relations of life* mentioned by my worthy friend. WIVES may "*adorn*
"*the doctrine of God*" by SUBMISSION to their "*own*
"*hufbands, as it is fit in the Lord.*" (See Coloff. iii.
18.) And HUSBANDS, by *love* to their *wives:* for they
are exprefsly charged in the following verfe "*not to*
"*be bitter againft them,*" that is, they muft, by *love*
and *fincere affection,* moderate and foften that fupreme
authority with which *hufbands* are entrufted, (by the
laws of God and man,) that they may *rule* rather by
the gentle influence of an inviolable *love* and *fidelity,*
as

to an abfolute *property* in their poor *brethren?* or that they " *do the will of*
" *God*

as fo good an example will feldom fail to produce
*due refpect*, and will certainly " *adorn the doctrine*" or
profeffion of the Chriftian. CHILDREN " *may adorn the*
" *doctrine of God*" by OBEDIENCE *to their* " *parents in*
" *all things, for this is well-pleafing* (fays the text) *unto*
" *the Lord.*" (v. 20.) And again, the reciprocal duty of
FATHERS is plainly pointed out to be a prudent modera-
tion of that *paternal* authority with which they are entrufted, for they are carefully warned againft an arbitrary feverity, " *Provoke not* (fays the apoftle) *your*
" *children to anger, left they be difcouraged.*" SERVANTS
are in the very next verfe (v. 22.) commanded to
" *obey in all things their Mafters according to the flefh,*
" *not with eye-fervice, as* MEN-PLEASERS, *but in*
" *finglenefs of heart,* FEARING GOD :" fo that the
SUBMISSION of the fervants was alfo to *adorn the*
" *doctrine of God,*" it being manifeftly enjoined only
for *God's fake,* and not on account of any fuppofed
" RIGHT OF DOMINION" invefted in the *Mafters,*
which the following verfes (v. 23, and 24.) when *applied
to* THE SERVANTS, fufficiently demonftrate,——" And
" *whatfoever ye do, do it heartily as to the Lord, and*
" NOT UNTO MEN : *knowing, that of* THE LORD
" *ye fhall receive* THE REWARD OF THE INHE-
" RITANCE : *for* YE SERVE THE LORD CHRIST."
And to the fame eternal and unerring Difpenfer of *Rewards* (and not to *temporal Mafters)* is attributed
the power of punifhing the " *doing wrong,*" mentioned
in the very next verfe ; which, according to my learned
friend's notion, is *oppofed* to *obeying in all things the*
                                                    *Mafters*

" *God from the heart,*" (Ephefians vi.
5, &c.) when they retain their *neighbour*

*Mafters;* — " *he that* DOETH WRONG (fays the text) *fhall*
" *receive for* THE WRONG *which be hath done: and*
" THERE IS NO RESPECT OF PERSONS." (v. 25.)

Such ftrict *impartiality* in the adminiftration of juftice
cannot always be attributed, with certainty, even to
the beft-regulated *human* tribunal, and much lefs is it
applicable to the decifions of uncontrouled *will* and
*pleafure,* in punifhing " *wrong doing,*" under the abfolute *dominion* of Slaveholders! No earthly *dominion*
whatever is conducted with fuch an equal diftribution
of *rewards* and *punifhments,* as that it may always with
truth be faid, " *there is no refpect of perfons,*" for this
is the proper characteriftic of the *judgements and dominion* of GOD and CHRIST alone. " *For* THE LORD *is*
" JUDGE, *and with him is* NO RESPECT OF PERSONS,"
Ecclefiafticus xxxv. 12. " *For there is* NO RESPECT
OF PERSONS *with* GOD." Rom. ii. 11. And, therefore, we may fairly conclude that the punifhment, not
only of SLAVES, but that alfo of MASTERS, that
" *do wrong,*" is to be underftood in the text which
my friend has cited to fupport his notion of a " *right*
" *of dominion*" vefted in the *afters*; fo that the faid
fuppofed *right* has, indeed, but a very " *flippery*"
foundation! Agreeable to my laft remark on this text,
(Coloff. iii. 24.) the learned Dr. Whitby has com-
mented upon it, as if he thought it exactly parallel
to another declaration of the fame apoftle, (viz. Ephef.
vi. 8 and 9.) wherein not only both *Mafters* and *Servants* are unqueftionably included, but alfo the *dominion,* or *judgement,* in which " THERE IS NO RESPECT
" OF

*bour* in an involuntary unrewarded fervitude for life? If they can do this, I
E 2         fhall

" OF PERSONS," is exprefsly attributed to our " MAS-
" TER IN HEAVEN." — " *Chrift, in judging men at*
" *the laft day,* (fays the Doctor,) *will have* NO RESPECT
" *to the quality or external condition of any man's perfon* ;
" *but,* WHETHER HE BE BOND OR FREE, *he fhall*
" *receive recompence* FOR THE GOOD THAT HE HATH
" DONE, *in obedience to him* ; *whether he be* MASTER *or*
" SERVANT, *he fhall be punifhed for* THE WRONG THAT
" HE DOTH *in thofe relations.*"

If all thefe circumftances be duly confidered, it will
manifeftly appear, I truft, that the Mafters fuppofed " *right of dominion*" (which, certainly, is *not*
EXPRESSED in the text) cannot even be *implied* in
thefe contexts, nor in any of the parallel paffages already recited! Can the Mafter *adorn the* " *doctrine of*
" *God our Saviour,*" (as in the other indiffoluble relations of life,) by continuing the unnatural *connection*
of *Mafter* and *Slave,* and by *exacting* involuntary labour
from his *brethren, without wages* or *reward,* agreeable
to my friend's notions of the fuppofed implied " *right*
" *of dominion?*" The reciprocal duty of the Mafter is
mentioned, indeed, in the next chapter, (Col. iv. 1.)
but it is of fuch a nature as muft neceffarily lead Chriftian Mafters to abhor any fuch fuppofed " *right of*
" *dominion*" as that which is tolerated in the Britifh
colonies, and which my friend feems defirous to defend !
The *Mafters* are not directed by the apoftle to claim
as their own, by " *right of dominion,*" the *labour* of
their fervants WITHOUT WAGES, but, on the contrary,
are exprefsly commanded to " GIVE *unto* (their) *fer*
" *vants*

fhall have reafon to be filent. But if,
on the contrary, it fhould evidently appear

" *vants that which is* JUST *and* EQUAL ;" which com-
prehends (as I have fully fhewn in the preceding tract)
fuch a meafure of *generofity, recompence,* and *benevolence,* on
the part of *the Mafter,* as is totally inconfiftent with
the claims and views of modern *Slaveholders!* and, if
put in practice, would neceffarily effect the entire
abolition of flavery!

The Mafters are likewife carefully reminded, in the
laft mentioned text, that they " *alfo have a Mafter*
" *in Heaven.*" (Col. iv. 1 ) — A *Mafter,* by whofe
example they are bound to regulate their conduct, fo
that this confideration alone is a fufficient antidote a-
gainft *flavery;* for the principal doctrine of *that heavenly Mafter* was LOVE, which cannot fubfift with the
contrary *exaction of involuntary fervitude! " This is my*
" *commandment,*" (faid that glorious and gracious
MASTER,) " *That ye* LOVE *one another* AS *I have*
LOVED *you.*" The nature of *his love* (which we are
to imitate, that is, to LOVE *as he hath* LOVED *us)* is
then immediately defcribed as exceeding all bounds
of comparifon, " *Greater* LOVE" (faid he) " *hath*
" *no man than this, that a man lay down his life for his*
" FRIENDS. *Ye are my* FRIENDS, *if ye do whatfoever*
" *I command you.* HENCEFORTH I CALL YOU NOT
" SERVANTS." Here is an exprefs *enfranchifement* of *his
Servants* for our example! The univerfal *Lord* and
*Mafter* of all men delights in promoting *the dignity of
human nature;* which cannot be faid of the temporal
*Slaveholder,* who enforces an imaginary " *right of do-
minion,*" by exacting an *involuntary fervice,* and that
for

pear that a *very different behaviour* is required of *Christian Masters*, " *that* " *the*

for no other purpose than for the sake of a little pecuniary gain, by depriving the *labourer of his hire*; which favours of no other *love* but *self-love*; whereas, our disinterested Lord and Master hath even *laid down his life* through *love* and *compassion* to his SERVANTS. and hath *declared us free*, as before recited. — " *Hence-* " *forth I call you not* SERVANTS ; *for the Servant*" (said he) " *knoweth not what his Lord doeth* ; *but I have* " *called you* FRIENDS ; *for all things that I have heard* " *of my Father I have made known unto you.*" (John xv. 12–15.) And, in the 17th verse, he again enforces his doctrine of LOVE : " *These things I command you,* (said he,) *that ye* LOVE *one another.*" The measure of this indispensible LOVE is expressly declared in the Scriptures, " *Thou shalt* LOVE *thy neighbour* AS THYSELF. " LOVE *worketh no ill to his neighbour : therefore* LOVE " (is) *the fulfilling of the law.*" (Rom. xiii. 9 and 10.)

Such LOVE, therefore, is clearly incompatible with the arbitrary claims of the Slaveholder, who can neither be *said* to LOVE *his neighbour as himself*, nor to cherish that LOVE *which worketh no ill to his neighbour*, whilst he strenuously contends for such " *a right of* " *dominion*" as may enable him to exact, not only the *involuntary* service of his *neighbours* and *brethren*, contrary to the law of nature, but also to rob them of the *fruits of their own labours,* " GIVING THEM NOT " FOR THEIR WORK ;" against which practices a severe denunciation of WOE is expressly declared in the Scriptures ; as I have fully demonstrated in my tract on " *the Law of Retribution*," as well as in the preceding

" *the name of God and his doctrine be*
" *not blasphemed,*" (1 Tim. vi. 1.) they
muſt be obliged to allow that the " *rea-*
*ſon, or life of the law*" is againſt them;
and, conſequently, that none of theſe
texts, relating to Chriſtian ſervants, are
capable of affording them the leaſt excuſe for their ſelfiſh pretenſions. They
will find alſo, upon a more careful examination of the Scriptures, that they
themſelves are as much bound by the goſpel to bear perſonal injuries with patience
and humility, as their Slaves. Becauſe
the benevolent principles of the *goſpel*
*of peace* require all men, *freemen* as *well*
*as ſlaves,* to return " *good for evil.*"
" *Bleſs them that* CURSE *you,*" (ſaid our
Lord,)

---

ding tract: and, therefore, as it is neceſſary to con-
ſtrue difficult or dubious paſſages of *Scripture* conſiſt-
tently with the general tenour of *Scripture* evidence,
it would be highly improper to admit this *oppoſite doc-*
*trine* of a ſuppoſed " RIGHT OF DOMINION," eſpecially as the ſame *is not expreſſed* in the text which my
learned friend has cited for it, but is merely drawn
forth by an imaginary *implication !*

Lord,) " *and* PRAY *for them which* DE-
" SPITEFULLY USE YOU. *And unto*
" *him that* SMITETH *thee on the one*
" *cheek, offer also the other; and him*
" *that* TAKETH AWAY *thy cloke, for-*
" *bid not* (to take thy) *coat also*," &c.
Luke vi. 28, 29. But, though *submis-*
*sion* and *placability* are thus unquesti-
onably enjoined to the *sufferers* in all
the cases above recited in the text, yet
surely no reasonable man will pretend
to alledge, from thence, that *tyrants* and
*oppressors* have thereby obtained a legal
*right.* under the gospel, to *curse others,*
and use them *despitefully* ; or that the
unjust oppression of *strikers and robbers*
is thereby authorized or justified! In the
*same light exactly* must we view the *Slave-*
*holders* claim of *private property in the*
*persons of men,* whenever an attempt is
made to support it on the foundation of
any such texts as I have quoted, wherein
servants or slaves are exhorted to submit

*with*

*with paffive obedience,* &c. to their Mafters; becaufe the *right* (as it is impro-
perly called) or pretenfion of the Mafter may with the greateft propriety be
compared to the pretended *right* or authority of oppreffing or robbing others,
which is too often exercifed by imperial
tyrants and defpotic princes, as well
as by *their brethren in iniquity* of a lower
clafs, viz. pirates, highwaymen, and
extortioners of every degree! The gofpel
of peace cannot authorize the oppreffion
of thefe lawlefs men, though it clearly
enjoins patience, fubmiffion, and acqui-
efcence, to the individuals that are en-
jured, whether freemen or flaves! The
*placability* and *abfolute fubmiffion,* commanded by the laft-cited text, to Chriftians *in general,* are manifeftly founded
on the very fame principles with that
*particular* fubmiffion which the gofpel
requires of *Chriftian flaves;* and is farther parallel to the latter, by being *e-*
*qually*

*qually paſſive*; ſo that the *oppreſſion* of the *Slaveholder* can no more be juſtified by any text of the New Teſtament, that I am able to find, than the *oppreſſion* of the *ſtriker* and *robber*.

Unhappily for the Chriſtian world, the duties of *patience, ſubmiſſion,* and *placability,* enjoined by the goſpel to *perſons injured,* are too commonly either miſunderſtood or rejected; though the *temporal,* as well as the *eternal,* happineſs of mankind greatly depends upon a conſcientious and proper obſervation of theſe duties: for even the moſt rigid obedience to the letter of the command would be far from being productive, either of the *real evils* to which the pernicious doctrine of *a national paſſive obedience* apparently tends, or of the *imaginary inconveniences* apprehended by the advocates for *duelling,* becauſe the ſame benevolent principles, (viz. univerſal love and charity,

charity, founded on the great commandment, " Thou fhalt love thy neigh-
" bour as thyfelf,") which oblige the
true Chriftian, moft *difintereftedly*, to
forgive all injuries, and pafs over every
affront offered to his *own perfon*, will
neceffarily engage him, on the other
hand, as *difintereftedly*, to oppofe every
degree of oppreffion and injuftice, which
affects his *brethren and neighbours*, when
he has a fair opportunity of affifting
them ; and from hence arifes the zeal
of good men for *juft* and *equitable laws*,
as being the moft effectual means of
preferving the *peace* and *happinefs* of the
community, by curbing the infolence
and violence of wicked men. We have
an eminent example of this *loyal zeal* in
the behaviour of the apoftle Paul, who
could not brook an infringement of *the
Roman liberty* from any perfons whatever
in the adminiftration of government,
though he could endure *perfonal injuries*
from

from men unconnected therewith, and
the perfecutions of the multitude, with
all the *Chriftian patience* and *meeknefs*
which the gofpel requires. The Scrip-
ture-hiftory of this great apoftle affords
many proofs of his extraordinary humility and patience *under fufferings*, fo
that his fpirited oppofition to the illegal
proceedings of magiftrates cannot be attributed to *private refentment* on his own
account, but merely to his zeal for *the
public good*, founded upon the great
Chriftian principle of " *loving his neigh-*
" *bour as himfelf*," fince the maintaining
of *good laws* is, certainly, the moft effectual means of promoting the welfare
and happinefs of fociety. His refolute
and free cenfure of the magiftrates at
Philippi, in the meffage which he fent
by their own ferjeants, (2) his fpirited

F 2

re-

(2) " And, when it was day, the magiftrates fent the
" ferjeants, faying, Let thofe men go  And the keeper
" of the prifon told this, faying to Paul, The ma-
" giftrates

remonftrance to the chief captain at
Jerufalem, (3) and his fevere rebuke
to

" giftrates have fent to let you go : now therefore de-
" part, and go in peace.  But Paul faid unto them,
" *They have beaten us openly uncondemned, being Romans,*
" *and have caft* (us) *into prifon : and now do they thruft*
" *us out privily ? nay verily ; but let them come themfelves*
" *and fetch us out.*  And the ferjeants told thefe
" words unto the magiftrates : and they feared when
" they heard that they were Romans.  And they came
" and befought them, and brought *(them)* out, and
" defired *(them)* to depart out of the city."  Acts
xvi. 35 to 39.

(3) " The chief captain commanded him to be
" brought into the caftle, and bade that he fhould be
" examined by fcourging ; that he might know where-
" fore they cried fo againft him.  And, as they bound
" him with thongs, Paul faid unto the centurion that
" ftood by, *Is it lawful for you to fcourge a man that*
" *is a Roman, and uncondemned ?*  When the centurion
" heard *(that)*, he went and told the chief captain,
" faying, Take heed what thou doeft : for this man
" is a Roman.  Then the chief captain came, and faid
" unto him, Tell me, art thou a Roman ? he faid,
" **Yea.**  And the chief captain anfwered, With a great
" fum obtained I this freedom, and Paul faid, But I
" was free born.  Then ftraightway they departed
" from him which fhould have examined him : *and the*
" *chief captain was alfo afraid after he knew that he*
" *was*

to the high prieſt himſelf, even on the
ſeat of judgement, (4) are remarkable
inſtances of this obſervation.

In the laſt-mentioned inſtance, indeed, the apoſtle was charged, by thoſe
" *that ſtood by*," with *reviling God's
high*

"*was a Roman, and becauſe he had bound him.* On
" the morrow, becauſe he would have known the cer-
" tainty wherefore he was accuſed of the Jews, he
" looſed him from *(his)* bands, and commanded the
" chief prieſts and all their council to appear, and
" brought Paul down, and ſet him before them."
Acts xxii. 24 to 30.

(4) " And Paul earneſtly beholding the council,
" ſaid, Men and brethren, I have lived in all good
" conſcience before God until this day. And the
" high prieſt Ananias commanded them that ſtood by
" him to ſmite him on the mouth. Then Paul ſaid
" unto him, *God ſhall ſmite thee,* (thou) WHITED
" WALL ; *for, ſitteſt thou to judge me after the law, and
" commandeſt me to be ſmitten contrary to the law?* And
" they that ſtood by ſaid, Revileſt thou God's high
" prieſt ? Then ſaid Paul, I wiſt not, brethren, that
" he was the high prieſt, for it is written, Thou ſhalt
" not ſpeak evil of the ruler of thy people." Acts
xxiii. 1 to 5.

*high prieft,* which would have been a
notorious breach of the law, had there
not been circumſtances of juſtification
ſufficient to vindicate the ſeverity of
the Apoſtle's cenſure : theſe, however,
were not urged by the apoſtle himſelf,
who beſt knew how to behave towards
thoſe with whom he had to do.  He
readily allowed the principle (however)
on which the cenſure of his accuſers was
founded, but he by no means retracted
what he had ſo juſtly applied to the
perſon of the unworthy magiſtrate *who
ſat to judge him;* neither did he even
*acknowledge* him to be the *high prieft,*
though he was expreſſly queſtioned for
a ſuppoſed miſbehaviour to that digni-
tary!  His anſwer was cautiouſly word-
ed. — He did not ſay, —— *I knew not
that this perſon, whom I have cenſured,
was the high prieft,* but, —— ουκ ηδειν,
αδελφοι, ὁτι εϛιν αρχιερευς, *&c.* " *I knew*
" *not, brethren, that there is a high*
" *prieft.*"

" *prieſt.*" (5) Which anſwer, though on the firſt hearſay it ſeems to bear ſome affinity to an excuſe or apology for what had paſt, yet, in reality, includes a ſtill farther rebuke ; for it plainly implies that the *high prieſt,* in whoſe preſence the apoſtle then ſtood, was (in ſome reſpect or other) deficient or blameable in his deportment as chief magiſtrate, either that he did not duly ſupport the dignity of that ſacred and diſtinguiſhing public character, ſo that he did not ſeem to be *high prieſt,* and of courſe could not be known and honoured as ſuch ; or elſe that his behaviour had been ſo unjuſt and illegal that he did not deſerve to be conſidered as a *lawful magiſtrate,* who had publicly demeaned himſelf

(5) The learned Hugh Broughton has conſtrued the text as follows, — " *I knewe not, brethren, that there* " *was a high prieſt* ;" but the words, ουκ ηδειν, αδελφοι, ὁτι εϛιν αρχιερευς, are more literally rendered above. Castalio reads it, — " *Neſciebam, fratres, eſſe ponti-* " *ficem.*"—And Heinsius,—" *Summum eſſe ſacerdotem* " *ignorabam.*"

himfelf as *a tyrant*, by commanding a
prifoner to be beaten, *contrary to law*,
without hearing his defence! And, that
this latter fenfe is moft probable we
may learn by the following circumftance, viz. that the apoftle chofe to de-
cline the difpute, and to wave the accufation about *reviling the high prieft*, by
*acknowledging* the principle of law on
which it was manifeftly founded, viz.
*Thou fhalt not fpeak evil of the ruler of
thy people*. But, be pleafed to obferve,
he neither *acknowledged* that he himfelf had broken the faid precept by fo
feverely cenfuring the unjuft *ruler*, nor
did he *acknowledge* the prefence of *a
high prieft* in the perfon of Ananias;
neither did he allow the by-ftanders
time enough to criticife upon the true
literal meaning of his reply, (whereby
they would probably have been led to
demand fome exprefs recantation of the
*perfonal* cenfure which he had fo amply
beftowed

beſtowed upon the high prieſt,) but **he**
prudently changed the ſubjeƈt in debate
from *the* PERSON *of the high prieſt* (who
was a zealous overbearing SADDUCEE) (6)
to an avowed *cenſure of his whole ſeƈt,*
charging the SADDUCEES in particular
with the unjuſt perſecution, then before
the aſſembly, and openly appealing **to**
the oppoſite party, *the Phariſees,* in
order to divide his united enemies: " *I*
" *am a* PHARISEE, (ſaid he,) *the ſon*
" *of a* PHARISEE; *of the hope and re-*
" *ſurreƈtion of the dead I* AM CALLED
" IN QUESTION." Such a manifeſt
reflection againſt the whole body of
*Sadducees*

(6) Ὁ δε νεωτερος ΑΝΑΝΟΣ, ὁν την αρχιεροσυνην εφαμεν
παρειληφεναι, θρασυς ην τον τροπον, και τολμητης διαφεροντως.
Αἱρεσιν δε μετηει την ΣΑΔΔΟΥΚΑΙΩΝ, οἱπερ εισι περι τας
κρισεις ωμοι παρα παν]ας τες Ιεδαιους, καθως ηδη δεδηλωκαμεν·
ἁτε δη εν τοιετος ων ὁ ΑΝΑΝΟΣ, &c. But the younger
ANANUS, who, as we have ſaid, obtained the pontificate, was of a bold and daring diſpoſition, and followed
the ſeƈt of the SADDUCEES, who, with reſpeƈt to judgements, are more cruel than all the reſt of the Jews, as we
have already demonſtrated. Therefore, Ananias being
of this ſtamp, &c.

*Sadducees* cannot by any means favour
the fuppofition of an intended apology,
or recantation, in the preceding fentence,
to foothe the enraged leader of that very
party, whom he had publicly branded
as a hypocrite, with the fignificant appellation of *whited wall!* Let it be alfo
remembered that the fuppofed breach of
the precept (" *thou fhalt not fpeak evil of*
" *the* RULER *of thy people"*) could not reft
entirely on the circumftance of KNOW-
ING ANANIAS TO BE THE HIGH
PRIEST; for, whether the apoftle *did
know*, or *did not know*, that Ananias
was *high prieft*, yet he certainly *knew*,
before he cenfured him, that he was *a
ruler of the people*, and that he then fat
in *the quality of a judge*; (for this is
declared in the very cenfure itfelf, ——
" *fitteft thou to* JUDGE ME *after the*
" *law, and commandeft me to be fmit-*
" *ten* CONTRARY TO LAW ?") fo that
whether *Ananias* was really *high prieft*,

or

or not, yet he was manifeſtly cenſured
in his official capacity as a *ruler*, or *magiſtrate*, and not as a private individual,
through any inadvertency or miſtake of
the apoſtle, as ſome commentators have
conceived. And, even when the a-
poſtle was informed, by thoſe " *that*
" *ſtood by*," that the magiſtrate whom
he had cenſured was the *high prieſt*,
*("* revileſt *thou* God's *high prieſt ?") Yet
his reply, ("* I knew not, brethren, that
" *there is a high prieſt,") when fairly
compared with the preceding cenſure of
Ananias, as an *unjuſt* diſpenſer of God's
law, *("* ſitteſt *thou to judge me according
" *to law?* &c.) proves, as I before remarked, that the apoſtle neither acknowledged the dignity of *a high prieſt*,
nor that of a *legal ruler, in the perſon
of Ananias*, though he knew him at the
ſame time TO BE A RULER, and had
cenſured him as ſuch, for having notoriouſly proſtituted the power and authority

rity of a *ruler*, and violated the law, by commanding him to be *stricken contrary to law*, notwithstanding, that *he sat to judge* (as the apostle remarked) " AC- " CORDING *to the law;*" in which case no epithet whatever could be so apt and expressive to mark the true character of the dignified hypocrite in power, as *whited wall!* This proves, that the apostle knew well enough with whom he had to do. The censure was too just, and his prophecy in the accomplishment too true, *("* God *shall smite thee,*" thou *whited wall,)* (7) to be esteemed a mere unguarded sally of resentment! The latter supposition is, indeed, inconsistent with the remarkable *sagacity, prudence,* and *readiness* of *mind,* which always distinguished

(7) This denunciation of God's vengeance against Ananias was fully justified by the event; for, Josephus (as the learned monsieur Martin remarks) reports that he was killed in Jerusalem with his brother Ezechias. " Josephe rapporte," liv. 2. de la guerre des Juifs, " qu'il fut massacré dans Jérusalem avec son frère " Ezéchias."

guiſhed this apoſtle in bearing his teſtimony to the truth, on the moſt dangerous emergences! The apoſtle's known
character as *a choſen veſſel* for Chriſt's
ſervice, and as an exemplary preacher
of RIGHTEOUSNESS, will by no means
permit us to conceive that he was either
guilty of any *miſtake* or *inadvertency*
with reſpect to *the perſon* of the high
prieſt on this occaſion; or of any *illegal*
or miſbecoming behaviour to him as a
*ruler* or *judge* of the people! When theſe
ſeveral circumſtances are compared with
the general bad character of Ananias, (8)

as

(8) This malicious Sadducee very ſoon afterwards
gave ſo flagrant a proof of his injuſtice and cruelty
towards the Chriſtians, that even the *Jewiſh hiſtorian,*
Joſephus, has recorded it as an event which gave offence
to all good and loyal men at that time in Jeruſalem ; I
mean the murder of the apoſtle James, biſhop of Jeruſalem, whom Joſephus ſtiles *the brother of Jeſus, who
was call'd Chriſt*. The Jewiſh hiſtorian, therein, bears a
remarkable teſtimony in favour of Chriſtianity, — Ἅτε
δη εν τοιꞷτος ꞷν ὁ Ἀιανος, (for he is deſcribed, in the preceding quotation from Joſephus, as a bold daring man
of the moſt cruel ſect,) νομισας εχειν καιρον επιτηδειον,

δια

as a perfecuting zealot of the moſt virulent
and intolerant ſeɛt among the Jews, it
muſt appear that the apoſtle accounted
that perſon unworthy of any eſteem as a
magiſtrate, whom he had ſo publicly convicted

διὰ το τεθναναι μεν Φηϛον, Αλϐινον δε ἐτι κατα την ὁδον
ὑπαρχειν, καθιζει συνεδριον κριτων, και παραγαγων εις αυτο
ΤΟΝ ΑΔΕΛΦΟΝ ΙΗΣΟΥ ΤΟΥ ΛΕΓΟΜΕΝΟΥ ΧΡΙΣΤΟΥ,
ΙΑΚΩΒΟΣ ονομα αυτῳ, και τινας ἑτερους, ὡς παρανομησαν-
των κατηγοριαν ποιησαμενος, παρεδωκε λευσθησομενους· ὁσοι δε
εδοκουν επιεικεϛατοι των κατα την πολιν ειναι, και περι τους
νομους ακριϐεις, ϐαρεως ηνεγκαν επι τουτῳ, και πεμπουσιν προς
τον ϐασιλεα κρυφα παρακαλουντες αυτον επιϛειλαι τῳ Ανα-
νῳ, μηκετι τοιαυτα πρασσειν, μηδε γαρ το πρωτον ορθως
αυτον πεποιηκεναι. Which is tranſlated by Mr. Whiſton as follows, —— "When, therefore, Ananus was
"of this diſpoſition, he thought he had now a proper oppor-
"tunity (to exerciſe his authority). FESTUS was
"dead; and ALBINUS was but upon the road. So he
"aſſembled the ſanhedrim of judges, and brought before
"them THE BROTHER OF JESUS, WHO WAS CALLED
"CHRIST, whoſe name was JAMES, and ſome others,
"(or ſome of his companions,) and when he had formed
"an accuſation againſt them as breakers of the law, he de-
"livered them to be ſtoned. The MOST EQUITABLE OF
"THE CITIZENS, AND SUCH AS WERE THE MOST
"UNEASY AT THE BREACH OF THE LAWS, DIS-
"LIKED WHAT WAS DONE. They alſo ſent to the
"king, (Agrippa,) deſiring him to ſend to ANANUS,
"that he ſhould act ſo no more ; for that what he had
"already done was not to be juſtified."

victed of abufing and perverting the legal
authority with which he had been entrufted; and, indeed, a notorious breach
of the law, by any man in the capacity
of *a ruler*, may reafonably be efteemed
a temporary difqualification for fuch an
honourable truft; for, a *judge* without
*juftice* and *righteoufnefs*, who openly perverts judgement, does thereby unqueftionably degrade himfelf from the dignity of his ftation, and render himfelf
unworthy, for the time being, of that
refpect which is otherwife due to his
rank in office. The fame apoftle, indeed, upon another occafion, commands
us to give " *honour to whom honour*"
*is due*; but what *honour* can be due to
a convicted hypocrite, — a " *whited*
" *wall*," — a " *wolf in fheep's cloath-*
" *ing*," — to an " *Ananias on the feat*
" *of judgement?*" SUCH characters muft
expect SUCH treatment, as *Ananias* met
with, from all fenfible and difcerning
men ;

men; if the latter are also equally *loyal*
with the apoftle, I mean in the ftrict
and proper fenfe of the word *loyal*,
(which is fo frequently mifapplied and
perverted by fycophants,) that is, if
they are equally zealous with that a-
poftle for *law*, *juftice*, and *righteoufnefs*,
for the general good of mankind! So
that if we approve of the apoftle's advice, in the beginning of the fame fentence, viz. " RENDER, THEREFORE,
" UNTO ALL THEIR DUES,"—" *tri-*
" *bute, unto whom tribute,*"—" *cuftom,*
" *to whom cuftom,*"—" FEAR, *to whom*
" FEAR,"—" HONOUR *to whom* HO-
" NOUR;" we muft needs alfo allow,
that the apoftle's *practice* (even in his
behaviour to *Ananias)* was ftrictly confiftent with his own declared *precepts,*
and that he moft juftly *rendered* to *A-*
*nanias* HIS DUE, when he fo feverely
reprimanded his conduct *as a judge!*
When all thefe circumftances are duly
confidered,

confidered, the meaning of the apoſtle's reply, may, fairly enough, be para-phraſed in the words of LORINUS, (9)

as

(9) " *Neſciebam cum eſſe* PONTIFICEM, *quia, ex modo* " *loquendi furioſo, non videtur eſſe* PONTIFEX, ſed " TYRANNUS." Many of the moſt learned and cele-brated commentators have confidered the apoſtle's cenſure nearly in the ſame light. In the learned com-mentary, commonly called Affembly's Annotations, the ſame ſenſe is applied to the apoſtle's reply to the charge of having *reviled God's high prieſt,* viz. " *I knew* " *him not to be a lawful high prieſt,* WHO THUS VIO-" LATETH THE LAW ; and, indeed," (ſays the Com-mentary,) " *he was but an uſurper.* — For proof of which they refer us to " Joſephus, Ant. l. 20. c. 3. 5. " Chr. Helvic. Theat. Hiſt. Anno Chriſti, 46."

The learned MATHIAS FLACIUS FRANCOWITZ remarks, that the famous *Auguſtine,* biſhop of Hippo, thought this reply of the apoſtle IRONICAL, * " *and* " *truly,* (ſays he,) *it borders upon* IRONY ; *for, when he* " *ſaw him* (Ananias) *ſit in the chief place among the* " *prieſts, to judge according to the law, he neceſſarily* " *knew*

* " IRONIAM eſſe putat Auguſtinus. Eſt ſane quiddam vicinum " ironiæ. Cum enim videret eum ſedere inter ſacerdotes loco præci-" puo, et ſecundum legem judicare ; neceſſariò ſcivit eum eſſe " pontificem : tametſi et alioqui etiam minimi pueri neceſſariò id " illic vel ex ſola ejus pompa et aſſeclis vulgoque jactatis vocibus " ſciverunt, nedum Paulus homo tam vigilans et diligens. Senſus " ergo eſt : Ego *non agnoſco in hoc homine pontificem Dei :* ſed *hypocritam,* " *ſeductorem, et veritatis perſecutorem.* Alioqui bene ſcio principi " maledicendum non eſſe."

as I find him quoted by CORNELIUS A
LAPIDE, viz. " *I knew not that he*
" *was*

" *knew him to be the high prieſt : for even the little*
" *children knew that by his mere pomp and attendants;*
" *and much leſs could a man, ſo watchful and diligent*
" *as Paul, be ignorant of it ; the ſenſe therefore, is,*" (ſays
the learned Francowitz,) " *I do not acknowledge, in this*
" *man, the high prieſt of God,* but a hypocrite, a de-
" ceiver, and a perſecutor of the truth. Otherwiſe,
" I well know that *a ruler* is not to be ſpoken againſt
" or reviled." To the ſame effect, alſo, the learned
monſieur Martin, — " *as St. Paul*" (ſays he †) " *was*
" *not ignorant, nor could be ignorant, that this was*
" *the high prieſt, eſpecially as he ſaw him at the head of*
" *the ſanhedrim, it is better to tranſlate the term of the*
" *original, by I* DID NOT THINK, *&c. as in Mark ix.*
" *6. and ſo to underſtand this reply of St. Paul as a*
" *grave and ſtrong irony, by which he would make thoſe*
" *underſtand, by whom he was accuſed of the want of*
" *reſpect for the high prieſt, that this perſon was a man*
" *unworthy of that character, and that he did not be-*
" *lieve, that a vicious and wicked man, ſuch as Ananias,*
" *who*

† Comme St. Paul n'ignoroit pas, et ne pouvoit pas même
ignorer, que ce ne fût le ſouverain ſacrificateur, puis qu'il le voyoit
à la tête du ſanhédrin, il vaut miéux traduire le term de l'original
par *je ne penſois pas,* comme Marc ix. 6. et prendre ainſi cette
répartie de St. Paul comme une grave et forte ironie, par laquelle il
vouloit fair ſentir à ceux qui l'avoient repris de manquer de reſpect
pour le ſouverain ſacrificateur, que c'étoit un homme indigne de ce
caractère ; et qu'il ne croyoit pas qu'un vicieux et un impie, comme
étoit Ananias, qui avoit uſurpé le pontificat en l'achetant des Romains,
méritat d'être regardé comme *le ſouverain ſacrificateur de Dieu.*

" *was the high prieſt.* becauſe, from his
" furious manner of ſpeaking, he did
" not ſeem to be a HIGH PRIEST, but
" a TYRANT." This ſenſe is ſtrictly
conſonant to *reaſon* and *natural right!*

*Juſtice* and *righteouſneſs* are ſo in-
ſeparably connected with the proper
character of a CHIEF MAGISTRATE or
RULER, that any notorious perverſion of
thoſe neceſſary principles, in the actual exerciſe of that official power with
H 2     which

" *who had uſurped the pontificate by purchaſing it of the*
" *Romans, could deſerve to be eſteemed as the high prieſt*
" *of God!*"
It would be tedious to quote all the authorities that
may be found to this purpoſe; the evidence, however,
of the learned Dr. Whitby, as it includes more au-
thorities than his own, is worthy the readers notice.—
" Dr. LIGHTFOOT *and* GROTIUS (ſays he) *think as*
" *I do, that St. Paul does* NOT *go about* TO EXCUSE
" HIS MISTAKE, *but rather ſaith, I* KNOW WELL
" ENOUGH THAT GOD'S HIGH PRIEST IS NOT TO
" BE REVILED, *but that this* ANANIAS *is a* HIGH
" PRIEST, *I know not, i. e. I* DO NOT OWN HIM AS
" SUCH *who hath procured this title by bribery: our*
" *celebrated* RABBINS *having declared that ſuch an one* IS
" NEITHER A JUDGE, *nor* TO BE HONOURED AS
" SUCH," &c.

which a magiftrate is entrufted for *legal*
(and not for *illegal*) purpofes, muft un-
avoidably diftinguifh the *contemptible
hypocrite,* THE WHITED WALL, from
the honourable MAGISTRATE, and deprive the former of the refpect which is
due only to the latter ! " *Sitteft thou to*
" *judge me* ACCORDING TO THE LAW,
" *and commandeft me to be fmitten* CON-
" TRARY TO LAW ?" Thus the a-
poftle clearly explained the fitnefs and
propriety of the reproachful figure of
fpeech, *(whited wall,)* by which he
had expreffed the true character of the
unworthy judge!

An appellation fimilar to this was
given, even by our Lord himfelf, to *the
Scribes and Pharifees,* who were the
teachers and magiftrates of the people :
" *Wo unto you,* SCRIBES *and* PHARI-
" SEES, HYPOCRITES ; *for ye are like*
" *unto* WHITED SEPULCHRES, *which,*
" *indeed,*

" *indeed, appear beautiful outward, but*
" *are within full of dead mens bones*
" *and of all uncleannefs.*" (Matth. xxiii.
27.)—And, in the context, he calls
them " *blind guides,*" (v. 24 )—" *hypo-*
" *crites,*" (v. 25.)—" *full of hypocrify and*
" *iniquity,*" (v. 28.)—" *partakers in the*
" *blood of the prophets,*" (v. 30.)—" *fer-*
" *pents,*"— " *generation of vipers,*"—
" *how can ye efcape the damnation of hell?*"
&c. (v. 33.) Nay, Herod himfelf, the
tetrarch of Galilee, was not exempt-
ed from the feverity of our Lord's cenfure, when there was a proper occafion to declare it; for, though our Lord
lived, for the moft part, under Herod's
temporal jurifdiction, that is, in GALI-
LEE, yet he openly characterifed the *craf-*
*ty, bafe,* and *felf-interefted,* difpofition
of the TETRARCH, by expreffly calling him *a* FOX,—(10) " *Go ye, and tell*
" *that*

(10) " *The meffage, our Lord here fends to Herod,*"
(fays a fenfible and learned commentator, the Rev. Mr.
*Francis*

" *that* FOX," &c. (Luke xiii. 32.) and,
though our Lord endured the moſt
provoking

*Francis Fox*, in his edition of the New Teſtament,
with references ſet under the text in words at length,)
" *is no breach of that command which forbids the*
" SPEAKING EVIL OF THE RULER OF THE PEOPLE,
" *and conſequently is no blemiſh* (ſays he) *in our Lord's ex-*
" *ample.* For our Lord here acts AS A PROPHET, *as*
" *one who had received an extraordinary commiſſion from*
" *God: and thoſe, who were truly* PROPHETS, *were, in*
" *the* EXECUTION *of their* COMMISSION, *above the*
" *greateſt* MEN *and moſt powerful princes, whom they*
" *were not to ſpare when God ſent them to reprove for ſin.*"
All this is certainly true with reſpect to the real authority of Chriſt to cenſure Herod, and that his applying ſo harſh and ſevere an expreſſion to the tetrarch " *is*
" *no blemiſh in our Lord's example :*" but yet this is not,
I apprehend, the proper method of reconciling the
ſeeming difficulty, which ariſes from this example, of
our Lord's applying a ſevere and reproachful epithet
to a chief *ruler*, (in calling Herod a FOX,) when it is
compared with that precept of the law, which forbids
the *ſpeaking evil of the ruler of the people* ; for, though
our Lord had ample ſuperiority and authority to reprove whomſoever he pleaſed, even the greateſt *ruler*
upon earth, yet, with reſpect to *his own perſonal be-*
*haviour,* as *a man* among *men*, he claimed no authority to diſpenſe with the poſitive precepts of the Mo-
ſaic law, on account of his own real dignity, or ſuperiority over the reſt of mankind, but ſtrictly obeyed
the law in all things, and publicly declared his ſtrict
conformity thereto. " *Think not,*" (ſaid he,) " *that*
" I

provoking indignities from the licentious
foldiery and reviling multitude, *in filence*, anfwering not *a word*, agreeable
to that ftriking character of a fuffering
Meffiah,

" *I come to deftroy the* LAW *or the* PROPHETS : *I am*
" *not come to deftroy, but to fulfill.*" Matth v. 17.

" *By* THE LAW AND THE PROPHETS" (fays the
fame ingenious commentator above cited) " *are*
" *meant the great rules of life, delivered in the writings of*
" MOSES *and the* PROPHETS, *or in the* Old *Teftament,*
" *more efpecially the duties of the* MORAL *or* NATURAL
" LAW ;" (from whence thofe, refpecting our behaviour to RULERS, cannot with propriety be excluded ;)
" *Thefe, our Lord affures us,* HE DID NOT COME *to* DE-
" STROY *or* DISSOLVE : *It was not his defign to* FREE
" *men from the obligation they were under to practife the*
" MORAL LAWS *of* GOD, *but to fulfil and perfect them.*
" *This our Lord did,* BY LIVING UP TO THOSE
" LAWS HIMSELF," (which totally excludes the idea
of his difpenfing, on account of his own real fuperio-
rity, with that *moral* law refpecting behaviour to rulers,) " *and becoming thereby* AN EXAMPLE TO US,
" *by freeing them from the corrupt gloffes, which the*
" *teachers among the Jews put upon them, and by expound-*
" *ing them in their fulleft fenfe, and according to their juft*
" *latitude, fhewing that they command not only an* OUT-
" WARD OBEDIENCE, *but* THE OBEDIENCE *even of*
" *the* MIND *and* THOUGHTS, *as appears in what our*
" *Lord delivers in the following verfes : — Thefe laws*
" *have their foundation in the reafon and nature of things,*
" *and therefore their obligation will never ceafe.*"

Meffiah, fo minutely defcribed, many
ages before, by the prophet Ifaiah ; (11)
yet he made an apparent diftinction between the VIOLENCE *and* INJUSTICE
of thefe, as *individuals*, and the INJUS-
TICE of a man in a *public character*, as a
*chief magiftrate*; for even, in our Lord's
ftate of extreme humiliation, when his
hour of fufferings was come, he did not
fail to rebuke *the* INJUSTICE of the *high
prieft* in his judicial capacity, becaufe,
inftead of proceeding againft him by
the legal method of *examination by witneffes*, he had attempted to draw out
matter of accufation from his own
mouth, againft himfelf, by INTERRO-
GATORIES, according to the baneful
method of arbitrary courts!

But,

(11) " *He was oppreffed, and he was afflicted*, YET
" HE OPENED NOT HIS MOUTH: *he is brought as a*
" *lamb to the flaughter ; and, as a fheep before her fhearers*
" IS DUMB, SO HE OPENED NOT HIS MOUTH. *He*
" *was taken from prifon, and from judgement : and who*
" *fhall declare his generation ? for he was cut off out of the*
" *land of the living : for the transgreffion of my people*
" *was he ftricken!*" Ifaiah liii. 7, 8.

But our Lord foon put a ftop to his impertinent QUESTIONS, by referring him to the legal method of finding evidence by witneffes : —*Why* ASKEST " *thou me?* ASK *them which heard me,* " *what I have faid unto them: behold,* " *they know what I faid."* John xviii. 21. Upon which, a time-ferving officer, who probably had not accuftomed himfelf to diftinguifh the different degrees of refpect that are due to *good* and *bad* magiftrates, " gave *Jefus a* " *blow, or rap with a rod,"* (εδωκε ῥαπισμα τῳ Ιησȣ,) faying, " *Anfwereft thou the* " *high prieft fo?"* (v. 22.) which open injuftice, to a perfon uncondemned, (even while he ftood in the prefence of the magiftrate, who ought to have protected him,) drew a farther *remonftrance,* even from the meekeft and humbleft man that ever was on earth, though the fame divine perfon afterwards fuffered much greater indignities *in filence!* For, " *Je-*
" *fus*

" *fus anſwered him,*"——" *If I have ſpo-*
" *ken evil,*" (ſaid he,) " *bear witneſs of*
" *the evil: but, if well, why ſmiteſt*
" *thou me?*" (V. 23.)

This ſhews that the reprehenſion of magiſtrates and their officers, for *in-juſtice* and *abuſe of power*, is not incon-ſiſtent with the ſtricteſt rules of *Chriſti-an* PASSIVE OBEDIENCE: and, though the apoſtle Paul. in a ſimilar caſe, uſed much harſher language, yet his cenſure was undoubtedly *juſt* and *true*, and the ſeverity of his expreſſions was plainly juſtified (as I have already ſhewn) by the event! i. e. *by the fatal cataſtrophe of* ANANIAS. The law, therefore, which forbids *the ſpeaking evil of the ruler of the people*, is certainly to be underſtood with proper exceptions, ſo as not to ex-clude any juſt cenſure of *rulers*, when their *abuſe of office*, and the cauſe of *truth* and *juſtice*, may render ſuch cen-

ſure

fure expedient and feafonable. That
the apoſtle Paul thus underſtood the text
in queſtion, is manifeſt from his manner of quoting it, when he was charged
with *reviling God's high prieſt,* if the
feverity of his cenſure be compared with
the indifference which he ſhewed, immediately afterwards, towards the offended *Sadducee,* by openly profeſſing
himſelf to be of an oppoſite party, and
by throwing an oblique charge againſt
the whole body of Sadducees, as the
principal authors of the unjuſt perſecution againſt himſelf,—" *I am a* PHARI-
" SEE," (ſaid he,) " *the ſon of a* PHA-
" RISEE; *of the hope and reſurrection of*
" *the dead am I called in queſtion.*" (Acts
xxiii. 6.) Thus he manifeſtly threw
the whole blame upon *the Sadducees,* and
thereby ſhewed no inclination to apologize for the feverity of his ſpeech to their
dignified chief!

I muſt

I muſt farther remark, that the a-
poſtle's behaviour, in openly oppoſing
the *high prieſt*, (who, as ſuch, was alſo
a *chief magiſtrate* and *judge,)* is by no
means inconſiſtent with that excellent
advice which the ſame apoſtle has laid
down in the thirteenth chapter of his
Epiſtle to the Romans, though it is
frequently cited by the advocates for arbitrary power, in order to juſtify their
falſe notions concerning the neceſſity of
*abſolute ſubmiſſion and entire paſſive obe-
dience !*

To an inattentive reader, indeed, the
apoſtle's expreſſion may ſeem too much
to favour ſuch doctrines, if the ſenſe
and connexion of the whole context are
not carefully weighed together; but
though he ſaid,—" *Let every ſoul be*
" *ſubject unto the higher powers. For*
" *there is no power but of God: the pow-*
" *ers that be are ordained of God. Whoſo-*
" *ever*

" *ever, therefore, refifteth the power, re-*
" *fifteth the ordinance of God: and they,*
" *that refift, fhall receive to themfelves*
" *damnation.*" Yet he immediately afterwards fignifies what kind of *rulers* he
fpoke of " that were not to be refifted."
" *For* RULERS" (fays he in the very next
verfe) " ARE NOT A TERROR TO
" GOOD WORKS, BUT TO THE EVIL.
" *Wilt thou then not be afraid of the*
" *power? do that which is* GOOD, *and thou*
" *fhalt have praife of the fame; for he*
" *is the* MINISTER *of* GOD *to thee for*
" GOOD." (But ANANIAS, as *a ruler,*
was certainly the very reverfe of this
defcription, fo that the practice of the
apoftle, with refpect to him, was by no
means oppofite to this doctrine.) " *But*"
(fays he) " *if thou do that which is* EVIL,
" *be afraid; for he beareth not the fword*
" *in vain: for he is* THE MINISTER
" OF GOD, *a revenger to* (execute)
" *wrath upon him that doeth evil. Where-*
" *fore* (ye) *muft needs be fubject, not only*
" *for*

" *for wrath,  but also* FOR CONSCI-
" ENCE SAKE. *For this cause pay ye*
" *tribute also : for they are* GOD'S MINI-
" STERS, *attending  continually  upon*
" *this very thing.  Render, therefore, to*
" *all their dues : tribute, to whom tri-*
" *bute* (is due); *custom, to  whom  cus-*
" *tom; fear  to whom fear ; honour* (12)
" *to whom honour.*" (Romans xiii. 1 to
7.)  Now, be pleased to remark, that
the apostle has expressly and repeatedly
assigned the reason why so much respect
and obedience is due to the *higher pow-*
*ers*, or to the *ruler*, or *magistrate* ; " *for*
" *he is*" (says the apostle) *the* MINISTER
" OF GOD TO THEE FOR GOOD," *&c.*
and again,—" *for he is the* MINISTER OF
" GOD, *a  revenger  to  wrath  upon  him*
" *that doeth evil :*" and again,—" FOR
" THEY ARE GOD'S MINISTERS;" ——
that is, they are *God's ministers* while
                                                    they

(12) See pages 55, 56, and 71, concerning the kind
of magistrates to whom honour is or is not *due!*

they maintain *juſtice* and *righteouſneſs* in the execution of their *public* charge, howſoever deficient their characters may be in other reſpects, as *private* individuals; but, on the other hand, ſuch an unjuſt *ruler* as *Ananias,* for inſtance, who *ſat to judge* ACCORDING TO LAW, *and yet commanded a perſon to be beaten* CONTRARY TO LAW, ſuch *a ruler,* I ſay, cannot be eſteemed *a miniſter of God to us* FOR GOOD, or *a miniſter of God* in any reſpect whatſoever. A man, who is notoriouſly guilty of perverting the laws, and of abuſing the delegated power, with which he is entruſted, by acts of *violence* and *injuſtice,* is ſo far from being " *the miniſter of God,*" that he is manifeſtly " *the miniſter of the devil;*" which is the expreſs doctrine of *the common law of this kingdom,* according to the moſt approved and moſt antient authorities ; wherein we find it applied not merely to inferior *rulers,* but to the ſupreme

preme magiſtrate, even to the *king*
himſelf, (13) if he *rules* contrary to
law,

(13) The celebrated and learned *Henry de Bracton*
ſays,—" *that a king can do nothing elſe upon earth, as*
" *he is* THE MINISTER *and* VICAR OF GOD, *but*
" *that only which* BY LAW *he may do,*" &c. And, a
little farther, he adds,—" *His power, therefore,*" (ſays
he,) " *is of right,* (or law,) *and not of wrong,* (or in-
" jury,) &c.*" -—" *That a king ought, therefore, to exer-*
" *ciſe the power of right,* (or LAW,) *as* THE VICAR AND
" MINISTER OF GOD *on earth, becauſe that power is*
" *of* GOD ALONE; *but the power of* WRONG (or INJU-
" RY) *is of the* DEVIL, *and* NOT OF GOD, *and the*
" *work of which ſo ever of theſe the king ſhall do,*
" *of him* HE IS THE MINISTER * *whoſe work he ſhall do.*
" *While,*

* This is perfectly agreeable to the doctrine of holy Scripture;
—" *Whoſoever committeth ſin*" (ſaid OUR LORD HIMSELF) " *is the*
" *ſervant*" (or miniſter) " *of ſin.*" John viii. 34. Here is no
exception or excluſive privilege allowed on account of *temporal dig-*
*nity,* or *offices* of worldly power! All men that wilfully *do evil,*
(be they *high* or *low.)* are not only *ſervants of* SIN, but alſo SONS
(as well as ſervants) OF THE DEVIL, as our Lord himſelf declared,
" *Ye do the deeds of* YOUR FATHER," &c. Ibid. ver. 41. And, when
thoſe men, to whom he addreſſed himſelf, ſtill contended (notwithſtanding their wicked deeds) that they were *the ſons and ſervants of*
*God:* Chriſt replied, " *Why do ye not underſtand my ſpeech?*" &c. —
" *Ye are of* (your) *father,* THE DEVIL, *and the luſts of your father*
" *ye will do.* He was a murderer from the beginning, and abode not in
" *the truth, becauſe there is no truth in him. When he ſpeaketh a lye,*
" *he ſpeaketh of his own: for he is a lyar, and the father of it.*" Ibid.
ver. 43 and 44. And, in like manner, THE DEVIL is certainly *the*
FATHER, or PROMOTER, of every other immorality among men, as
much

law, by violating, corrupting, or perverting, in any refpect, the powers of
K   go-

" *While, therefore, he does* JUSTICE, *he is the* VICAR
" (or MINISTER) *of the* ETERNAL KING ; *but he is the*
" MINISTER *of the* DEVIL *while he turns afide to* IN-
" JUSTICE, *for he is called king* (REX) *from* WELL
" RULING, *and not from* REIGNING ; *becaufe he is*
" KING *while he* RULES WELL, *but a* TYRANT *while*
" *he oppreffes the people committed to his charge with vio-*
" *lent* (or oppreffive) *government*." " Nihil enim aliud
" poteft rex in terris, CUM SIT DEI MINISTER ET
" VICARIUS, nifi id folum quod *de jure* poteft, &c.
" Poteftas itaque fua *juris* eft, et non *injuriæ*, &c.
" Exercere igitur debet rex poteftatem *juris*, ficut
" DEI VICARIUS ET MINISTER *in terra*, *quia illa*
" *poteftas folius Dei eft*, poteftas autem *injuriæ* DIA-
" BOLI, *non* DEI ; et cujus horum opera fecerit rex,
" ejus MINISTER erit, cujus opera fecerit. Igitur *dum*
" *facit juftitiam*, VICARIUS EST REGIS ÆTERNI;
" MINISTER AUTEM DIABOLI, *dum declinet ad inju-*
" *riam*. Dicitur enim rex a bene regendo et non a
" regnando, quia rex eft dum bene regit, tyrannus
" dum populum fibi creditum violenta opprimit
" dominatione." Henrici de Bracton de Legibus et
Confuetudinibus Angliæ lib. iii. c. ix.   And nearly
the fame doctrine in fubftance is laid down in Fleta,
lib. i. c. 17.

much as he is of *murder, lying,* and *deceit,* howfoever dignified the
vifible agents therein may be by the inveftiture of temporal honours,
titles, and power, or royal commiffions! — " *Know ye not*'' (faid the
apoftle Paul) " *that to whom ye yield yourfelves* SERVANTS *to obey,*
" HIS SERVANTS" (or MINISTERS) " *ye are to whom you obey;*
" *whether of fin unto death, or of obedience unto righteoufnefs!*'' Rom.
vi. 6.

[ 74 ]

government! And that excellent conſtitutional lawyer, *Lord Sommers*, informs us, that St. Edward's law even goes farther, (14) viz. " *That, unleſs the* " *king performs his duty, and anſwers* " *the end for which he was conſtituted,* " *not ſo much* AS THE NAME OF A " KING *ſhall remain in him.*" Now, when theſe conſtitutional principles of *the Engliſh law* are collated and duly compared with the precepts before cited from the apoſtle Paul, they are ſo far from being contradictory, that the full and clear meaning of them all may be maintained together without the leaſt inconſiſtency or diſcrepance of doctrine ; for we may ſurely ſay, with the apoſtle, " *Render to all their dues,*" &c. without ſeeming to favour the pernicious and dangerous doctrine of an *unlimited paſ-*

*ſive*

(14) The judgement of whole kingdoms and nations, concerning the rights, power, and prerogative, of KINGS, and the rights, privileges, and properties, of the PEOPLE, &c. See the 61ſt paragraph.

*five obedience!* " *Render, therefore, to*
" *all their dues; tribute, to whom tri-*
" *bute* (is due); *cuſtom, to whom cuſtom;*
" *fear, to whom fear; honour, to whom*
" *honour.*"—For, though *cuſtom, tribute,*
*fear,* and *honour,* are certainly due to
him who is the MINISTER OF GOD *to*
*us for good,* yet, ſurely, no honour is
*due,* or ought to be *rendered,* to THE
MINISTER OF THE DEVIL, to the
perjured violater of a public truſt, who,
in the eye of the Engliſh law, is not
even worthy of " *ſo much as the name*
" *of a king!*"

*Fear,* indeed, may too often be ſaid
to *be due* to ſuch men when in power;
but it is a very different ſort of *fear*
from that reverential *fear* which *is due*
to him who " *is the miniſter of God to*
" *us for good!*" It is ſuch *a fear* only as
that, which men have of a *wild beaſt* that
devours the flock! He is *fierce* and
*ſtrong,*

*ſtrong*, ſay they, and, therefore. each individual, through fear of *perſonal inconveni-
ence to himſelf*, is induced to wink at the
ruinous depredations made upon *his neighbours* and *brethren*, ſo that, for want of a
prudent and timely oppoſition, the vora-
cious animal (which in a ſtate is a many-
headed monſter) becomes ſtronger and
more dangerous to the community at
large, till the unwary time-ſervers themſelves perceive (when it is too late) that,
by their own ſelfiſh connivance, re-
ſpectively, as individuals, they have been
acceſſaries to the general ruin; and, as
ſuch, muſt one day be anſwerable to
God for their ſhameful breach of that
LAW OF LIBERTY, (15) *(" Thou ſhalt
" love thy neighbour as thyſelf,")* in which
we are aſſured *all the law is fulfilled,* (16)
and

(15) See my Tract on the *Law of Liberty.*

(16) " *For all the law is fulfilled* in one word, even
" in this; *thou ſhalt love thy neighbour as thyſelf.*" Galatians v. 14.

and by which, we are alfo affured, *we fhall be judged!* (17)

This heavenly *principle* is the true and proper ground for *patriotifm,* and undoubtedly has always been the predominant motive of great and good men, (fuch as the difinterefted and loyal apoftle Paul, following his Lord's example,) in their oppofition to the injuftice of *rulers* and *magiftrates,* though they *paffively* fubmit to perfonal injuries from other hands! for, in this, as I have already remarked, confifts the due diftinction between the neceffary *Chriftian fubmiffion to perfonal injuries,* and the doctrine of an *unlimited paffive obedience.*

The SUBJECTION and OBEDIENCE to MAGISTRATES, enjoined by the fame apoftle in his Epiftle to Titus, (c. iii. 1.) muft certainly be underftood with the fame

(17) " So fpeak ye, and fo do, as they that fhall be " JUDGED *by the law of liberty.*" James ii. 12.

fame neceffary limitations,—" *Put them*
" *in mind* (fays the apoftle) TO BE SUB-
" JECT TO PRINCIPALITIES AND
" POWERS, TO OBEY MAGISTRATES,"
(πειθαρχειν, fays he, but then he immediately fubjoins,) " *to be ready to e-*
" *very good work.*" —— And no man
can be efteemed " *ready to every good*
" *work,*" if he is *obedient* to magiftrates
when their commands exceed the due limits of the law; or if (contrary to the example of the apoftle himfelf) he neglects a
fair opportunity of publicly difcounten-
ancing and cenfuring any notorious perverfion of *juftice and right* by a magiftrate!

The fame neceffary limitation of the
doctrine of *obedience* muft alfo be underftood when we read the exhortation
of another apoftle on this head, viz.
" *Submit yourfelves to every ordinance*
" *of man for the Lord's fake: whether*
" *it be to the* KING, *as fupreme*; *or*
" *unto*

" *unto* GOVERNORS, *as unto them that*
" *are sent by him* FOR THE PUNISH-
" MENT OF EVIL DOERS, *and for the*
" PRAISE OF THEM THAT DO WELL.
" *For so is the will of God, that with*
" WELL-DOING *ye may put to silence*
" *the ignorance of foolish men : as free,*
" *and not using* (your) *liberty for a cloke*
" *of maliciousness, but as the servants of*
" *God!*" (1 Peter ii. 13-16.) GOVER-
NORS are here declared to be sent *for the*
*punishment of evil doers,* and for the
*praise of them that do well*; to such, therefore, as answer this description, the *sub-*
*mission* and *honour* enjoined in the context
are undoubtedly due; but, whenever the
governors themselves become *the evil do-*
*ers,* and, like *Ananias,* instead of praising
and encouraging " *them that do well,*"
do notoriously abuse, oppress, and murder, them, *as he did,* (18) it would be a
manifest

(18) The apostle Paul was so far from retracting
any part of his severe censure and remonstrance against
Ananias

manifest perverfion of the text to fuppofe that we are required thereby to
" *fubmit ourfelves to every ordinance of*
" *man,*"

Ananias, that he afterwards (before Felix) defied
Ananias and the reft of his accufers to fhew that he had
been guilty of any the leaft mifdemeanour ever fince
his laft arrival at Jerufalem, and more particularly
while " *he flood before the council,*" (meaning the time
when he foretold that God fhould fmite that *whited*
*wall,* Ananias,) " or elfe" (faid he to Felix) " let thefe
" fame here fay," (meaning the high prieft *Ananias,*
the elders, and their orator, Tertullus, mentioned in
the fiift verfe of the chapter,) " *if they have found any*
" EVIL DOING * IN ME WHILE I STOOD BEFORE THE
" COUNCIL, *except it be for this one voice,*" (now he
once more provokes the malicious Sadducee,) " *that*
" *I cried, flanding among them, Touching* THE RESUR-
" RECTION OF THE DEAD *I am called in queftion by*
" *you this day.*" (Acts xxiv. 20.) This is a manifeft
declaration that there was nothing reprehenfible either
in his *behaviour* or *words* on that day " *before the*
" *council,*" becaufe his declaration concerning the *re-*
*furrection of the dead* was the only *one voice* (or expreffion) which he fuppofed thefe Sadducees could call
in queftion and lay to his charge!

---

* The word in the original is αδικημα, fignifying rather *irjuftice,*
or *unrighteoufnefs,* than EVIL-DOING; and as the former may be effected
by *words* as well as by *deeds,* this public challenge from the mouth of
the apoftle includes a complete juftification of all that he either *faid*
or *did* on that day *before the council.*

" *man*," (19) without admitting fuch juft
and neceffary exceptions to the doctrine
L as

(19) The apoftles and difciples of Chrift were fo far
" from *fubmitting themfelves to every ordinance of man*,"
that they boldly rejected the *unjuft* commands even of the
high prieft and the whole national council of the Jewifh
ftate! The great council, called SANHEDRIM, i. e.
συνεδριον, (the commands of which they rejected,) included at that time all perfons of their nation that bore
any public authority or dignity among them, for the
text exprefsly informs us that " *their* RULERS, *and*
" ELDERS, *and* SCRIBES, *and* ANNAS, THE HIGH
" PRIEST," (and the *high priefts* fince the time of the
Maccabees were generally confidered as a fort of princes,) " *and Caiaphas, and John, and Alexander, and as*
" *many as were of the kindred of the high prieft, were*
" *gathered together at Jerufalem.*"
No power, therefore, amongft the Jews, could be
more refpectable (in regard to temporal authority)
than this great national council: and the apoftle Peter accordingly acknowledged their legal authority
at firft, by refpectfully addreffing them, faying,—" *Ye*
" *rulers of the people and elders of Ifrael*," &c.
Yet, notwithftanding the temporal authority of this
awful affembly of *rulers* and *elders*, (or fenators,) they
were publicly difregarded and contradicted by the a-
poftles even in their prefence, upon the very firft propofal of an *unreafonable* and *unlawful* ORDINANCE ; for
" *they called them*," (the apoftles,) " *and* COMMANDED
" THEM *not to fpeak at all, nor teach in the name of*
" *Jefus.*"—But " *Peter and John anfwered and faid*
" *unto them, whether it be right in the fight of God to*
" *hearken*

as I have already cited from the example of the apoſtle Paul, and even from that of our Lord himſelf.

And, therefore, though the apoſtle Peter adds,—" *Honour all* (men): *love* " *the brotherhood: fear God: honour* " *the king:*" yet he muſt neceſſarily be underſtood to mean, with the apoſtle Paul, that we muſt render " *honour* " *to whom honour*" is DUE, and not to

*honour*

" *hearken unto you more than unto God, judge ye. For we* " *cannot but ſpeak the things we have ſeen and heard.*" (Acts iv. 19 and 20.) And afterwards, when they were brought a ſecond time before the ſaid great council to anſwer for their breach of this " ORDINANCE OF " MAN," " *the high prieſt aſked them, ſaying,* DID NOT " WE STRAIGHTLY COMMAND YOU *that you ſhould* " *not teach in this name, and behold ye have filled Jeru-* " *ſalem with your doctrine, and intend to bring this man's* " *blood upon us. Then Peter and the other apoſtle an-* " *ſwered and ſaid,—*WE OUGHT TO OBEY GOD RA- " THER THAN MEN," &c. This ſentence, in effect, holds good with reſpect alſo to the rejection of *every public ordinance* that is contrary to *reaſon, juſtice,* or *natural equity,* as well as thoſe that are contrary to *the written word of God!* This I have ſhewn more at large in my Declaration of the People's Right.

*honour* such *men* and such *kings* as are
unworthy of *honour!* (20)

But

(20) To the example of the patriotic apostle, Paul,
upon this point, I must now add that of another chosen vessel of Christ, the protomartyr *Stephen :* this
excellent man, " *full of the Holy Ghost and wisdom,*"
(Acts vi. 3.) " *full of faith and power,*" (v. 8.) " *and*
" *whose wisdom and spirit none were able to resist :*"
(v. 10.)—This excellent man, I say, has left us by
his own example an unquestionable precedent on record to demonstrate that HONOUR IS NOT DUE to the
highest temporal authority on earth, not even to a
*great national council of rulers and elders,* while they exercise their authority in *unjust* prosecutions, and abuse
their power by enacting *unreasonable and tyrannical or-
dinances.* The great council of the Jewish state had
" *straightly commanded* " the apostles and disciples of
Christ (as I have already remarked in a preceding
note) " *not to speak at all, nor teach in the name of*
" *Jesus* ;" which command, it seems, was given lest
their preaching should " *bring this man's blood* " (said
the high priest, meaning the blood of our LORD JESUS)
" *upon us:*" but *Stephen* paid so little regard either
to the *unlawful* command itself, or to the reason of it,
that he afterwards publicly upbraided the whole council, with the high priest at the head of it, (in the most
stimulating and unreserved terms,) as the betrayers and
murderers of that just One!—" *Ye stiff-necked, and un-*
" *circumcised in heart and ears,*" (said he to their faces
in the public assembly,) " *ye do always resist the Holy*
" *Ghost : as your fathers* (did), *so* (do) *ye. Which of*
" *the prophets have not your fathers persecuted? And they*
" *have*

But what men (it will be faid) are to be efteemed the proper *judges of defert* in fuch cafes, fo as to determine with propriety when *honour* is or is not to be rendered? To which I anfwer, — *Every man* is a judge of it if he be not an idiot or mad man! *Every man* of common fenfe can diftinguifh *juftice* from *injuftice*, *right* from *wrong, honourable*

---

" *have flain them which fhewed before of the coming of the* " JUST ONE, *of whom ye have been now the* BETRAY-" ERS *and* MURDERERS," &c. (Acts vii. 51 and 52.) Words could not well be *fharper* than thefe, which is manifeft from their *effect*; for the text teftifies that " *when they heard thefe things they were* CUT TO THE " HEART, *and they gnafhed on him with* (their) *teeth*." (V. 54.) Thus it clearly appears that the holy, inno-cent, and meek Stephen did not think himfelf bound (like our undiftinguifhing *paffive-obedience* men) to " *fub-* " *mit to every ordinance of man*," &c. nor to " *honour all* " *men*," without making reafonable and due excep-tions! Nay, fo far from *honouring* men merely on account of their *temporal dignity*, it is manifeft that he treated the whole *body of rulers* with the utmoft feverity and contempt, while he thought them *unworthy of honour*, and yet there is no doubt but that he moft confcienti-oufly, on every occafion, rendered " *honour to whom* " *honour*" WAS DUE!

[ 85 ]

*honourable* from *diſhonourable,* (21) whenever he happens to be an eye or ear
witneſs of the proper circumſtances of
evidence for ſuch a judgement! *Every
man,* (except as above,) be he ever ſo
poor and mean with reſpect to his
rank in this life, inherits *the knowledge
of good and evil,* or REASON, from the
common parents of mankind, and is
thereby rendered anſwerable to GOD
for *all* his actions, and anſwerable to
MAN for *many* of them!

In this *hereditary knowledge,* and in
the proper uſe of it, (according to the
different ſtations of life in which men
ſubſiſt in this world,) conſiſts the *equality*
of ALL MANKIND in the ſight of GOD,
and alſo in the eye of *the law,* I mean
the *common law* and rules of *natural juſtice,* which are formed upon the ſelf-
evident

(21) See my Tract on " *the Law of Nature and the*
" *Principles of Action in Man,"* wherein, I hope, this
point is fully demonſtrated.

evident conclufions of *human reafon*, and
are the neceffary refult of the abovementioned *hereditary knowledge in* MAN.
Every man *knows*, by what we call
*confcience*, (which is only an effect of
*human reafon* upon the mind,) whether
his own actions deferve the *cenfure* of
the *magiftrate, who* " *bears not the*
" *fword in vain!*" And the fame principle of *hereditary knowledge* enables
him to judge alfo concerning the outward actions of *other men*, whether they
be *juft* or *unjuft*; whether they be *praife-
worthy* or *cenfurable!*

But, if a man abufes his own *natural
reafon*. and fuffers himfelf to be blinded
by private intereft, by paffion, or unreafonable refentment, or by pride, envy, or perfonal partiality, and is thereby led to mifconftrue the actions of his
fuperiors, to behave unfeemly towards them, and to cenfure them publicly

licly without a juſt cauſe, the *conſcience* of ſuch an offender againſt *reaſon* will ſpeedily inform him that he
has cauſe to *fear the magiſtrate,* and
that he is liable to ſuffer for his miſbehaviour " *as an evil doer :*" but, when
the like faults are diſcoverable on the o-
ther ſide, that is, on the ſide of the
ſuperior or magiſtrate, (as it happened
in the caſe of Ananias,) a *juſt* cenſure of
the *unjuſt* magiſtrate, even though it
comes from the pooreſt and meaneſt
man that happens to be preſent, will
have its due weight in the opinion of
all unprejudiced and diſintereſted perſons, and may occaſion a conſiderable
check to the progreſs of *injuſtice ;* and,
therefore, if any man neglects ſuch an
opportunity (when he has it in his
power) of making a perſonal *proteſt* (as
Paul did) againſt the public injuſtice
of a wicked magiſtrate, he ſtrengthens
the hand of iniquity by his timidity
and

and remiſſneſs, and becomes acceſſary
to the public diſgrace by refuſing his
endeavours, according to his abilities,
(howſoever ſmall,) to vindicate the *laws*
*of God*, and maintain the *common rights*
*of his neighbours and brethren*. Such
an one unhappily demonſtrates that he
has more *fear* of MAN than of GOD,
and much more *love* for *himſelf* than he
has for his *neighbour* and *country*, and,
conſequently, in that awful day, when
he " *ſhall be judged by the law of liber-*
" *ty*," (22) muſt be liable, (unleſs a
timely repentance ſhould have previouſly
reſtored him to a better uſe of that *he-*
*reditary knowledge* for which all men
are accountable,) muſt be liable, I ſay,
" to be caſt with *the unprofitable ſer-*
" *vant into outer darkneſs: there ſhall*
" *be weeping and gnaſhing of teeth!*"
Matth. xxv. 30.

ALL

(22) James ii. 12. See alſo my Tract on *the Law*
*of Liberty*.

ALL MEN, therefore, be they ever
so *rich*, or ever so *poor* and *mean*, are
REQUIRED to vindicate the cause of
*truth*, *justice*, and *righteousness*, whenever they have a favourable opportunity of
doing so; they ARE REQUIRED, I say,
because they ARE ENABLED by their
NATURAL KNOWLEDGE of GOOD and
EVIL to discern and judge concerning
the *fitness* or *unfitness* of human actions,
and of the *justice* or *injustice* of all mea-
sures and proceedings that happen to
fall within the reach of their inspection
and consequent observation. He, who
denies this, is ignorant of the *true dignity of human nature*, and wants a teacher
to point out to him not only *the equality
of mankind before God*, but also *the universal conditions of man's subsistence in the
world!*——THE HEREDITARY KNOW-
LEDGE OF GOOD AND EVIL may, at
least, be esteemed as the ONE TALENT
for

for which *all mankind* are accountable
to the univerſal Lord! And, therefore,
if they wilfully *abuſe* or *bury* THIS
TALENT, they have ſurely nothing to
expect but the condemnation abovementioned of the *unprofitable ſervant!*

Shall we blame the patriotic apoſtle,
then, for his zeal in vindicating *the natural rights of mankind* againſt an UNJUST
JUDGE, when he had ſo fair an opportunity of proteſting againſt his iniquity? God forbid! Let us, on the
contrary, revere his example, which,
in reality, affords no oppoſition to the
doctrine laid down in the beginning of
this Tract concerning the neceſſity of
" *Chriſtian ſubmiſſion to perſonal inju-*
" *ries.*" If he, ſometimes, freely and
courageouſly expreſſed his *reſentment
for perſonal ill uſage*, (23) it was always

(23) In purſuing the examination of this ſubject concerning *reſentment for perſonal ill uſage*, I was gradually
led

ways in vindication of *the law,* on which (next to the providence of God) the fafety, liberty, and happinefs, of the community depend; whereas, the *hafty revenger of his own caufe* is fo far from being a friend to the community, or a *lover of liberty,* that he himfelf is actually *a tyrant*; becaufe he neglects the neceffary doctrine of " *Chrif-* " *tian fubmiffion to perfonal injuries,"* and on every occafion is ready to revenge his *own caufe* with his *own hand,* and to ufurp all the diftinct offices of

M 2                        judge,

led to confider the prefent unnatural though prevailing practice of DUELLING; and this occafioned my " *Re-* " *marks on the Opinions of fome of the moft eminent Wri-* " *ters on* CROWN LAW, *refpecting the due diftinction* " *between* MANSLAUGHTER *and* MURDER," (printed in 1773,) which Remarks were, at firft, intended as a continuation of this tract; but finding, foon afterwards, that fome publication, to correct the common miftaken doctrines concerning *manflaughter* and *duelling,* was become more immediately neceffary, I thought it advifeable to detach what I had written on that fubject from this tract, and to print it as foon as poffible, (with fome few alterations and additions,) rather than to wait for the publication of thefe other tracts.

judge, jury, and executioner! He is so far from vindicating *the law*, like the generous and patriotic apostle, for the sake of *national liberty*, that he manifestly sets himself up *above the law*, (which is *the first characteristic of a tyrant,*) and thereby renders himself in fact an open enemy to *liberty*, and consequently *a disgrace to society!*

GRANVILLE SHARP.

" GLORY to GOD in the Highest!
" And on Earth — PEACE,
" GOOD WILL towards Men!"

INDEX

# I N D E X

OF

Texts referred to in the foregoing Work.

LEVITICUS.

| Chap. | Verses. | Pages. |
|---|---|---|
| XXV. | 52. | 18. |

DEUTERONOMY.

| | | |
|---|---|---|
| XV. | 12, 14. | 21. |

ECCLESIASTICUS.

| | | |
|---|---|---|
| xxxiii. | 12. | 34 n. |

ISAIAH.

| | | |
|---|---|---|
| liii. | 7, 8. | 64 n. |

MATTHEW.

| | | |
|---|---|---|
| v. | 17. | 63 n. |
| xxiii. | 24, 25. | 61. |
| | 27, 28. } | 61. |
| | 30. 33. } | |
| xxv. | 30. | 88. |

MARK.

| | | |
|---|---|---|
| ix. | 6. | 58 n. |

LUKE.

| Chap. | Verses. | Pages. |
|---|---|---|
| vi. | 28, 29. | 39. |
| xiii. | 32. | 62. |

JOHN.

| | | |
|---|---|---|
| viii. | 34. | 72 n. |
| | 41. | 72 n. |
| | 43, 44. | 72 n. |
| xv. | 12 to 15. | 37 n. |
| xviii. | 21, 22. | 65. |
| | 23. | 66. |
| | 36. | 7. |

ACTS.

| | | |
|---|---|---|
| iv. | 8. | 83 n. |
| | 10. | 83 n. |
| | 19, 20. | 83 n. |
| vii. | 51, 52. | 84 n. |
| | 54. | 84 n. |
| xvi. | 30 to 39. | 44 n. |
| xxii. | 24 to 30. | 45 n. |
| xxiii. | 1 to 5. | 45 n. |

[ 94 ]

## ACTS *continued.*

|---|---|---|
| xxiii. | 6. | 67. |
| xxiv. | 20. | 80 n. |

### ROMANS.

|---|---|---|
| ii. | 11. | 34 n. |
| vi. | 6. | 73 n. |
| xiii. | | 68. |
| | 1 to 7 | 70. |
| | 9, 10. | 37 n. |

### 1 CORINTHIANS.

|---|---|---|
| vi. | 19, 20. | 23. |
| vii. | 21. | 7. |
| | 20, 21. | 16. |
| | 21 to 23. | 12 n. |
| | 21. | 17. |
| | 22. | 17. |
| | 23. | 17. 20. |

### GALATIANS.

|---|---|---|
| v. | 14. | 76 n. |

### EPHESIANS.

|---|---|---|
| vi. | 5 to 8. | 7. 15. |
| | 5, &c. | 34. |
| | 8, 9. | 34 n. |

### COLOSSIANS.

|---|---|---|
| iii. | 2. | 15. |

## COLOSSIANS *continued.*

|---|---|---|
| iii. | 18. | 32 n. |
| | 20. | 33 n. |
| | 22. | 33 n. |
| | 22, 23. | 7. |
| | 23, 24. | 33 n. |
| | 24. | 34 n. |
| | 25. | 31 n. 34 n. |
| iv. | 1. | 35 n. 36 n. |

### 1 TIMOTHY.

|---|---|---|
| vi. | | 32 n. |
| | 1 to 8. | 11. |
| | 1. | 14. 38. |
| | 2. | 24. 28. |

### TITUS.

|---|---|---|
| ii. | 9. | 32 n. |
| | 9, 10. | 11. |
| | 10. | 14. 32. |
| iii. | 1. | 77. |

### JAMES.

|---|---|---|
| ii. | 12. | 77 n. 84 n. |

### 1 PETER.

|---|---|---|
| ii. | 13 to 16. | 79. |
| | 18. | 15. |

INDEX

# I N D E X

## OF THE

## Different Authors referred to.

### A.

ASSEMBLY's ANNOTATIONS, 57 n.
Ananias, 49 n.
Ananus, 49 n.
Auguſtine, biſhop of Hippo, 57 n.

### B.

Benſon, (Dr. Geo.) 25 n.
Borner, 26 n.
Brafton, (Hen. de,) 72 n. 73 n.
Broughton, (Hugh,) 47 n.

### C.

Caſtalio, 47 n.
Cornelius a Lapide, 58.

### F.

Fleta, 73 n.
Fox, (reverend Francis,) 59 n.
Francowitz, (Mat. Flac.) 57 n. 58 n.

**G.**

Grotius, 59 n.

**H.**

Hammond, 28.
Heinſius, 47 n.

**J.**

Joſephus, 52 n. 53 n. 57 n.
Judgement of whole kingdoms and nations, &c. 74 n.
Juſtin Martyr, 21.

**K.**

Kuſter, 26 n.

**L.**

Law of Liberty, 76 n. 86 n.
Law of Nature, 85 n.
Lightfoot, 59 n.
Lorinus, 57.

**M.**

Martin, (monſ.) 58 n.
Mill, (Dr.) 26 n.

**P.**

Pet. 2 and 3. MSS. ſo called, 26 n.

**S.**

Sommers, (lord,) 73.
Syriac verſion, 25 n.

**T.**

Tertullian, 21.

**W.**

Whiſton, 54 n.
Whitby, (Dr.) 59 n. 21. 25 n. 34 n.

INDEX

# I N D E X

## OF THE

## Various Topics difcuffed in this Work.

A.

*ANANIAS.* See FRANCOWITZ, MARTIN, alfo *high prieft, judge,* and *magiftrate.* St. Paul's denunciation againft him juftified by the event, 52 n. his injuftice and cruelty towards the Chriftians, 53 n.

*Apoftles.* Did not fubmit themfelves to every ordinance of man without exception, 78 & feq.

*Author.* A learned and reverend correfpondent differs from him in his notions of flavery, 4 ; his character of that correfpondent, 5 ; conceffions of his, 6, 13; reafons for not anfwering a letter from him at the time of receiving it, ib. his defign in this treatife is to demonftrate the abfolute illegality of flavery among Chriftians, 7 ; efteems both mafter and flaves as brethren, 12 ; his reafons for printing his Remarks on the Crown Law prior to this tract, 91 n.

B.

*Believers.* God alone their judge, 26.

C.

## C.

*Chrift.* His difciples had no commiffion to alter the temporary conditions of men, 7 ; claimed no authority to difpenfe with the Mofaic law, 62 n.

*Confcience.* Only an effect of human reafon, 86.

*Correfpondent* of the Author's. See *Author.* Does not think Chriftianity releafed flaves, &c. 6 ; an opinion of his examined, 18 n. & feq. another, 30 n. & feq.

## D.

*Duties* of placability, fubmiffion, and patience, too commonly mifunderftood or rejected by the Chriftian world, 41.

## E.

*Edward,* (St.). The ftrictnefs of his law concerning kings, 74 & feq.

*Egyptian bondage.* A type of our fpiritual fervitude to -the enemy of mankind, 20.

## F.

*Fear.* That we have of a tyrant very different from that we have of a good magiftrate, 75.

*Francowitz,* (Mat. Flac.). His opinion of St. Paul's anfwer to Ananias, 57 n.

*Freedom.* The attainment of it legally enjoined fervants by St. Paul, 12 n. 16.

## G.

GOD. Submiffion in fervants enjoined for confcience fake towards him, 15 & feq. mafters and fervants equal in his fight, 17. See *Believers, Judge.*

*Good and evil,* See *Reafon.*

*Good*

[ 99 ]

*Good men.* From whence their zeal arises for just and equitable laws, 42.

*Grotius.* Quoted by Dr. Whitby concerning St. Paul's reply to Ananias, 59 n.

#### H.

*High priest.* St. Paul's spirited but cautious behaviour before him, 46 & seq. did not attempt to excuse or apologize for it, 47 & seq. 67; the justness of that behaviour, 56. 60. 90; Lorinus' paraphrase of the apostle's reply to him, 57; which is strictly consonant to reason and natural right, 59; our Lord's behaviour, in the same predicament, exactly similar. 60 & seq. the apostle's behaviour not inconsistent with his doctrine, Rom. xiii. 68 & seq. which behaviour he afterwards defended before Felix, 79 n.

#### J.

*Jews.* Not to be sold as bondmen, 18, 19, 20. See *Slavery.*

*Injustice.* Censuring bad magistrates may tend to check its progress, 87; which is the duty of every man, 89.

*Interrogatories.* Their illegality, 64.

*Judge.* One who perverts judgement degrades himself from his office, 55; our Saviour's character of such, 61 & seq. who cannot be deemed ministers of God in any respect, 71.

#### K.

*Kings.* Are not *ministers of God* when they act contrary to law, 72; and see the notes on that and the succeeding page. See *Edward* (St.); not worthy the name of a king, 75; but are *ministers of the devil,* and unworthy of *honour* while they do evil, ib.

L.

**L.**

*Law.* A notorious breach of it by a ruler is a temporary difqualification, 55. See *Kings, Edward* (St.).
*Loyal.* What it is to be really fo, 56.


**M.**

*Magiftrates.* Their reprehenfion not inconfiftent with
Chriftian paffive obedience, 66 & feq. good one.
See *Fear, Injuftice.*
*Martin,* (monf.). Agrees with M. Flac. Francowitz,
Grotius, Whitby, &c. concerning St. Paul's reply
to Ananias, 58 n.
*Mafters.* See GOD, *Slavery.*
*Minifters of God.* See *Kings.*
*Minifters of the devil.* See *Kings.*


**O.**

*Obedïence.* See *Servants.*
*Oppeffion.* That practifed by the flave-holders no
more juftified by the New Teftament than that of
ftrikers or robbers, 41.


**P.**

*Paffive obedïence.* See *Magiftrates.* Not due to evil
magiftrates, 77 & feq.
*Patience.* See *Duties.*
*Patriotifm.* The proper ground for it, 77.
*Paul,* (St.). His zeal for the Roman liberty, 42 ; his
Chriftian patience and meeknefs under perfonal in-
juries, 43. 44 n. See *high prieft.* His injunction,
Tit. iii. 1. explained, 77.
*Peter,* (St.). His injunction, 1 Pet. ii. 13 to 16. ex-
plained, 79.
*Price.* The meaning of that word in 1 Cor. vii. 23.
examined, 21 & feq.

Q.

## Q.

*Questions.* Serious ones to the slave-holders, 30 & seq.

## R.

*Reason.* Inherited by all men, except idiots or mad men, 84. 89 ; which renders all men equal in the sight of God and the law, 85. See *Conscience.* The talent for which all men are accountable, 90.

*Royal law.* No single text to be depended on, which will not bear the test of it, 27.

*Ruler.* See *Law.*

## S.

*Sanhedrim.* Its power and dignity, 81 n.

*Scriptures.* Their honour what the author has most at heart, 4.

*Servants,* (Christian,). Their obedience frequently insisted on by St. Paul, 8 & seq. the submission required of them does not imply the legality of slave-holding, 11 ; on what principles that submission is founded, 13 & seq. 24 n. which do not admit of any right or property in the master, 15 ; submission enjoined by St. Peter both to the good and bad master, for conscience' sake towards God, 15 & seq. See GOD, *Slavery, Slave-holders, Tyranny.*

*Slave-holders.* Cannot avail themselves of any of the texts relating to Christian servants, 29. 38. See *Questions, Oppression.*

*Slavery.* Some particular texts seem to prove the toleration of it amongst the primitive Christians, 3. See *Author.* No more than a state of hired servitude among the Jews, 19 n. 21 n. the text 1 Tim. vi. 2. no argument in favour of it, 24 & seq. that text intended for servants, not masters, 26 ; so understood by by Dr. Hammond, 26 ; the texts which juftify the flave's fubmiffion do not authorize the mafter's tyranny, 30. (See the whole note in that page.) 40.

*Subjection* (unlimited). Inconfiftent with the dignity of a Chriftian, 17 ; and intirely illegal, ib. See *Duties*.

### T.

*Texts.* See *Price, Slavery, Whitby, Paul, Peter.*

*Tyrants.* See *Fear.* The folly and wickednefs of abetting them, 76 ; characteriftics of one, 91.

*Tyranny.* The fubmiffion enjoined in the gofpel no plea for it, 39.

### W.

*Whitby,* (Dr.). Miftakes the meaning of the text 1 Cor. vii. 23, 21 ; is of the fame opinion with Grotius concerning St. Paul's reply to Ananias, 59 n.

*Whited wall.* The propriety of that expreffion of St. Paul, 52.

# THE END.

### ERRATUM.

Page 47, line 2, for hearſay, read hearing.

T H E

# L A W OF L I B E R T Y,

O R,

# R O Y A L L A W,

By which *all Mankind* will certainly *be judged!*

# THE

# LAW OF LIBERTY,

OR,

# ROYAL LAW,

BY WHICH

*ALL MANKIND* WILL CERTAINLY *BE JUDGED!*

EARNESTLY RECOMMENDED TO THE

SERIOUS CONSIDERATION

OF ALL

*SLAVEHOLDERS* AND *SLAVEDEALERS*.

By GRANVILLE SHARP.

" *So ſpeak ye, and ſo do, as they that ſhall be* JUDGED
" *by* THE LAW OF LIBERTY." Jam. ii. 12.

LONDON:

Printed for B. WHITE, at Horace's Head, in Fleet Street; and E. and C. DILLY, in the Poultry.

MDCCLXXVI.

T H E

LAW of LIBERTY,

O R,

R O Y A L   L A W.

IN two former Tracts I have attempted
to defcribe the JUST LIMITATION OF
SLAVERY IN THE LAWS OF GOD, and
THE LAW OF PASSIVE OBEDIENCE,
with refpect more particularly to the due
SUBMISSION of *Chriftian Servants* or
*Slaves* to their *Mafters*.

The purpofe of the prefent Tract is
not only to point out the reciprocal duty
of *Chriftian Mafters* to their *Servants*,
and all other perfons with whom they
are connected, but alfo more particularly

to

to enable our *Britiſh American* Slaveholders to examine or *meaſure* (with
very little trouble) by *the Rule* of God's
Holy Word, *the Legality* or *Illegality of
Slavery among Chriſtians.* For this purpoſe ſome of the cleareſt and moſt eſſential *Maxims* or *Principles* of Scripture are
ſelected and compared with each other
in the following pages.

" *So ſpeak ye, and ſo do, as they that*
" *ſhall be* JUDGED *by* THE LAW OF
" LIBERTY."

This the earneſt advice of the Apoſtle
James in his General Epiſtle; (ii. 12.)
and as it is therefore manifeſt that we
ſhall certainly BE JUDGED by " THE
" LAW OF LIBERTY," it becomes a
buſineſs of the utmoſt importance to
aſcertain what particular Law is thereby
to be underſtood, that we may *write it
on our hearts,* ſince our everlaſting happineſs

pinefs depends upon it, and the peril
of eternal damnation feems to attend a
breach of it; " *for he fhall have* JUDG-
" MENT WITHOUT MERCY" (fays the
Apoftle in the following verfe) " *who*
" *hath fhewed* NO MERCY !" The neceffary premifes for the examination of
the queftion are nothing lefs than the
fundamental moral Principles of Chriftianity ; and if I am rather prolix in
defining them, I hope *the importance of
the fubject* will be confidered as a fufficient excufe ; for indeed *the fubject* is
not only *important* to thofe perfons for
whofe ufe this Tract is particularly intended (*I mean thofe perfons who defire to
be fatisfied concerning* THE LEGALITY
*or* ILLEGALITY OF SLAVERY AMONG
CHRISTIANS) but to all Mankind befides of every rank and denomination.

All the moral duties of the Gofpel
are briefly comprehended in *two fingle
Prin-*

*Principles* of the Law of Mofes, viz.
THE LOVE OF GOD, and THE LOVE OF
OUR NEIGHBOUR. Nothing, therefore,
can be efteemed truly *lawful* under the
Gofpel, that is, in the leaft, repugnant
to either of thefe; and we need never be
at a lofs to diftinguifh what is, or what
is not fo, if we will but carefully confider the proportion or degree of *that Love*,
which is clearly expreffed to be *due*, both
to *God* and our *Neighbour* in thefe two
comprehenfive and eternal maxims. The
degree of *Love due to God* exceeds all
comparifon or confideration of other
things; for it muft (fays the text) be
" *with* ALL *thy heart, and with* " ALL
" *thy foul, and with* ALL *thy might."*
(Deut. vi. 5.) which neceffarily implies a
moft fervent zeal for the glory of GOD,
far exceeding all worldly confiderations.
And with refpect to the degree or true
proportion of *Love due to our Neighbour,*
we have no pretence to plead ignorance,
fince

since the appointed *meafure* of it is contained in *every Man's Breaſt*—" THOU
" SHALT LOVE THY NEIGHBOUR AS
" THYSELF. (Lev. xix. 18.) " *On*
" *theſe two Commandments*" (faid the
Eternal Judge) " *hang* ALL THE LAW
" *and* THE PROPHETS." (Mat. 22. 40.)
The fame Eternal Judge of Mankind
made alfo, on another occaſion, a fimilar
declaration concerning the *Sum or Com-*
*pendium* " OF THE LAW AND THE
" PROPHETS"—" *All things whatſoever*
" *ye would that Men ſhould do to you*"
(faid he) " *do ye even ſo to them; for*
" *this is* THE LAW AND THE PRO-
" PHETS." (Matth. vii. 12.) This
moſt excellent rule of conduct and behaviour towards *our Neighbours,* which
includes the whole Subſtance or Spirit
of " THE LAW AND THE PROPHETS,"
fo perfectly correfponds with the fecond
great Commandment, to LOVE *our Neigh-*
*bours as ourſelves* (viz. to manifeſt our
LOVE,

Love, *by* DOING *to them, as we ourselves might* WITH REASON AND JUSTICE *expect and desire* THEY WOULD DO UNTO US) that it seems intended like a sort of paraphrase to explain the true tenour of it; for though the mode of expression is different, yet the effect of the doctrine is undoubtedly the same; because the Apostle Paul has in like manner declared this second great Commandment to be *the Compendium of* " *all the Law.*" " *All* " *the Law*" (says he) " *is fulfilled in one* " *word, even in this* : *Thou shalt* LOVE " *thy Neighbour* AS THYSELF." (Gal. v. 14.

SELF-LOVE, therefore, must be the RULE or MEASURE (not of Self-gratification, or private Interest, but) *of our Conduct and Behaviour towards other Men!* It must not be SOLE TENANT of the heart; but is always to leave *equal* room for a due balance of *that Love which we*

*owe*

*owe to our Neighbour,* whenever the prefent circumftances (whatever they may
be) require a confcientious regard to the
*publick Good,* or a fympathetick confideration for *the Feelings and Sufferings of
Individuals,* to enable us to fulfil *our
Duty to our Neighbour.* SELF-LOVE is
not hereby *excluded;* for *Self-prefervation,*
and a prudent regard for our own
fupport and happinefs, may ftill be allowed an *equal Share* of our confideration, without a Breach of *this fecond great
Commandment,* which would otherwife be
too hard and difficult for *Human Nature*
to receive : we are not commanded therein to love our Neighbours MORE *than
ourfelves,* but only (ὡς) AS *ourfelves;* fo
that SELF-LOVE is apparently the *true
Meafure of our Conduct and Behaviour towards other Men:* and though an exalted
Senfe of *Duty to God* (according to the
*firft great Commandment*) may, in fome
particular cafes, prompt Men to noble
actions,

actions, wherein SELF-LOVE may seem
to be loft in a generous and benevolent
regard to others (of which there are
several inftances in Scripture, as I have
elfewhere fhewn (1); and alfo though the
like admirable generofity and perfect dif-
intereftednefs may, poffibly, upon fome
unforefeen occafion, become likewife the
peculiar duty of any one of us, viz.
" *to lay down* (our) *Lives for the Bre-*
" *thren* (2), 1 John iii. 16. yet as this
far exceeds the meafure of *Love* laid
down

(1) See my Tract on *the Law of Nature, and Principles
of Action in Man.* P. 79—105.

(2) *Hereby perceive we* (or rather, it fhould be rendered, *Hereby have we perceived*) " the LOVE (of God),
" *becaufe he laid down his Life for us*" (faid the Apoftle,
and then he immediately informs us of the duty which
arifes from that extraordinary manifeftation of LOVE)
" AND WE OUGHT (fays he) TO LAY DOWN (our)
" LIVES FOR THE BRETHREN." 1 John iii. 16.
This plain declaration of our duty (ἡμεῖς ὀφείλομεν, &c.
" WE OUGHT *to lay down our Lives*," &c.) fufficiently
enables us to account for the many extraordinary examples
of SELF-LOVE *being fuperfeded by more noble Principles,*
fome of which I have cited in my Tract on *the Law of
Nature,*

down in the second great Commandment, which is given us as the *general*
or

*Nature, and Principles of Action in Man*, p. 79—105, to
which also the following may be added.

THE GRATITUDE of the *Galatians* to their Teacher
*Paul*, is expressed by that Apostle in the strongest terms—
" *I bear you record* (says he) *that if it had been possible, ye*
" *would have plucked out your own eyes, and have given*
" *them to me.*" Gal. iv. 15.

Not inferior to this was the LOVE of that same Apostle
himself towards *the Corinthians*, though they were so far
from returning a *mutual affection* like *the Galatians*, that
the Apostle, it seems, had reason to complain of their
INGRATITUDE—" *I will very gladly* SPEND, AND BE
" SPENT *for you* (literally " *for your Souls,*" said he)
" *though the more abundantly I* LOVE *you, the less I be*
" LOVED." 2 Cor. xii. 15.

To " SPEND, AND BE SPENT" for others, and that
" *very gladly !*" is the strongest expression of *disinterested*
LOVE that could have been chosen ! It implies a chearful
sacrifice of every thing that is dear in this world (LIFE
ITSELF NOT EXCEPTED !) " *and greater Love hath no*
" *Man than this, that a Man lay down his Life for his*
" *friends.*" John xv. 13. So that, as *no Man can have*
*greater Love than this,* we may certainly esteem it the
highest demonstration of " *perfect Love* ;" and as the sentence last quoted from the Apostle John relates, in its pri-
mary application, to the voluntary sacrifice which Christ
made of himself to save Mankind, it leads us to the true
foundation of that " *perfect Love*" enjoined in the Scriptures,

or *ordinary* Rule of Life, we may be assured, that such a very difficult duty,

as

tures, which (as the preceding examples demonstrate) does occasionally overcome the general Principle of " *Self-* " *love*," and every other *interested* Motive natural to " MAN !

The Apostle John informs us, no less than *twice* in *one* chapter, that " GOD IS LOVE !" (ὁ Θεος αγαπη εςιν. 1 John iv. 8. ὁ Θεος αγαπη εςί. ibid. v. 16.)

This information is introduced in an argument, whereby the Apostle endeavours to inculcate a due sense of the necessity we are laid under, *to love one another*, because GOD hath first *loved us* : so that GRATITUDE TO GOD must be the foundation of our " *Love to one another* :" and we are therefore bound to imitate (and will certainly endeavour to imitate, if " GOD DWELLETH IN US." See 1 John iv. 13. 16.) that glorious Attribute of the *Divine Nature*, LOVE (" GOD IS LOVE") which he has manifested towards us, by sacrificing all that could be *truly perfect* and *dear* in his sight, even his only begotten Son, who also *voluntarily submitted himself* (for our happiness and *eternal* welfare) to the most severe *temporal* sufferings, and trials, *even unto death !*

To GOD, and to the ETERNAL WORD, therefore, (to whom we are indebted, not only for that extraordinary manifestation of LOVE, but for all other things that we enjoy, even for our very existence) our return of LOVE, must be UNLIMITED ; and the *natural Principle* of SELF-LOVE, which is given as the measure of our LOVE *to our Neighbour* in the *Law of Liberty*, or *second great Command-ment*,

[ 15 ]

as that of *laying down our Lives for the Brethren*, can only be required of us on
very

*ment*, muſt be entirely ſuppreſſed whenever it falls in competition with *the Love of God* enjoined in the *firſt great
Commandment* ; and though this doctrine is very hard and
difficult to be received, and much more difficult to be
practiſed, as it includes the moſt exalted *Heroiſm* and
*Greatneſs of Soul* that Human Nature is capable of attaining, yet we have ample reaſon to hope and truſt (as the
diſcharge of our *Duty to our Neighbour* includes and fulfils
the moſt eſſential part of *our Duty to God*) that thoſe men,
who carefully endeavour to make " *the Law of Liberty*,"
(I mean *the ſecond great Commandment*) their *general* or
*ordinary* Rule of Conduct IN LIFE, will nòt want due
aſſiſtance from the Almighty to enable them to fulfil alſo
the duty which ariſes from *the firſt great Commandment*, even
UNTO DEATH, if any extraordinary emergency ſhould
require ſuch a manifeſtation of their LOVE ; becauſe we
are aſſured by the Scriptures, that " GOD *dwelleth*" in
thoſe men, who maintain the proper meaſure of *Love* and
*Benevolence* for the reſt of mankind.

" BELOVED" (ſaid the *beloved* Apoſtle) " *let us* LOVE
" *one another : for* LOVE *is of* GOD, *and every one that*
" LOVETH *is born of* GOD, *and knoweth* GOD. *He that*
" LOVETH NOT *knoweth not God*, FOR GOD IS LOVE.
" *In this was manifeſted the* LOVE OF GOD *towards us*,
" *becauſe that* GOD *ſent his only begotten Son into the world*,
" *that we might live through him. Herein is* LOVE, *not*
" *that* WE LOVED GOD, *but that he* LOVED US, *and ſent*
" *his Son to be the propitiation for our ſins*. BELOVED, IF
" GOD SO LOVED US, *we ought alſo to* LOVE ONE ANO-
" THER.

[ 16 ]

very extraordinary occasions, as in times
of persecution, or on other such pressing
emergencies, when some very singular
Good or Benefit to our *Friends,* our
*Country,* or *Mankind in general,* apparently depends upon our perseverance
*unto death* for their sakes, in a just cause
*to the Glory of God;* or to the manifestation of his revealed *Truth,* for their
confirmation and example! This is, indeed, the best and most noble foundation, not only for true PATRIOTISM
in all Men, *as Members,* respectively, *of
some particular Nation,* but also for UNI-
VERSAL BENEVOLENCE, *as Citizens of
the World;* which latter Duty should
always regulate and limit the former (viz.
PATRIOTISM) by the eternal Rules of

" THER. *No man hath seen God at any time. If we love*
*one another,* GOD DWELLETH IN US, *and his* LOVE
" *is perfected in us.*" 1 John iv. 7—12. And again, in
the 16th verse—" *We have known and believed the* LOVE
" *that God hath to us.* GOD IS LOVE, *and he that dwelleth*
" *in* LOVE, DWELLETH IN GOD, AND GOD IN HIM.
" *Herein is our* LOVE MADE PERFECT, &c.

natural

natural Equity and Juſtice. But though a chearful obedience in this ultimate Duty of *laying down our Lives,* and ſacrificing *Self-love,* and every temporal Bleſſing *for the Good of others,* does undoubtedly exalt HUMAN NATURE to the higheſt pitch of *Heroiſm* and *real Dignity,* let us all, neverthelefs, pray God (as in effect we do by that comprehenfive expreſſion in our daily prayers— " *Lead us not into temptation*") to preſerve us from any ſuch ſevere trials of our Obedience and LOVE to him as the neceſſity of of " *laying down our Lives* " *for the Brethren*;" left, through the want of preſence of mind, or unwarineſs, or through weakneſs and natural infirmity, any of us ſhould unhappily ſhrink back from that ultimate Duty, and thereby incur the dreadful condemnation of thoſe that *deny Chriſt before Men !* Let us alſo be truly thankful, that the *abſolute Command,* in the
fecond

second great Branch of our Duty, by which *all Mankind are to be* JUDGED (as shall hereafter be shewn) extends no farther than to limit SELF-LOVE by a sympathetick Consideration or *Fellow-feeling* for our *Neighbour*'s welfare, left the former (*Self-love*) should be considered as the proper and " *universal* " *Principle of Action*," and thereby endanger the peace and happiness of Society by its *partial* instigations : let me add too, that if SELF-LOVE is not thus restrained, it will defeat its own Purpose and fixed Principles of *Self-preservation*, by incurring a dreadful and eternal Doom !

The OMISSION of an Act of *Mercy* and *Benevolence* towards our Neighbour, when it is in our power, and occasion requires it, *is declared by our Lord, the Saviour of the World*, to be as gross an affront, *even to himself*, as if *he* had been

*personally*

*perfonally* neglected and denied by us!
" *Inafmuch* (fays he) *as ye did it not to*
" *one of the leaft of thefe,* YE DID IT
" NOT TO ME." Matt. xxv. 45. And
if SINS of OMISSION, even towards *the*
*meaneft of our Brethren,* are by OUR
LORD efteemed as a *perfonal Affront*
*to himfelf,* we may be affured, that the
actual COMMISSION of Injuries will be
infinitely more heinous in his fight, and
cannot efcape his juft Vengeance. We
muft remember alfo, that *this Declara-*
*tion* of our Lord will be made to thofe
miferable wretches, who fhall ftand " *on*
" *the Left Hand,*" after the tremendous
final fentence is paffed upon them!
" *Depart from me ye Curfed, into ever-*
" *lafting Fire, prepared for the Devil*
" *and his Angels!*" See verfe 41.

It is manifeft therefore, that *a Viola-*
*lation of* THE LOVE THAT IS DUE TO
OUR NEIGHBOUR, is a Violation alfo of
THE

THE LOVE OF GOD; and, on the contrary, *the latter is perfected* by a ſtrict
obedience *to the former*—" *If we* LOVE
*one another*" (ſays *the beloved* Apoſtle)
" *God dwelleth in us, and* HIS LOVE IS
" PERFECTED IN US." (1 John iv. 12.)
So that the two great Commandments
appear to be reciprocally included and
blended together in their conſequences;
by which we may more readily perceive
the propriety of our Lord's declaration,
that the *ſecond great Commandment is like
unto the firſt* (3); and this reciprocal
connexion between them enables us alſo
to comprehend the reaſon why *the ſecond*
is given *alone* (when BOTH are undoubtedly neceſſary) as the grand teſt of Chriſtian obedience, and as the ſum and eſ-

(3) " *Thou ſhalt love the Lord thy God with all thy*
" *heart, and with all thy ſoul, and with all thy mind.*
" *This is the firſt and great Commandment.* AND THE
" SECOND IS LIKE UNTO IT, *Thou ſhalt love thy Neigh-*
" *bour as thyſelf. On theſe two Commandments hang all*
" *the Law and the Prophets.*" (Matt. xxii. 37. to 40.)

ſtian

fence of the whole Law of God. " *For* " *all the Law is fulfilled*" (fays the Apoſtle Paul) " *in one word,* (even) *in this, Thou* " *ſhalt love thy Neighbour as thyſelf.*" (Gal. v. 14.)

Now a continued multiplication of Statutes (as in England, where the number exceeds the capacity of the human Memory) affords matter only for *Equivocation, Doubt,* and *Evaſion,* whereby SOUND LAW is vitiated and corrupted; and the loathſome *Proſtitute,* ſtill retaining *the Name of* LAW, *ariſes* (like the Harlot POPERY from pure CHRISTIANITY) *in another Dreſs !* She is clothed with the many-coloured garment of miſconſtruction, and feats herſelf at the right hand of the unjuſt judge, prompting him with wily Subterfuges, and *bad Precedents* inſtead of LAW; whereby he is enabled to enſnare the innocent, and ſcreen the guilty. But, on the other hand, when we conſider that " ALL LAW" is

reduced

reduced to fo fmall a compafs, that it
may be accounted, comparatively, as ONE
WORD, there is no room left for offenders to plead *Ignorance,* as an excufe for
having violated the general Laws of
Morality, and the *natural Rights of Mankind.* Let me therefore exhort my op-
ponents, as they regard their own eternal welfare, to take this fubject into
their moft ferious confideration, and no
longer refufe to acknowledge this glorious WORD or *Maxim,* as the TRUE
MEASURE (except a ftill greater meafure
of LOVE is required (4) of all their actions,
and more efpecially with refpect to the
prefent point before us, the *Legality or
Illegality of Slavery among Chriftians !* For
this queftion, by infallible neceffity,
falls under the decifion of *this very
Law* ; becaufe it fets before us our own
*perfonal Feelings,* as *the proper Meafure
or Standard of our Behaviour to other*

(4) This exception relates only to fuch extraordinary
cafes of emergency as are mentioned in pages 12 to 17.

*Men* ;

*Men*; for Tyrants, Slaveholders, Extortioners, and other Oppreſſors, would
moſt certainly diſlike to be treated as
as they treat others; ſo that this compendious Law neceſſarily excludes *the
leaſt Toleration of Slavery*, or of any other
*Oppreſſion*, which an *innocent Man* (5)
would be unwilling to experience in his
own perſon from another.

We

(5) On the other hand, *notorious offenders*, that are
clearly convicted of their crimes by the laws of the land,
may, conſiſtently *with reaſon and juſtice*, be puniſhed with
a temporary DEPRIVATION OF LIBERTY, provided
they be not *ſold to ſtrangers*, nor even to *their own countrymen*, to be ſubjected to *private dominion*, or the *abſolute
rule of individuals*, which is dreadfully baneful to morality! The community at large (and *that community only
whoſe Laws they have broken*) can alone have any RIGHT
to detain them in *bondage*; and this RIGHT of detaining
ſhould be moderated by ſuch wholeſome regulations for
the religious *inſtruction*, as well as *employment*, of the unhappy convicts, as ſhould apparently tend more to their
*reformation*, (to render them worthy of being ſpeedily reſtored to *Liberty*) than to any other object; and no perſons whatſoever ſhould be entruſted with the care, inſtruction, or employment of ſuch *public delinquents*, without being ſubject to the inſpection and *legal* controul of
the king's judges, and of other regular *crown officers* of the
*Law department* (but of no other *crown officers* as ſuch
whatever) as alſo of the county courts of aſſizes and ſeſſions,

courts

We muſt therefore acknowledge this
heavenly maxim to be the true ſtandard,
not only of *mutual Benevolence* among
MEN, but alſo, of *our Love and Duty*
to GOD ; ſince it includes the firſt great
Commandment, by " *perfecting the Love*
" *of God in us,*" as I have before remarked (ſee p. 20.); ſo that it muſt neceſſarily
be eſteemed the moſt ſure and beſt foundation " of PERFECT LIBERTY." And
accordingly we find it expreſſly diſtinguiſhed in Scripture by the title of
" *the Law of Liberty.*"

" *So ſpeak ye, and ſo do,*" (ſays the
Apoſtle James) " *as they that ſhall be*
" *judged by* THE LAW OF LIBERTY."
(James ii. 12.) This title properly belongs, indeed, to the *whole Law,* or

courts of inqueſt, grand juries, juſtices of the peace,
ſheriffs, and of ſuch other *legal* guardians of the public
peace, for and in behalf of the public, left the cauſe of
*liberty* ſhould ſuffer by the influence of any innovation
in that reſpect.

*Goſpel*

*Gospel of Christ*, and seems to be so applied by the same Apostle in the preceding chapter (25th verse) wherein he
speaks of " *the perfect* LAW OF LIBER-
" TY."—Yet the *general* application of
the title does not lessen the propriety of
that *particular* application, which I conceive to have been intended by the
Apostle in this 2d chapter, because the
precept in question is *a complete Compendium of Christian Morality,* containing
(as I have before observed) the *very
Essence of the whole Gospel,* or *general*
LAW OF LIBERTY, with respect to our
*Duty towards Men,* and has, therefore,
an indisputable Right, also, to the *general Title of the whole.* But there are
other reasons to justify the application
of this *general Title of the Gospel* to that
*one* comprehensive *Word,* or Maxim, in
which " *all the Law is fulfilled.*"—
Though the Apostle James seems to
mean the *whole Gospel* in that passage of
his

his firſt chapter, wherein he mentions
" THE PERFECT LAW OF LIBERTY."
—Yet the whole tenor of his argument
in the 2d chapter, where he again mentions THE LAW OF LIBERTY, is apparently founded on the Principles of
the glorious Maxim in queſtion——
" THOU SHALT LOVE THY NEIGH-
" BOUR AS THYSELF ;" for the *Subject,*
in the beginning of the chapter, particularly relates to *the Duty we owe to* OUR
NEIGHBOURS, being a warning againſt
" *Reſpect of Perſons,*" or *Partiality* ; and
as the Maxim in queſtion forbids even
*Self-preference,* by directing us *to* " *love*
" *our Neighbours* (ὡς) AS *ourſelves,*" it is ſo
apparently ſuitable to the Apoſtle's *ſub-
ject,* that he expreſſly cites it under the
eminent title of the " *Royal Law* (νομον
Βασιλικον) to enforce his argument. " *My*
" *Brethren*" (ſays he) " *have not the*
" *Faith of our Lord Jeſus Chriſt*" (the
Lord) " *of Glory,* WITH RESPECT OF
" PER-

" Persons ;" and then, after charging
them in the 2d and 3d verses with *Partiality*, in *preferring* a well-dreſſed Man
in their aſſemblies to the *Poor*, and after
appealing to them thereupon in the 4th
and 5th verſes, ſaying, " *Are ye not*
" *partial in yourſelves*," &c. and alſo,
after reproving them (in the 6th and 7th
verſes) for *deſpiſing the Poor*; he adds,
in the 8th verſe—" *If ye fulfil*," (ſays he)
" *the* Royal Law (νομον Βασιλικον) *according to the Scripture*, Thou shalt
" love thy Neighbour as thy-
" self," (which is the very Maxim in
queſtion) " *ye do well : But if ye have*
" respect to Persons," (ſays he,
thereby plainly pointing out this Partiality as a direct breach of the ſaid
Royal Law) " *ye commit Sin, and are
" convinced of the Law as Tranſgreſſors.
For whoſoever ſhall keep the whole Law*,"
(continues the Apoſtle) *and yet offend in*
" *one* (point) *he is guilty of all. For he*
" *that*

" *that faid do not commit Adultery* ; *faid*
" *alfo, Do not kill.  Now if thou commit*
" *no Adultery, yet if thou kill, thou art*
" *become a Tranfgreffor of the Law.  So*
" *fpeak ye, and fo do ye, as they that fhall*
" *be* JUDGED *by the* LAW OF LIBERTY,"
(manifeſtly referring us to the *indifpen-*
*fible Principle of doing as we would be done*
*by*, or to that which is exactly parallel
—*the loving our Neighbours as ourfelves*)
" FOR HE SHALL HAVE JUDGMENT
" WITHOUT MERCY" (faid the Apoſtle)
" THAT HATH SHEWED NO MERCY ;
" *and Mercy rejoiceth againft Judgment.*"
(James ii. 1. to 13.)

This abſolute neceſſity that we are
laid under *to fhew Mercy, that we may*
*obtain Mercy*, is apparently founded on
the very fame *Principle*, which our Lord
declared to be ' *the Law and the Pro-*
' *phets* ;' that is, the fum and eſſence of
the whole Scriptures, as I have before
remarked

remarked—" ALL THINGS WHATSO-
" EVER YE WOULD THAT MEN SHOULD
" DO TO YOU, DO YE EVEN SO TO
" THEM: FOR THIS IS THE LAW AND
" THE PROPHETS;" (Mat. vii. 12.)
and I have already fhewn (in p. 3.)
that this comprehenfive Maxim is exactly
the fame in effect (though expreffed in
different words) as the fecond great
Commandment of our Lord, " THOU
" SHALT LOVE THY NEIGHBOUR AS
" THYSELF;" in which (as the Apoftle
Paul has exprefsly declared) " *All the*
" *Law is fulfilled*," viz. " *All the Law*
(fays he) " *is fulfilled in* ONE WORD (even)
" *in this*, THOU SHALT LOVE THY
" NEIGHBOUR AS THYSELF." (Gal.
v. 14.)

This *one Word* (as the Maxim is
efteemed by the Apoftle Paul) is therefore undoubtedly that glorious " LAW
" OF LIBERTY" by which *we fhall all*
*be*

*be judged,* as the Apoſtle James hath fairly warned us—" *So ſpeak ye, and ſo* " *do*" (ſays he) " *as they that* SHALL " BE JUDGED BY THE LAW OF LI- " BERTY." And therefore, if what has already been ſaid be duly conſidered, the propriety of citing this glorious and comprehenſive LAW OF LIBERTY, in vindication of the NATURAL LIBERTY OF MANKIND *againſt the Tyranny of Slaveholders,* cannot be doubted or called in queſtion ; for though this SUPREME LAW virtually prohibits every other kind of *Oppreſſion,* yet its very title leads us to a more particular and exprefs appli- cation of it AGAINST THE TOLERA- TION OF SLAVERY AMONG CHRISTI- ANS : becauſe it feems to be thus emi- nently diſtinguiſhed by the appointment of God himſelf in his Holy Word, as *the peculiar Antidote* againſt that *baneful Evil* (SLAVERY) which is moſt oppoſite and repugnant to its glorious title—

" THE

" THE LAW OF LIBERTY." This " LAW OF LIBERTY," this SUPREAM, this " ROYAL LAW," muft therefore be our guide in the interpretation and examination of all Laws which relate *to the Rights of Perfons*, becaufe it ex-cludes *Partiality*, or *Refpect of Perfons*, and confequently removes all ground for the pretence of any *abfolute Right of Dominion inherent in the Mafters* over their Slaves : for as all Ranks of Men are EQUAL *in the Sight of God* (the Chriftian *Slave*, or Servant, being *the Freeman* of the Lord, and the Chriftian *Mafter* the *Servant* of Chrift, 1 Cor. vii. 22.) there is no doubt but that the fame *Chriftian* Qualities are neceffary to be maintained by the *Chriftian* MASTER, that are required of the *Chriftian* SERVANT ; as *Humility, Forgivenefs of Trefpaffes* or *Debts, and* (though not *Submiffion*, yet certainly) *Brotherly Love towards Inferiors,* with *unfeigned Charity* and *univer-*

*fal*

*fal Benevolence*, founded on the glorious Maxim, or *Royal Law*, " THOU SHALT " LOVE THY NEIGHBOUR AS THY- " SELF." All which are as indifpenfably neceffary to form the difpofition of a *true Chriftian Mafter*, as they are abfo- lutely incompatible with the oppreffive and tyrannical Claims of our American Slaveholders! " *Quod tibi fieri non vis,* " *alteri ne feceris. What thou wouldeft* " *not have done to thee, do not thou to* " *another,*"—was the favourite Maxim of the Emperor *Alexander Severus*, ac- cording to the Report of *Lampridius* quoted by the learned Jof. Mede, Book 3. p. 550. This Principle was probably deduced from " THE ROYAL LAW," " or LAW OF LIBERTY;" for *Lam- pridius* relates, that the Emperor heard it either from fome Jews or Chriftians: (" *Quod à quibufdam five Judæis five* " *Chriftianis audierat, et tenebat,*" &c.) and

and it cannot be denied, that the doctrine of it is neceffarily included in that great and indifpenfable Commandment. The doctrine was expreffed even by Chrift himfelf nearly to the fame effect, which I have already quoted :—" *All things* " *whatfover ye would that Men fhould do* " *to you, do ye even fo to them :* FOR THIS " IS THE LAW *and* THE PROPHETS." (Mat. vii. 12.) So that Slavery is abfolutely inconfiftent with Chriftianity, becaufe we cannot fay of any *Slaveholder*, that he *doth not* to another, what he would not have done to himfelf! For he is continually exacting *involuntary Labour* from others *without Wages*, which he would think monftroufly unjuft, were he himfelf the Sufferer! Nay, many of them are fo befotted with Avarice, that they are not content with reaping *the whole Fruit of other Men's Labour upon Earth* WITHOUT WAGES;

Wages (3); but would deprive their poor Labourers even of their *eternal Comfort*, if they could exact a little more Work from them, by reducing them nearer to the State of Brutes!—What I advance cannot be denied; for it is notorious, that *many Mafters* oppofe the inftruction of their *Slaves* in Chriftian Knowledge; and *but very few* promote it as they ought; fo that the Iniquity of the ignorant Slave muft reft *with double Weight* on the guilty head of the owner, to fill up the meafure of his fins!

Suppofe a reverfe of fortune—that an Englifh or Scotch *Slaveholder*, or *Slavedealer*, is fhipwrecked on the Barbary Coaft, and is retained, *as a Slave*, by the Moors, who feize him; or is *fold, as fuch*, to another Perfon, accord-

(3) " *Woe unto him that buildeth his Houfe by Unright-* " *eoufnefs, and his Chambers by Wrong*; *that* USETH HIS " NEIGHBOUR'S SERVICE WITHOUT WAGES, AND " GIVETH HIM NOT FOR HIS WORK." Jer. xxii. 13.

ing

ing to the deteſtable cuſtoms of that
Savage people!—Would he eſteem himſelf the *lawful Property* of his tawney
Maſter, becauſe the wretched police of
thoſe Barbarians, *in tolerating Slavery*, is
ſimilar to his own former practices as
an *American Slaveholder*, or *African
Trader?* Would he not think it cruel
treatment to be eſteemed *a mere Chattel*;
and, as ſuch, to be ranked with the
horſes and oxen of his African Maſter?
*Like them*, to be compelled by ſtripes
to perform the moſt ſervile and abject
Labour? *Like them*, to receive *no Wages*,
or other *Reward* for his Service, except
a little *coarſe Provender*, merely to keep
him in working Order for his Maſter's
Benefit? Would he not think himſelf
grievouſly injured by being forcibly detained and prevented from working for
himſelf? And would he not think himſelf abſolutely *robbed of the Fruits of his
own Labour?* He would certainly have
ample

ample reafon to lament the Mahometan's Ignorance of the heavenly Precept,
" THOU SHALT LOVE THY NEIGH-
BOUR AS THYSELF ; for he would then
be taught, by his own Sufferings, to
comprehend the full Force, Extent,
and meaning of that benevolent Command, which, in his profperity, he was
never *willing* to underſtand, though the
doctrine is fo plain and obvious, that
there can be no excufe for mifunder-
ſtanding it ; for unleſs the Slaveholder
can make it appear, *that his* SLAVE *is
not his* NEIGHBOUR. he muſt neceſſarily
acknowledge *this* " LAW OF LIBERTY"
to be *the true Meafure* of his conduct
and behaviour *towards his* SLAVE, as
well as *towards all other* MEN !

Let not *Slaveholders* or *African Traders*
conceive, that they are at liberty to
receive or reject this glorious Precept,
according as it may fuit their intereſt

or

or convenience! But rather let them carefully examine (for they are particularly interefted in the determination of the queftion) whether obedience to the doctrine of the great " LAW OF LIBER- " TY," is not abfolutely indifpenfable ? And whether the violation of it is not dangerous to falvation ?

If they think there is any room to flatter themfelves, that they do not offend God by tolerating Slavery among them, let them but examine their Actions by this " ROYAL LAW," and they will clearly perceive both their *Guilt and Danger, unlefs they have Con- fciences feared with a hot Iron!*"

" *If ye have refpect unto Perfons*" (fays the Apoftle James, when he enforces the Obfervation of the ROYAL LAW) " *ye* " *commit Sin, and are convinced of* THE " LAW AS TRANSGRESSORS," &c. ii. 9.

Now

Now this Offence of " *having Respect* " *unto Persons,*" is a mark which strongly characterizes *Slaveholders* as Violaters of " THE ROYAL LAW."

They are courteous, friendly, and hospitable enough, in general, to Persons *of their own Rank,* as, indeed, they ought to be; but, at the same time, they look down upon their *Slaves* (who are *equally their Brethren*) as if they were *not Human Beings,* and rank them as *mere Chattels* with their Horses and Dogs; so that there needs no Argument to prove them guilty of " *having Respect* " *unto Persons*" in a most notorious degree, whereby they surely " *commit Sin,*" and are " *convinced of the Law as Transf-* " *gressors.*" What therefore have such Men to expect, when they shall be judged by " THE LAW OF LIBERTY !" especially as the Apostle adds, " *they* " *shall*

" *ſhall have Judgment without Mercy,*
" *that have ſhewed no Mercy!"* &c.

And even our Lord himſelf has declared the very ſame doctrine, though
in different Words—" *With the ſame*
" Measure *that ye* mete" (ſays he)
" *ſhall it be* measured *unto you again."*
Τῳ γαρ αυτῳ μετρῳ ῷ μετρειʃε αντιμετρηθησεται ὑμιν.
Luke vi. 38. Mat. vii. 2. Mark iv. 24.

What Measure of *Benevolence,* therefore, have theſe Men to expect, who
endeavour to enrich themselves by *en-
ſlaving* and *oppreſſing* their Brethren?
For Men, who, " *without Mercy,"* or
Fellow-feeling, have violated " The
" Royal Law of Liberty," can
neither be ſaid to *love God,* nor *their
Neighbour,* as directed in the two great
Commandments, and conſequently are
Violaters of " *the whole Law ;"* by which
they abſolutely deprive themſelves of
the

the Benefit of Chrift's Redemption !
This feems to be the neceffary meaning
of that dreadful Doom before-men-
tioned ; " *He fhall have* JUDGMENT
" *without* MERCY, that *hath fhewed* NO
" MERCY."

But let no Man conceive, that I prefume to charge Individuals, or *any Perfon in-particular,* with the want of this
MERCY, fo neceffary to Salvation, even
though they are apparently guilty of
that oppreffive treatment of their *Neighbour,* which I now oppofe ; for this
would feem like fetting bounds to the
*Mercy of God,* whereby I fhould be liable
to involve myfelf, as an *uncharitable
Judge,* in the fame condemnation. And
there are, certainly, a variety of circumftances, beyond the reach of human
knowledge, that may extenuate the guilt
of *particular Perfons,* of which the great
Searcher of Hearts alone can judge !

It

It is not, therefore, *the Perfons*, but *the uncharitable Practices* of Slaveholders and Slavedealers, that I now venture *to condemn*; and thefe I can with confidence affirm to be really *damnable*, or *dangerous to Salvation*, as being the moft notorious violations of that Chriftian Charity, or LOVE OF OUR NEIGHBOUR, which God indifpenfably requires of us, and without which, the higheft Gifts are vain, and even *Faith itfelf!* For, *tho' I have* " ALL FAITH" (faid the Apoftle Paul) " *fo that I could remove Mountains, and have* " *no* CHARITY, *I am nothing.*" I Cor. xiii. 2. The nature of this indifpenfable CHARITY is more particularly defcribed by the fame Apoftle under the appellation of LOVE (ἡ αγαπη). " LOVE," (fays he) " *worketh no* ILL *to his Neighbour: there-* " *fore* LOVE *is the fulfilling of the Law.*" Rom. xiii. 10. But, as the being detained in *an involuntary Slavery* is one of the greateft ILLS, or EVILS, that can

happen

happen to *our Neighbour*, it muſt neceffarily be allowed, that he who *cauſes*, or
*continues* fuch an *unnatural Oppreſſion* of
poor unfortunate *Strangers*, who never
injured him, nor his, nor ever voluntarily contracted to ſerve him, ever for
the ſhorteſt term, much leſs for life;
fuch a Man, I ſay, moſt certainly
" *worketh* ILL *to his Neighbour* ;" and,
confequently, violates that *ſaving* LOVE,
which is required for " *the fulfilling of*
" *the Law.*" For " *he that* LOVETH
" *another*" (ſays the Apoſtle in a preceding verfe of the fame chapter) " *hath*
" *fulfilled the Law :*" and after repeating
the feveral Articles of the Decalogue,
refpecting *our Duty towards our* NEIGH-
BOUR, he adds, " *and if there be any*
" *other Commandment, it is briefly com-*
" *prehended in this,* THOU SHALT LOVE
" THY NEIGHBOUR AS THYSELF."
Rom. xiii. 8—10. We may therefore
fairly conclude, that this glorious MAX-
IM

IM is the touchſtone or proof of *that ſaving* LOVE, which is THE FULFILL- ING OF THE LAW, and without which " FAITH IS DEAD," as declared by *the Apoſtle Paul*; that it is alſo " THE ROYAL LAW," being thus eminently diſtinguiſhed from all other Precepts of the Goſpel, by the *Apoſtle James*; and if it *is not* alſo particularly ſignified (though I am fully convinced that it *is*) under the Title of " THE LAW OF " LIBERTY," by the *ſame Apoſtle*, in his 2d Chapter; yet it is ſurely one of the moſt eſſential and comprehenſive Principles of that " LAW OF LIBERTY," by which *we ſhall all be judged*; be- cauſe the Apoſtle at the ſame time de- clares, that " *he ſhall have Judgment* WITHOUT MERCY, *who hath ſhewed* NO MERCY;" (chap. ii. 13.) by which he manifeſtly refers to the Breach of that particular Precept, which ought to re- gulate the Conduct of all Mankind to- wards

wards each other; and therefore, laftly, we muft acknowledge this fame Precept to be alfo THE TRUE MEASURE OF Teft on which our eternal Doom will depend in that awful Day, when it " *fhall be* " MEASURED *unto us again,*" *according to* THE MEASURE of our Actions, as declared by the *eternal Judge himfelf,* (Mat. vii. 2. Mark iv. 24. Luke vi. 38.) whofe Words cannot fail! And if even a mere *Neglect* or *Omiffion* in our Duty towards our *Neighbour* is fo *offenfive* to our bleffed Lord, that he efteems it as a Denial and Affront to his *own Perfon,* (which I have already obferved) how *much more offenfive* to him muft be *the actual Commiffion* of the groffeft Injuries, fuch as the Exaction of *an involuntary Service* from our poor Brethren " WITH- " OUT WAGES," and the various Cruelties ufually practifed to enforce the fame, which are the neceffary and unavoidable Attendants on *Slavery*—What a dreadful

a dreadful MEASURE of RETRIBUTION,
then, may obſtinate and unrepenting
*Slaveholders* and *Slavedealers* juſtly expect
from the righteous Judge! Surely there
is but too much Cauſe to apprehend,
that Chriſt will one Day PROFESS UNTO
THEM—" *Inaſmuch as ye have done it unto*
" *one of the leaſt of theſe my Brethren,*
" *ye have* DONE IT UNTO ME!" (Mat.
XXV. 40.)

This Sentence, indeed, is applied in
the Text to thoſe who ſhall have DONE
GOOD to their Brethren; yet by necefſary Conſequence it is equally applicable
(as in the 45th verſe) to thoſe who have
neglected, or ſhewn them *no Brotherly*
LOVE and CHARITY!—" *Inaſmuch* (ſaid
our Lord) " *as ye did it not to one of*
" *the leaſt of theſe, ye did it not to me.*
" *And theſe* (by which our Lord plainly
referred to all that ſhould neglect or
violate that indiſpenſible *Brotherly Love*
and

and *Charity* which he enjoined) " *shall*
" *go away* INTO EVERLASTING PU-
" NISHMENT : *but the Righteous into*
" *Life eternal !*"

But alas !—to *worldly* minded Men
the Judgments of *another World* feem
too far diftant to awaken their Attention, though they are liable to be called
away, in the very next Hour, to a State
of Exiftence, wherein the moft pun-
gent Remorfe will avail them nothing !
From fuch therefore, and from thofe
unrepenting Individuals, that will ftill
perfift in violating the LAW OF LIEERTY
by *Slave-dealing* and *Slave-holding*, it is
time to turn away ! I have already beftowed too much labour upon them, I
mean, with refpect to themfelves ! But
this Warning was not intended for them
alone;—the whole Community—every
Individual (without excepting even thofe
who never had the leaft Concern in pro-
                                    moting

moting *Slavery*) is perfonally interefted in the Confideration of this Subject! For if a Breach of God's Command, even in the *hidden* Crime of a fingle Individual, as in the Cafe of *Achan*, could involve a whole Nation in Trouble (4), and deprive them of God's Blefling, how

(4) " —*For Achan the Son of Carmi*,"—*took of* THE " ACCURSED THING," (i. e. of that which was *devoted to Deſtruction* by God's exprefs Command) : " *And the " Anger of the Lord was kindled againſt the Children of " Iſrael*." Joſhua vii. 1.—Thus the whole NATION was involved in the Confequences of Achan's Guilt! Nay, *Jehovah* himfelf exprefsly imputed the Action of that one Individual to the NATION at large, until a folemn and public Exertion of NATIONAL Juftice had expiated that prefumptive Breach of his Command! For when Joſhua and the Elders of Ifrael lay proſtrate before God, lamenting the public Calamity and Difgrace, which a late Defeat of their Army had brought upon the NATION.— " *the Lord* (Jehovah) *ſaid unto Joſhua, Get thee up ; " wherefore lieſt thou thus upon thy Face ?* ISRAEL *hath " ſinned, and* THEY HAVE *alſo* TRANSGRESSED *my Cove- " nant which I commanded them : for* THEY *have even taken " of* THE ACCURSED THING, *and have ſtolen*, (that is, THEY *have ſtolen* גנבו) " *and* THEY *have diſſembled " alſo, and* THEY *have put* (it) *even among their own " Stuff*." (Yet this general Crime, for fo it was imputed, was

[ 48 ]

how much more hateful in the Sight
of God muſt be a *public* Infringement
of his ROYAL LAW, THE PERFECT
LAW OF LIBERTY, by *national* Authority !

The AFRICAN SLAVE TRADE, which
includes the moſt contemptuous Violations of *Brotherly Love* and *Charity* that
men can be guilty of, is openly encouraged
and promoted by the Britiſh Parliament!
And the moſt deteſtable and oppreſſive

was perpetrated by *a ſingle Individual*, though the *whole*
NATION was doomed to ſuffer for it, till the actual Ag-
greſſor ſhould be brought to *public Juſtice* ; and this ſhould
teach us, that the Welfare of NATION greatly depends
on a ſtrict Adminiſtration of public *Juſtice* and *Righteouſneſs*, leſt the State ſhould be accountable for the Crimes of
Individuals.)  " *Therefore the Children of Iſrael*" (ſaid
Jehovah himſelf) " *could not ſtand before their Enemies,*
" (but) *turned* (their) *Backs before their Enemies, becauſe*
" *they were* ACCURSED." (Thus the CURSE was tranſ-
ferred to the People from THE ACCURSED THING, until
*public Juſtice* could trace and transfer it to the devoted
Head of the guilty Perſon !) " *Neither will I* (ſaid Jehovah) "; *be with you any more, except ye deſtroy* THE
" ACCURSED *from among you.*"  See the whole Chapter.

*Slavery,*

*Slavery,* that ever difgraced even the unenlightened Heathens, is notorioufly *tolerated* in the Britifh Colonies by the *public Acts* of their refpective Affemblies, —by Acts that have been ratified with the Affent and Concurrence of British Kings!

The horrible Guilt therefore, which is incurred by *Slave-dealing* and *Slave-holding,* is no longer confined to the few hardened *Individuals,* that are immediately concerned in thofe baneful Practices, but alas! the whole British Empire is involved!

By the unhappy Concurrence of *National Authority,* the Guilt is rendered *National;* and *National* Guilt muft inevitably draw down from God fome tremendous *National* Punifhment (which, I truft, is fully demonftrated in my Tract on the Law of Retribution) if we do not fpeedily " *take away the accurfed*
" *Thing*

" *Thing from among us*,"—if we do not carefully reform and redrefs at leaft every *public* and notorious Violation of GOD's " *Royal Law*," " *the perfeƐt Law of* " *Liberty !*"

GRANVILLE SHARP.

" GLORY to GOD in the Higheft !
" And on Earth—PEACE,
" GOOD WILL towards Men !"

# TEXTS of SCRIPTURE

## QUOTED or ILLUSTRATED

## IN THE FOREGOING TRACT.

### LEVITICUS.

| Chapter. | Verse. | Page. |
|---|---|---|
| XIX. | 28. | 9 |

### DEUTERONOMY.

| | | |
|---|---|---|
| VI. | 5. | 8 |

### JOSHUA.

| | | |
|---|---|---|
| VII. | | 48, n. |
| | 1. | 47, n. |

### JEREMIAH.

| | | |
|---|---|---|
| XXII. | 13. | 34, n. |

### MATTHEW.

| | | |
|---|---|---|
| VII. | 2. | 39. 44 |
| | 12. | 9. 29. 33 |
| XXII. | 37—40. | 20, n. |
| | 40. | 9 |
| XXV. | 40. | 45 |
| | 41. | 19 |
| | 45. | 19. 45. |

### MARK.

| | | |
|---|---|---|
| IV. | 24. | 39. 44. |

### LUKE.

| | | |
|---|---|---|
| VI. | 38. | 39. 44 |

### JOHN.

| | | |
|---|---|---|
| XV. | 13. | 13, n. |

### ROMANS.

## ROMANS.

| Chapter. | Verse. | Page |
|---|---|---|
| XIII. | 8—10. | 42 |
|  | 10. | 41 |

## I CORINTHIANS.

| VII. | 22. | 31 |
| XIII. | 2. | 41 |

## II CORINTHIANS.

| XII. | 15. | 13, n. |

## GALATIANS.

| IV. | 15. | 13, n. |
| V. | 14. | 10. 29 |

## JAMES.

| I. |  | 26 |
| II. |  | 26. 43 |
|  | 13. | 43 |
|  | 1—13. | 28 |
|  | 2, 3, 4, 5, 6, 7, 8. | 27 |
|  | 9. | 37 |
|  | 12. | 6. 24 |
|  | 13. | 7. 43 |
|  | 25. | 25 |

## I JOHN.

| III. | 16. | 12 |
| IV. | 7—12. | 16, n. |
|  | 8. | 14, n. |
|  | 13. 16. | 14, n. |
|  | 16. | 16, n. |

INDEX.

# I N D E X.

## A.

*AFRICAN Slave-trade*, encouraged by parliament, page 48.

*Alexander Severus* (emp.) his favourite maxim, 32

*Author*, his defign in this tract, 5. And for whofe ufe it is intended, 7. The confideration of which every man is interefted in, 7. 46. & feq. See *Slaveholders.*

## B

*Benevolence* (univerfal) its beft foundation, 16.

*Brethren*, the duty of laying down our lives for them explained, 12, & feq. The higheft demonftration of perfect love, 13 *note*. Only required on very extraordinary occafions, 16.

## C

*Charity*, an indifpenfable duty, 41.

*Chriftian Mafter*, his qualifications, 32.

*Corinthians*, their ingratitude to St. Paul, 13 *note*.

## G

*Galatians*, their gratitude to St. Paul, 13 *note*.

GOD, the extent of our love to him, 8. Is love, 14 *note*. Our love to him perfected by that to our neighbour, 20. All men equal in his fight, 31.

*Gofpel*, its moral duties comprehended in two fingle principles, 7. Is properly the law of liberty, 24, & feq.

*Gratitude* to God, the foundation of our love to one another, 14 *note*. See *Self-love.*

J.

J

*Juſt Limitation of Slavery in the laws of God,* 5.

L

*Lampridius,* 32.
*Law.* See *Statutes.*
*Law of Liberty,* recommended as a rule of action by
 St. James, 6. Defined, 24. See *Goſpel, Slavery.*
 Obedience to it, indiſpenſable, 37, & ſeq.
*Law of Nature,* and *Principles of Action in Man,*
 12 *note,* 13 *note.*
*Law of Paſſive Obedience,* 5.
*Liberty,* notorious offenders may be temporarily de-
 prived of, 23 *note.*
*Life,* laying it down for our brethren. See *Brethren.*
*Love,* of God and our neighbour, the two moral
 principles of the goſpel, 8. See *Neighbour.*

M

*Mede* (Joſ.) 32.
*Morality,* ignorance no excuſe for having violated its
 laws. 22.

N

*Neighbour,* our love to him explained, 8. Enforced
 by our Saviour, 9. And by St. Paul, 10. Omiſſion of it, declared by our Saviour an affront to
 himſelf, 18. A violation of it violates our love
 to God, 19. See GOD. The Royal Law, 26.
 43. The neceſſity thereof proved, 27, 28. The
 Law of Liberty, 43. The teſt on which our eternal doom will depend, 44.

P

*Patriotiſm* (true) its nobleſt foundation, 16.
*Paul* (St.) his love to the Corinthians, 13 *note.*
*Popery,* how it differs from pure Chriſtianity, 21.

R.

[ 55 ]

R
*Royal Law.* See *Neighbour.*

S

*Self-love,* the rule of our conduct towards other men, 10, 11. But not the univerfal principle of action, 18. Muft be fuppreffed when it comes in competition with the love of God, 15 *note.*

*Slaveholders,* the legality or illegality of their practices among Chriftians confidered, 6, & feq. Their practices contrary to the laws of Chrift, in doing that to others, which they would not have done to themfelves, 33. A ftriking appeal to their confciences, 34, & feq. The finfulnefs of their conduct, 38, & feq. Their practices, not their perfons, condemned by the author, 41. The injuftice of thofe practices, *ibid.* The dreadful confequences to be expected from them, 44.

*Slavery,* the inveftigation of its legality or illegality among Chriftians, the defign of this tract, 6, 7. Not defenfible on Chriftian principles, 23. Exprefsly againft the Law of Liberty, 30. Abfolutely inconfiftent with Chriftianity, 32.

*Statutes,* their multiplicity in England only affords matter for equivocation, doubt, and evafion, 21.

F I N I S.